About the reviewers

John Maschke is a technology business analytics consultant and leader, with over 25 years of experience leveraging BI environments to create insightful analytics, visually strong dashboards, and enhanced reporting capabilities. Communications and data literacy are just as important as the tools and technology, and he's enthusiastic about it all. Extremely passionate and knowledgeable about transitioning organizations into a data-driven culture, John has refined his skill sets by directly working within industries such as retail, financial services, real estate, education, and innovation.

Special thanks to my great friends and mentors Jerrard Gaertner and Ramkumar Krishnan, who have been instrumental to my passion and love of this industry.

Lindsay Langehoven is an experienced content specialist, creating and editing content in the communications and digital space for over 20 years. She has a particular passion for technology, data literacy, education, and empowerment. Her continual curiosity to discover and learn new things inspires her to craft the stories of today's human and technological evolution.

Table of Contents

3

Understanding the Four-Pillar Model   51

4

Implementing Organizational Data Literacy   69

5

Managing Your Data Environment   93

Part 2: Understanding How to Measure the Why, What, and How

6

Aligning with Organizational Goals   117

7

Designing Dashboards and Reports   139

8

Questioning the Data   183

9

Handling Data Responsibly   205

Part 3: Understanding the Change and How to Assess Activities

10

11

14

Appendix A – Templates   331

15

Appendix B – References   355

Index   361

Other Books You May Enjoy   372

Preface

Data is more than a commodity in our digital world. It is the ebb and flow of our modern existence. Individuals, teams, and enterprises that work confidently with data unlock a new realm of possibilities. The resultant agility, growth, and inevitable success have one origin: data literacy.

Data Literacy in Practice is a comprehensive guide that will build your understanding of data literacy basics, and accelerate your journey to independently uncovering insights with best practices, practical models, and real-world examples.

Discover the four-pillar model that underpins all data and analytics. Explore concepts such as measuring data quality, setting up a pragmatic data management environment, choosing the right graphs for your readers, and questioning your insights.

This guide is written by two data literacy pioneers, each with a thorough footprint within the data and analytics commercial world, including their lectures at top universities in the US and the Netherlands.

By the end of the book, you'll be equipped with a combination of skills and mindsets, along with tools and frameworks, that allow you to find insights and meaning within your data to enable effective and efficient data-informed decision-making.

Who this book is for

This book is for data analysts, data professionals, and data teams starting or wanting to accelerate their data literacy journey. Discover the skills and mindset you need to work independently with data, along with the tools and frameworks to build a solid knowledge base, and start making your data work for you today.

What this book covers

Chapter 1, The Beginning – The Flow of Data, covers the process of going from data to insights and action and shows how it is a multi-step process. Understanding this process is critical for anyone who is leveraging data to make decisions. This chapter will introduce the flow of data through this process, as well as common pitfalls that can get in the way at each step.

Chapter 2, Unfolding Your Data Journey, shows how, to be able to properly turn data into actionable insights, individuals need to be able to leverage multiple steps in analytics maturity: descriptive, diagnostic, predictive, prescriptive, and semantic. This chapter will introduce those steps with practical examples of what insights you can get from each step in the process.

Chapter 3, Understanding the Four-Pillar Model, looks at the four elementary pillars of data and analytics that we need to address in our businesses. Everybody knows and understands what data or a dashboard is. From that point of view, we see more demand and acceptance for data and analytics projects and the need for data literacy knowledge.

Chapter 4, Implementing Organizational Data Literacy, focuses on best practices related to organizational strategy and culture to support data literacy and data-informed decision-making. For individuals and organizations to be able to elicit insights and value from their data, there needs to be widespread adoption of data-informed decision-making. Despite many organizations having tools, technologies, and technical abilities, they are often unable to become data-informed due to their lack of a data literacy culture.

Chapter 5, Managing Your Data Environment, looks at how low-code/no-code solutions are maturing in an interesting way, giving all the benefits to their users in building rapid data lakes, data warehouses, and data pipelines. If we compare this technology against the more traditional solutions, we notice that we are able to get a better "race pace" in developing a data and analytics fundament. Due to the enormous growth (1.7 Mb of data is created every second for every person on earth) and complexity of data and data environments, a good and solid data strategy and taking care of a shared data vision was never as important as it is now. But in the last 2 years, there has been a shift occurring, and the necessity of a managed data environment has become more important.

Chapter 6, Aligning with Organizational Goals, explains how **Key Performance Indicators (KPIs)** are extremely vital in helping organizations understand how well they are performing in relation to their strategic goals and objectives. However, understanding what a KPI truly is versus what is just a measurement or a metric is important, along with understanding the right types of KPIs to track, including leading and lagging indicators.

Chapter 7, Designing Dashboards and Reports, talks about how visualizations provide a vital function in helping to describe situations. Visualizations can be used for both finding insights and also for communicating those insights to others. Choosing the right visualization depends on both the data you are using and what you are trying to show. This chapter will focus on choosing the right chart type, as well as designing charts to make it easier for people to interpret relevant parts.

Chapter 8, Questioning the Data, covers learning to ask questions, analyze outliers (supporting story by Dr. Snow – *Death in the Pit*), exclude bias, and so on so that you will be able to ask the right questions and develop your curiosity. You will understand the difference between correlation and causation. By addressing those topics, you will be able to understand what signals and noise are, and how to analyze the outliers by addressing hypothetical questions. You will be able to recognize the good, the bad, and the ugly insights.

Chapter 9, Handling Data Responsibly, explains how ethics is a science in which people try to qualify certain actions as right or wrong. However, there are no unequivocal answers to ethical questions because they are often very personal. Today, data and analytics are everywhere, touching every waking moment of our lives. Data and analytics, therefore, play an enormous role in our daily lives

– for example, Amazon knows what we buy and suggests other articles that we may be interested in; applications show us how we will look when we are older, and Netflix and Spotify know what we watch or listen to and give us suggestions of what else to watch or listen to.

Chapter 10, Turning Insights into Decisions, explores how many individuals and organizations come up with insights from their data. However, the process of turning insights into decisions and acting on them is much more difficult. This chapter focuses on what is required to support this step in the process, including introducing a six-step framework, which is both systemic and systematic. The chapter also includes how you can manage the change related to your decisions and how you can communicate effectively to all stakeholders via storytelling with data.

Chapter 11, Defining a Data Literacy Competency Framework, explains how the first step to increasing your own data literacy via education is to learn what exactly are the competencies that support data literacy. This chapter describes a data literacy competency framework, which includes the right hard skills, soft skills, and mindsets for data literacy. It also discusses how competencies have various levels, and you can progress up the levels as you become more experienced with data literacy. This chapter also focuses on best practices for getting started learning these competencies.

Chapter 12, Assessing Your Data Literacy Maturity, introduces how you can assess your own data literacy skills and then explains how to interpret the results of the assessment to personalize your educational journey. Before you begin your educational journey for data literacy, you should start by assessing your current level, and then using that assessment to understand what competencies to focus on next.

Chapter 13, Managing Data and Analytics Projects, explains the ways you can approach a data and analytics project and how you can manage it as a project leader and keep track of the business case and the value that it can bring. It all starts with the development of a data and analytics business case, in which you define the project scope, goals, and risks but also the beneficial value that it can bring to your organization. Data and analytics projects are often across organizations, departments, and processes of business units. They mostly contain a mix of strategic goals or have high political content and hidden stakeholders and have specific data and analytics risks that you should take care of.

Chapter 14, Appendix A – Templates, provides the materials to help you get started on your data literacy journey. All materials are also available on www.kevinhanegan.com.

Chapter 15, Appendix B – References, provides a summary of the references, books, and articles that we've read over the years. All of them inspired us and helped us to teach and write.

Conventions used

There are several text conventions used throughout this book.

Bold: Indicates a new term, an important word, or words that you see onscreen. For instance, words in menus or dialog boxes appear in **bold**. Here is an example: "In the **Create the default IAM role** pop-up window, select **Any S3 bucket**."

> **Tips or important notes**
> Appear like this.

Get in touch

Feedback from our readers is always welcome.

General feedback: If you have questions about any aspect of this book, email us at customercare@packtpub.com and mention the book title in the subject of your message.

Errata: Although we have taken every care to ensure the accuracy of our content, mistakes do happen. If you have found a mistake in this book, we would be grateful if you would report this to us. Please visit www.packtpub.com/support/errata and fill in the form.

Piracy: If you come across any illegal copies of our works in any form on the internet, we would be grateful if you would provide us with the location address or website name. Please contact us at copyright@packt.com with a link to the material.

If you are interested in becoming an author: If there is a topic that you have expertise in and you are interested in either writing or contributing to a book, please visit authors.packtpub.com.

Share Your Thoughts

Once you've read *Data Literacy in Practice* , we'd love to hear your thoughts! Scan the QR code below to go straight to the Amazon review page for this book and share your feedback.

https://packt.link/r/1-803-24675-8

Your review is important to us and the tech community and will help us make sure we're delivering excellent quality content.

Download a free PDF copy of this book

Thanks for purchasing this book!

Do you like to read on the go but are unable to carry your print books everywhere? Is your eBook purchase not compatible with the device of your choice?

Don't worry, now with every Packt book you get a DRM-free PDF version of that book at no cost.

Read anywhere, any place, on any device. Search, copy, and paste code from your favorite technical books directly into your application.

The perks don't stop there, you can get exclusive access to discounts, newsletters, and great free content in your inbox daily

Follow these simple steps to get the benefits:

1. Scan the QR code or visit the link below

https://packt.link/free-ebook/9781803246758

2. Submit your proof of purchase
3. That's it! We'll send your free PDF and other benefits to your email directly

Part 1: Understanding the Data Literacy Conceptss

Have you heard the buzz around data literacy? We define data literacy as a combination of skills and mindsets that allows individuals to find insights and meaning within their data to enable effective, efficient data-informed decision-making. During the first part of this book, we will help you understand the principles of being successful in your data literacy journey.

This section comprises the following chapters:

1

The Beginning – The Flow of Data

Data is the new gold of the 21st century, but what is it? Why is it important? Why should you know what data is and what you can do with it? More than ever, it's important to have data and make decisions based on that data. Everyone uses information every day.

In this chapter, we'll find out what data is, where it comes from, and how it's used to make decisions today. We'll also explain what data literacy is and why it's so important for both our everyday lives and our business lives. We'll show you some real-world examples and help you understand the basics of making decisions based on data or **Data-Informed Decision Making (DIDM)**.

By the end of this chapter, you'll recognize the most important parts of data and how we use it in our daily lives and at work. This will be explained with examples from the COVID-19 pandemic and stories from our own work lives.

In this chapter, we will cover the following topics:

- Understanding data in our daily lives
- Analyzing data
- An introduction to data literacy
- The organizational data flow

Understanding data in our daily lives

Data is a collection of observations or facts. Everything starts with data, and it's all around us. We know that every person on the planet creates 1.7 MB of data every second. Yet, many people are not even aware of all the data around them in their daily lives.

When we talk to people in our everyday lives, they always say, *We don't work with data. We know nothing at all about data.* But, let's look at the facts: data is all around us in the form of numbers, words, pictures, videos, maps, audio files, sensors, music, our phones, and even our wearable devices such as smartwatches and so on. Everything around us gives off data, and we don't even realize it most of the time. To give you an example, let's have a look at what kind of data we use when we wake up, as we show in *Figure 1.1*.

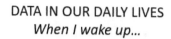

Figure 1.1 – Data in our daily lives

Let's think about this in terms of how we usually go about our workdays. We set an alarm, which is usually on our phones. When we pick up our phones, we create a movement, or *event*, and turn off the alarm. One of the next steps is to check the news and social media for information about the pandemic. This will help us get ready for the day to come. We'll also check the weather to see what it looks like and make sure we're wearing the right clothes for the day. We say *good morning* to Alexa or our Google home smart devices, and maybe we have a fancy coffeemaker that makes us a nice cup of coffee on its own. We might even be able to turn on the lights with an app on our phones. During coffee and breakfast, we check the traffic to decide whether to drive to work or take the bus or train.

Well, all these things or events are **data**. In fact, we have created a flow of data and don't even know it, and the story goes on: on the way to work, we can use our phones to check all kinds of things (we are connected to the world). Your social media followers on LinkedIn or Twitter; it's always fun to see how many people like your posts or replies. Let's be honest, when a message we post on LinkedIn gets more than 100 likes or has been seen more than 5,000 times, we get excited. When we like something, read an article, or share something on social media, we give information to the companies that make the social media software.

Analyzing data

In the process of making decisions, everyone now uses data. Let's look at an example for your next trip to Barcelona, which is a beautiful city in Spain. If you want to plan a summer trip to Spain and need a place to stay, you might look on Airbnb for a cool place to stay and set some parameters (called *filters* in the world of **data and analytics**).

Let's see what these filters, or parameters, are:

- The dates of our vacation period
- The number of people that are joining you
- Select a super host (we mostly do this because we have some experience)
- The area that you want to go to
- The type of accommodation
- Maybe even some special things that you want (swimming pool, air conditioning, and so on)

The following is a screenshot of Airbnb and how we set our filters to find a place to stay in Barcelona, for example:

Figure 1.2 – DIDM for the summer vacation using Airbnb

When the list has a lot of places you could go to, you might want to put the ones with the best prices or most reviews at the top, as shown in the following screenshot:

⭐ **4.62 · 71 reviews**

Cleanliness	4.7	Accuracy	4.6
Communication	4.7	Location	4.8
Check-in	4.7	Value	4.4

Cody
March 2022

Very nice place to stay in Barcelona with great restaurants and attractions near by!

Carlos
February 2022

This spot is located in a wonderful area of Barcelona that is safe, close to restaurants, and makes traveling to the nearby attractions easy. The metro line is nearby, there's a great bounty of restaurants to choose from and everything inside the room itself was as...

Show more >

Figure 1.3 – DIDM reviews to make a choice

From there, we'll read and think about some reviews, which will tell us a lot about the place we want to stay at. We will book a place to stay for our upcoming trip from there. In this case, we looked at data, sorted it, read about it, talked about it with the family, argued about it, and then decided where to stay during our vacation.

In this example, we've used data and the information that we found during our investigation (analysis) and created a decision together on where to go. In our line of work, we call this a data-informed decision.

To clarify the difference between data and information, data exists of data elements, and information is created from that data and put in context. We can't perceive anything from data unless we give meaning to that data. When we look at information, that is not the case.

Searching and finding information

First, we'll take a look at intentional or purposeful searching. Let's go over some of the things we've talked about in the first part. We noticed that we could answer some questions with a purpose and some answers we found by accident, or as we say, unintentionally. When we wake up, one of our first thoughts is mostly set on, *What should I wear today?* So, we checked the weather. This was done to answer the question, *What should I wear today?* The other question we were trying to answer with the data was about our upcoming trip to Barcelona, Spain. Our question, *Where should I stay in*

Barcelona? has been answered, and we're going to a nice place with lots of good reviews and a price we can afford. Those two questions had a purpose, a goal, and we were able to decide what to wear today and we found a cool place to stay.

Reading our social media messages on Twitter or other social media platforms, the news, and stories about the pandemic gives us information that has no purpose; we were just scrolling and reading without any purpose or meaning. We could also look at ads for clothes or other shopping items without meaning to. Those actions are unintentional; there is no underlying specific question that we want to answer.

This is where data literacy comes in. Everyone on earth has some data literacy skills, even if they don't know it. We all work with data, even if we don't know it.

Let's look at some of the apps we use every day to see what we mean. These apps use certain algorithms (using smart logic) to help organizations give us just the information they think we might be interested in:

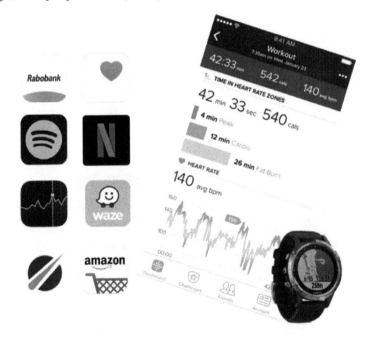

Figure 1.4 – How we use data during our days

Most of us use data and analytics every day in our personal lives. Here are some examples:

- **Personal health data**: The health app collects data about your health from your iPhone, Apple Watch, and other apps you already use. This way, you can see all your progress in one place. Health apps keep track of how far you walk, run, and how many steps you take. And if you have an Apple Watch, it keeps track of your activity data automatically.

- **Financial transactions**: A bank can tell you where you spend your money, but they can also use simple algorithms to check your credit card for any unusual charges. When a transaction is made and they think it might be a fraud because of their smart algorithms, they immediately block your credit card and send you a message telling you that someone tried to use your credit card in a fraudulent way. Also, don't forget that on the stock market, people buy and sell stocks by using information gathered from data.

- **Amazon**: When you shop on Amazon, it shows you products that it thinks you'll be interested in based on a lot of complicated math. As an example, when we ordered a whiteboard, two suggestions about whiteboard markers and a special wiper for cleaning the whiteboard popped up on our screens right away. All of this was done because we asked for *a whiteboard* as our first order.

- **Spotify**: It is used all over the world and it knows exactly what kind of music you like and gives you a list of your most played songs at the end of every year. It can even tell you what to listen to next and invite you to new podcasts based on what you've listened to in the past, among other things.

- **Netflix**: It has more than 203.67 million subscribers around the world. Since it started, it have become the most popular platform for streaming content. It grew even more than usual during the COVID-19 pandemic.

  How did it become so successful? It used sophisticated data and analytics, which helped in many ways, such as:

  - It was able to give users personalized suggestions for movies and TV shows

  - It was able to figure out how popular new content would be before it was approved (or not)

  - It could make marketing content such as trailers and thumbnail images to make the user experience more personal

  - It was able to improve its own production planning in-house

  - And, of course, it was able to improve business and technical decision making in general

- **Your Garmin watch**: The Garmin watch tells us how many steps we've taken (we experience it as a significant motivator to reach the 10K steps every day). Even though they say it's not 100% accurate, our nights of sleep are tracked. We can see when we're in REM sleep, when we're awake, or when we're sleeping in a light state. It also keeps track of our heart rate, how many times we climbed stairs (or mountains), and so on. It gives us a full picture of what we do 24 hours a day, including our stress level, heart rate, and how we do sports, in a fancy way.

  When we use it with an app such as My Fitness Pal, for example, we can link our data with the food we eat during the day, as shown in the following *Figure 1.5*:

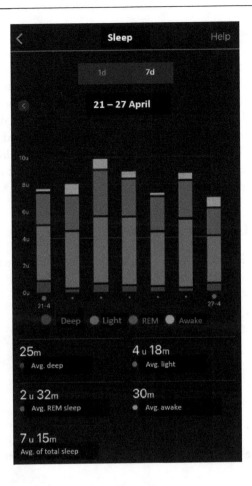

Figure 1.5 – Tracking your sleep

As you can see, all the activities that are measured serve a purpose, such as shopping, keeping an eye on our health, listening to our favorite music (and making playlists that we can share), and last but not least, watching movies and TV shows that we like. In *Chapter 9, Handling Data Responsibly*, we will talk about how we work with data, what you need to watch out for, and the risks that can happen when we share our *own* data.

Then, we get unintentional data use unintentionally. We use platforms such as Facebook, Instagram, LinkedIn, and Twitter to share news about our work or even our personal lives. We love that people are reading, liking, and even sharing our messages. Let's be honest, we get excited when people like something we've written.

However, reading the news through different apps on our devices (iPad, tablet, or laptop) to stay up to date on what's going on in the world is also an unintentional way we use data, especially since the COVID-19 pandemic hit us in 2020.

What does this intentional and unintentional data use mean? And how does it pertain to data literacy? Is data literacy the same for everyone? Well to be honest that depends what your role is within the Data and Analytics field of work. For a data analyst it would mean understanding the data related to a certain process, or transactional system, the tools that an organization uses and so on. For a data scientist, it would mean understanding the algorithms and data that is needed to create their models. For a marketing professional or a company that wants to grow, it is again different. The marketeer needs to understand how to read the created information from the data used from the website, social media platforms, and so on. But for someone who wants to take a vacation in Spain, the information they need is completely different. So, it depends on the role, the position that you are in when it comes to the understanding and level of Data Literacy.

An introduction to data literacy

So what is data literacy, and what does it mean to know how to use data? If we type `data literacy` into Google's search box, we will get a lot of results.

Figure 1.6 – Google search for data literacy

We and others think that the definition of data literacy is: *The ability to work with, analyze & argue with data…*

From our point of view, we'd like to add that *it means how a person uses data and understands the world around him (or her)*. It's also a matter of behavior, that people can work with data not because they must, but because they want to!

In his article *The Art of Questioning*, Kevin Hanegan explains the vital role questions play in data literacy:

"Asking the right questions of your data and knowing what you want to find is a key part of getting insights from your data that lead to specific actions."

Data isn't just black and white; you can do a lot with it. So, two people who look at the same data can come to very different conclusions. This is because a lot depends on the problem you're trying to solve and how you go about solving it. This is where communication comes in as a key soft skill. For that decision-making process, we need both technical skills (hard skills) and soft skills such as collaboration, organizational sensitivity, communication, and so on.

We'll use the pandemic, the news, the data, and the choices we and others had to make as examples in the next section and the later chapters.

The COVID-19 pandemic

To start learning about data literacy, we could look at some examples we've gathered from the news and different government organizations around the world.

When we look at the headlines in this picture, we might be surprised to see that only 2,000 of the 550,000 NHS workers were tested. And the headline next to it: "As two more brave doctors die, the same headline tells a story that only 0.16% of NHS staff have been tested for the virus and that the testing station is empty."

At first, we were all scared about what was going on in our world. There was no information about the topic, and there were no tests available. We saw every day, sad and horrifying news and stories told of people dying and being taken to the hospital, and that hospitals were full of people suffering from COVID-19.

Figure 1.7 – COVID-19 headlines

If we read those headlines without questioning them, it paints a scary picture. But what if you asked questions such as:

- Why are these numbers like this?
- What does *being tested* mean?
- What is a positive or a negative test?
- What does the *0.16%* mean?
- Compared with what?
- Can I trust this message?
- Which sources did they use? And so on.

All of this is based on the idea that we need to think carefully about what we think and how we should act on that. When we look at some news stories about the COVID-19 pandemic, we can see that there are many kinds of articles. Some are loud (with big headlines) and others are written in a calm way. It depends on which newspaper you read.

A basic understanding of data literacy

We'll walk through how to read a news story so we can start to understand how to use data to better understand the world around us. In this made-up example, we see how we can interact with data when we read the news online or in a paper news magazine.

Note that this news article is a mix of fact and fiction.

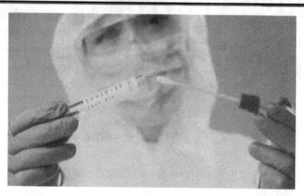

Amsterdam News
Latest news & updates

Tuesday March, 2nd 2021

x x
x x x
x x

Peter Woodward

Staggering increase in infections continues, the number of new corona patients in hospitals fluctuates!

The dramatic increase in infections continues, and the number of new corona patients in hospitals fluctuates, the number of new corona cases continues to rise dramatically now that the Omicron variant is most common.

Between Tuesday morning and Wednesday morning, 32,149 positive tests were reported. That is the highest number ever for a Wednesday. The number of new admissions of corona patients to the nursing wards has fluctuated in recent days. The experts say that most likely one of the reasons the numbers are rising this much is related to the increased testing capacity and the number of tests taken.

In the past seven days, the National Institute for Public Health was informed that the corona virus has been diagnosed 209,073 times. That equates to an average of 29,868 positive tests per day, the highest level ever. They even found in some areas a dramatic rise of 45%. This average is rising for the fifteenth day in a row during the COVID pandemic.

Figure 1.8 – News article about the COVID-19 pandemic

From what we can see and read, this article seems to be written for a wide range of people. If you look a little closer, the article also has data elements. These facts and figures can be hard to understand, and someone who doesn't have the right skills to do so might miss some important points in this news story. They might get the news wrong, and some people might even be scared by what they read. In all honesty, the same thing has happened all over the world. Most likely, everyone who reads this kind of article could have some questions such as:

- Am I safe?

- Should I stay in my house and not go outside?

- Shall I order my groceries online?

- Can I visit my mom and dad?

- Shall we invite people to our houses or not? And so on.

If we take out the information such as the figures we see in this news story, it might make more sense.

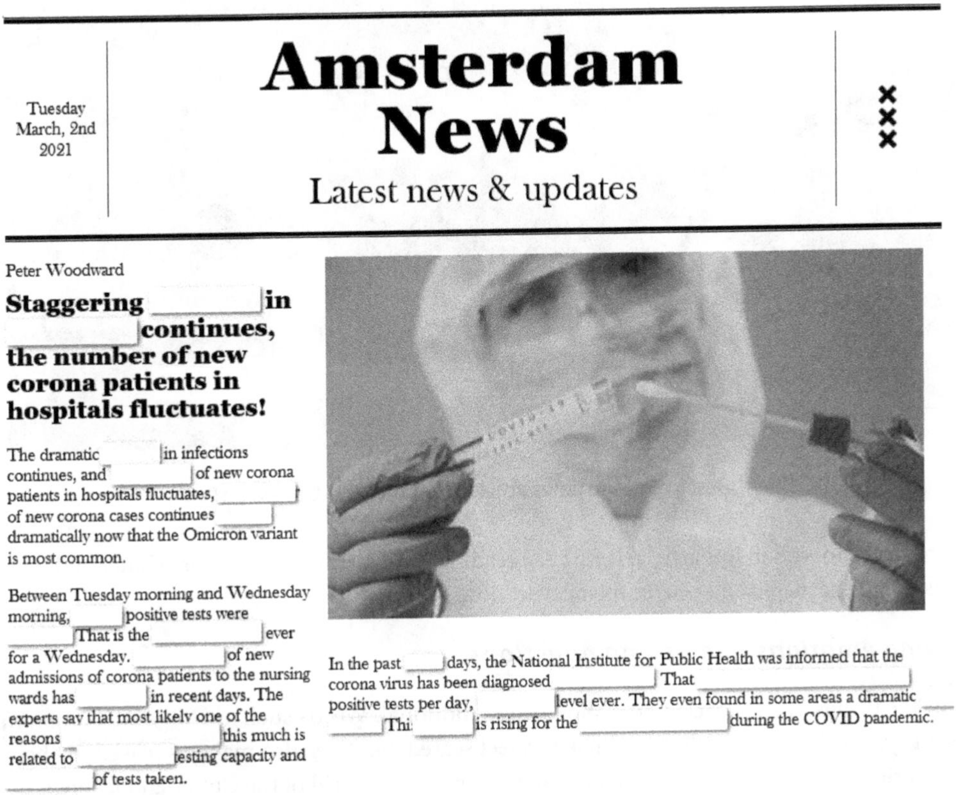

Amsterdam News
Latest news & updates

Tuesday
March, 2nd
2021

Peter Woodward

Staggering _____ in _____ continues, the number of new corona patients in hospitals fluctuates!

The dramatic _____ in infections continues, and _____ of new corona patients in hospitals fluctuates, _____ of new corona cases continues dramatically now that the Omicron variant is most common.

Between Tuesday morning and Wednesday morning, _____ positive tests were _____ That is the _____ ever for a Wednesday. _____ of new admissions of corona patients to the nursing wards has _____ in recent days. The experts say that most likely one of the reasons _____ this much is related to _____ testing capacity and _____ of tests taken.

In the past _____ days, the National Institute for Public Health was informed that the corona virus has been diagnosed _____ That _____ positive tests per day, _____ level ever. They even found in some areas a dramatic _____ This _____ is rising for the _____ during the COVID pandemic.

Figure 1.9 – News article removing data elements

We would understand more if we read the news article carefully and paid more attention to the facts.

We can read that the *"new positive cases are increasing."* But as stated in the article, that *"could be the result of the expansion of test locations."* We can draw the first conclusion that the increase in people who tested positive could be the result of expanding the test capacity.

Figure 1.10 – Questioning the news article to understand the message better.

But there's more to read in this article. If we keep reading, we'll see that there's more clutter and noise. Let's talk about the mess and noise in the next section.

Removing emotions and asking questions

Some of the things in the article being shown are emotional. Words such as *staggering*, *dramatic*, *dramatically*, and *highest level ever* can make us feel scared, but they also make us biased. By being able to get rid of these parts, we can read the article again and get rid of the clutter and feelings.

Most of the time, we start by coming up with questions and then looking for answers (or feedback) that will help us make decisions. Knowing which data is useful for answering our questions is also an important part of our data literacy skills. In this situation, we could ask things such as the following:

- How does the pandemic affect me?

- Can I go and visit my parents or my family?

- What do I have to take care of?

- Will our business survive?

- What are *some areas* and is this here in my hometown?

- What is a test, and what does being positive or negative mean? And so on.

As questions are an amazingly important aspect of our data literacy skill set, you will find more information in *Chapter 8, Questioning the Data.*

We use and see a lot of data in our everyday lives. Everyone needs to know how to read and understand data. Even during a pandemic and while reading the news, we need to be able to tell what information is useful and what is not. This is what we call *critical thinking.* Critical thinking is part of data literacy; it is the ability to question the logic of arguments or assumptions and examine evidence in order to determine whether a claim is true, false, or uncertain. In *Chapter 8, Questioning the Data,* we talk more about *questioning.* When COVID-19 hit us, at first, we mostly felt fear, hopelessness, and uncertainty, and we had many questions. As soon as the first cases came in, the first people were taken to the hospital or even the ICU. During the pandemic, we realized that we really needed to understand what data was and how we could use it to decide what to do or how to respond to the crisis. During this global crisis, we felt like we had to find out what was going on right away.

We needed to know and understand what was going on around the world. For example, we needed to know how many tests were being done, how many people were losing their jobs, and so on.

During the crisis, it was hard because some people also gave us false information. Some said all sorts of things that didn't make sense. In the following figure, you can see a picture that our friend Joe Warbington took of his TV.

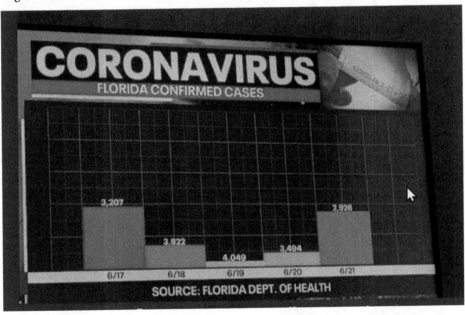

Figure 1.11 – Misleading graphs on TV

You may have noticed that the graph is a little strange, with high numbers and a small bar and low numbers and a bigger bar. We don't see any other information or context on the axes. People take the graph for granted instead of being critical and asking questions, which is a worry.

Noticing the problems with the graph and identifying that there are things wrong with it are an important part of your data literacy skills.

From here, we can learn the basics of data and how we can use it in our daily lives. Organizations also need data, and they need to know how to use data and be literate in data. So, let's look at the organizational data flow next to better understand this.

The organizational data flow

All beginnings are hard, and this is equally true when a company wants to start with **data-informed decision making** (**DIDM**). There are sometimes reports that give a general idea of how well the organization is doing financially. People often think, *We have some Excel reports, that's enough*. But when reality hits, they realize they need more information (for example, not only information about financial matters).

When new data projects start or new plans are made to add more information to existing reports, the projects take too long, the people who wrote the hard macros are no longer available, or the project methods are no longer good. With a *big bang* scenario, projects will take too long and more parts will be added as the project goes on. This is called **scope creep**.

Another common way organizations limit the effectiveness of their data is when business users in organizations just use the numbers on the **Key Performance Indicators** (**KPI**) reports as they are. In *Chapter 6, Aligning with Organizational Goals*, we help you understand the KPIs and how they should align with the strategic objectives. These business users do things such as hear, see, and be quiet. They seem to think, *Oh no, that's too bad. Let's hope the numbers are better tomorrow, next week, or next month*. To be honest, this is still a very serious problem in organizations. Most of the time, it's because business users can't make decisions that are based on facts. Many times, it is even worse when we don't know how to answer business questions even when we are in business and can't make a decision as simple as how to read graphs and reports or how to analyze. Still, it's important to keep track of your organization's goals and help people understand the insights that can be drawn from data. This will help them make decisions based on the data and not get lost in the data-insights jungle.

As mentioned at the beginning of this chapter, we have so much data in this digital age. Our data mountain is growing every day (1.7 MB per second per person on this planet), and data can help us be successful in what we do. So, we need to look at how information moves through an organization and what kind of knowledge and processes need to be taken care of. The following diagram represents a visualization of how the data grows, covering the flow of data and which disciplines are involved.

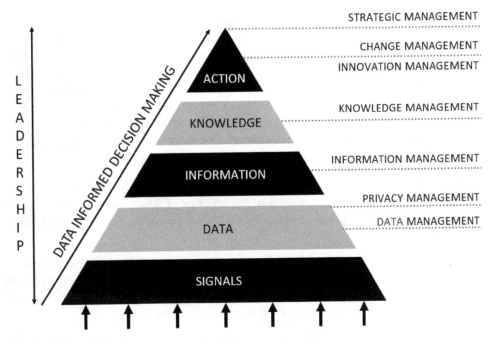

Figure 1.12 – The flow of data

If we look at how data-informed decision making works, we can see that it all starts with signals. There are a lot of signals around us right now. These signals are turned into data, and then that data becomes information (something we can do something with), and finally, knowledge. We'll use the following simple example of a traffic light to show how this works:

1. **Signal**: We are receiving light waves in our eyes.
2. **Data**: The data that we receive or see is that the light is red.
3. **Information**: The information that we have is that we know it's a traffic light.
4. **Knowledge**: The knowledge that we have is that we know we must stop.
5. **Action**: The action is that we will stop in front of the traffic light as we don't want to have an accident or get fined for passing the red traffic light.

One thing that can hinder the ideal flow of data in an organization is where data is stored and how it is managed. Data is kept in many places, for example, POS systems, CRM systems, and Excel documents, which keep track of sales data, marketing data, and financial data respectively. Multiple source systems are usually not a problem in smaller organizations, but in larger ones, they could be a problem and a potential risk.

When organizations don't pay attention to data management for simple things, such as different types of addresses or different definitions of fields, this could cause problems in how data flows through the organization. Data governance needs a place as well within your processes when we think of the usage of data. Do not confuse data governance with data management. Data management is about the day-to-day business when we use data in a company, whereas data governance looks at how the company can make more money using data in the future. The earlier *Figure 1.12* shows the different disciplines that an organization could use to set up a data and analytics environment, not just from a technical point of view, but also from a business point of view. To ensure data is managed effectively, businesses need the right skills and processes in place:

- **Data management**: Businesses deal with a lot of data. That data needs to be managed well so everyone can use it effectively. It is necessary to take care of things such as data entry, data registers, data quality, and so on. Today, we call this the *data office*, and a chief data officer usually runs it.

- **Privacy management**: Keeping personal, customer, or proprietary information safe and secure is vital. Privacy laws exist in many countries, covering things such as the right way to handle data. Most of the time, a data protection officer takes care of this. Later in this book, there will be more about privacy and how to handle data in an ethical and secure way.

- **Information management**: Information management is an important part of turning data into the insights that are needed. There are many ways to describe information management, but we think this is the best one: information management is the process that ensures that the information needs arising from various processes of an organization are translated into insights necessary for measuring and achieving the organizational objectives.

- **Knowledge management**: Businesses need to manage their information and knowledge effectively to avoid wasting people's time searching for the right information. Too much knowledge is stored in our (collective) brains, so we need to register and collect knowledge and plan for the future.

  On a small side note, some organizations in the Netherlands have a staff with an average age of 48. That means that information about processes, systems, designs, and other things needs to be kept for the future.

- **Change management**: Change management is a systemic approach to dealing with changes in a business. Every new dashboard, report, or change to an existing dashboard or report is overall a change, and we need to help the management and business stakeholders accept the change and work with the new dashboards and reports. There is more in this book about this subject.

- **Strategic management**: Strategic management is how an organization manages and achieves its overall goals. Data and analytics need to be embraced by the management or board of directors, and they need to set an example for the whole staff. If the people in charge don't take part in data and analytics projects, the idea will fail.

As you read through this book, there may be many concepts that are new to you. We'll help you gain a better understanding through case studies, such as the next one.

Intermezzo 1 – Is data management necessary?

This first story is from an organization that has a lot of complex systems. This organization wanted to set up a new source system for their registrations. Moreover, it was necessary to build connections between other systems. Of course, one of them was the connection to the data warehouse system.

Because no data management or data governance was in place, or no register for data elements was available in conversations that were held about common things such as how we arrange the connections, which protocols we need, and so on.

It would have been much better if we would have talked about the definition of attributes, formats of date fields, or other elementary data fields.

In fact (and this is something we say a lot during lectures and presentations), we all should speak the same data language! When one source system is in a different language than another system, we will run into problems when we want to extract data (or even connect data) or use data for dashboards and reports. You will get into problems if data management or data governance is not in place.

P.S. All the stories that are written in this book are real-life stories, and out of respect for the organizations, we will sometimes not mention any names.

The DIDM journey

Anyway, if we have data and are willing to use any tool, and we want to work with it, the data becomes *information*. Information management is an important part of the process because of this. In the end, information will become knowledge if we are willing to take in the information and go on that journey to understand the insights. The ideal flow of data or data journey will eventually look like this:

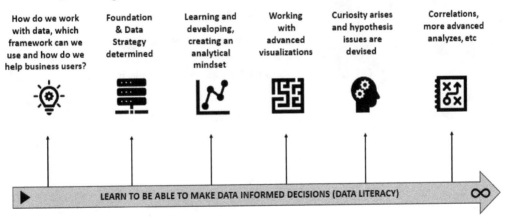

Figure 1.13 – The data-informed decision-making journey

The hardest part is to act on and make decisions based on what you've learned. This happens a lot in the places where we work or have worked. As we've already said, when the insights are actionable but we forget to deal with the change or forget to put them into action in our projects, we tend to take the insights for granted.

But how do you move forward? You can do this by analyzing the insights in small steps and slowly learning that data literacy and taking action go hand in hand.

In this book, we'll show you how to work with data, how to read and evaluate insights (be critical and ask questions), and how to make decisions based on what you learn. You must go on a journey, which starts with figuring out your (data) strategy, working with that data and gaining insights, and eventually starting to think about hypothetical questions and using more complex ways to show data. Put that dot on the horizon, start small, and grow quickly.

In the next section, we'll tell the story of *The Oakland A's* who did a great job of using data and analytics.

The success story of The Oakland A's

Let's go through the success story of *The Oakland A's* where we describe their journey when they started working with data-informed decision making. This story is a true, real-life story and they even created a movie about this success story, named *Moneyball*.

Billy Beane, general manager of the Oakland Athletics, is devastated by the team's loss to the New York Yankees in the 2001 American League Division Series. Some of the star players left the team and Beane needed to assemble a new competitive team for the 2002 competition with a limited budget.

During a scouting visit to the Cleveland Indians, Beane meets Peter Brand, a young Yale economics graduate with some amazing ideas about evaluating players.

Using Brand's method, Beane signed up undervalued players and traded another player.

Figure 1.14 – The Oakland A's

People are biased, and one of the things said in the movie was about Chad Bradford, who is one of the best pitchers. Bradford was not chosen by any big team, but with the analysis that Brand performed, they found out that he was highly underestimated; why? Because he threw the ball in a funny way (as they say in the movie, because he throws funny). Based on the analysis, they hired Bradford and he became a successful player for the team. This is a big reason why we're telling this story. He didn't get picked because of bias. But if you looked at his batting scores, he did well, so he was one of the most undervalued players.

The scouts for the Athletics didn't like the plan Beane had made, and in the end, Beane fired the head scout. Beane stuck with the new plan, and even though they lost the first 10 games, critics wrote of the new way of working with data.

As Brand says, math and statistics get rid of bias, and to be successful, you need to get things back to one number (one fact, one measure). They traded some players again, and then the team started to win.

The Athletics broke a record by winning 20 games in a row. Hatteberg's walk-off home run helped them do this. Beane tells Brand that he won't be happy until they win the World Series with their system and change baseball.

Fun fact

Billy Beane has helped a Dutch soccer team improve its statistical approach and use data to make decisions about players. He even bought some shares in the Dutch soccer team AZ Alkmaar.

Summary

After reading this chapter, we know more about data literacy and how we can use it in our everyday lives. With this skill set, we can do a better job of responding to the things we read and see around us, such as the pandemic; it also helps us decide how to respond in these conditions. We used an example to talk about how to get rid of noise, mess, and feelings.

Then, we talked about how data moves through an organization and which disciplines should be looked at. We talked about how these different fields can help make data and analytics projects successful.

We ended with a story about a baseball team in the United States. You learned that they became a successful team by using data, letting the insights speak for themselves, and taking bias out of decision making.

In the next chapter, we'll talk about the journey an organization can take. In practice, a journey doesn't always go as planned. Most of the time, we start with plain business intelligence (or performance management), but some organizations start with data science or advanced analytics. The problem is that these kinds of organizations don't even measure how well they're meeting their goals.

Unfolding Your Data Journey

Data is everywhere, both within and outside of your organization, and as we discussed in *Chapter 1, The Beginning – The Flow of Data*, it is growing rapidly. Because of recent global crises, the worlds digital transformation has advanced several years in a short period of time.. From this vantage point, we can see that organizations are leveraging the value of data more than ever before to strengthen their market position, increase profitability, reduce costs, and so on.

The structure of your organization, as well as the processes and systems in place, determines how you can make the best use of data within it. We know from experience that data and the information generated from that data can help your organization be more effective and efficient. The road to a data and analytics transformation can be started by properly applying those insights. In this manner, you will be able to develop into a high-performing organization that makes use of data and analytics.

To be able to properly turn data into actionable insights, individuals need to be able to leverage multiple steps in analytics maturity: descriptive, diagnostic, predictive, prescriptive, and semantic. This chapter will introduce those steps with practical examples of what insights you can get from each step in the process.

In this chapter, we will discuss the following topics:

- Growing toward data and analytics maturity
- Descriptive analyses and the data path to maturity
- Understanding diagnostic analysis
- Understanding predictive analysis
- Understanding prescriptive analysis
- Can data save lives? A success story

Growing toward data and analytics maturity

When organizations can provide context and meaning to their internal and external data, they can put data in place for data-informed decision-making.

With 1.7 megabytes per second per person, our data mountain is growing (*Chapter 1, The Beginning – The Flow of Data*). According to research (`statista.com`), the world will generate more than 180 zettabytes of digital data by 2025. We have added a table so that you are able to understand the data growth from kilobyte to yottabyte:

Name	Value in bytes
Kilobyte (KB)	1,000
Megabyte (MB)	1,000,000
Gigabyte (GB)	1,000,000,000
Terabyte (TB)	1,000,000,000,000
Petabyte (PT)	1,000,000,000,000,000
Exabyte (EB)	1,000,000,000,000,000,000
Zettabyte (ZB)	1,000,000,000,000,000,000,000
Yottabyte (YB)	1,000,000,000,000,000,000,000,000

Figure 2.1 – Understanding data growth

The growth was higher than previously expected, caused by the increased demand due to the COVID-19 pandemic; more people worked and studied from home and used home entertainment options more often.

Having a large amount of data to use is not a goal in and of itself; the ultimate goal is to use that data and get that information from the data mountain to make data-informed decisions.

In reality, the journey is frequently different; we see companies begin with **business intelligence (BI)** without a plan and fail, or get stuck and remain at a basic level. Sometimes it's even worse, and organizations begin with advanced analytics, or they fly in a team of data scientists, while others have no idea what is required, what it is, or whether the organizational objectives are measurable or defined.

To start with data and generate valuable insights is a difficult step; it all begins with some intriguing questions:

- What resources do we have?

- Should we use Excel or invest in tools?

- What data is available, and how can we use it?

- Where can I find the meaning of the data that will be used?

- What do I want to create or build?

Data projects (*Chapter 13, Managing Data and Analytics Projects*) include a strategic component as well as a technical component (*Chapter 6, Aligning with Organizational Goals*). Data and analytics projects, as with other maturity models, can be divided into several levels. There are numerous models, and we use a combination of them to highlight the differences in the following diagram to explain the path to analytical maturity:

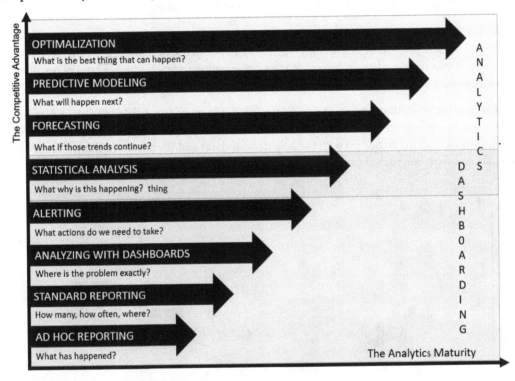

Figure 2.2 – Introducing analytical maturity

On the vertical axis, we note that working with various aspects of data and analytics can lead to a certain level of competitive advantage. However, all must grow, specifically in terms of analytics maturity as shown on the horizontal axis.

To begin, some level of BI maturity is required before investing in the use of advanced analytics or data science. It is necessary to investigate the commercial value of that journey toward **artificial intelligence (AI)**. Do organizations do this solely because others do it? This last approach is just like children often trying to get into the same streams or fields/classes in their schools only because their friends have opted for that class without knowing or understanding their own choices, skills, and aptitudes.

Descriptive analyses and the data path to maturity

To be truly transformative and use data and analytics throughout your organization, you must prioritize the following factors:

- Your organization's data and analytics ambitions, which will define your analytical maturity and allow you to be transformational

- Your organizational data and analytics goals must be aligned in order to progress from a transactional focus to adding business value to your organization

We will walk you through the maturity model's various stages using *Figure 2.3*. Each step has its own power, explanation, but—most importantly—actions and peculiarities, and the diagram represents the steps that you should take as a person or as an organization to reach a higher level of maturity, advancing in data and analytics.

You'll notice that we distinguish two areas, and we can define more as our field of work in data and analytics grows and changes on a daily basis. However, for the purposes of this book, we will limit ourselves to BI (looking backward with the help of your data) and the advanced things we can do with data and analytics, such as (advanced) analytics and data and science:

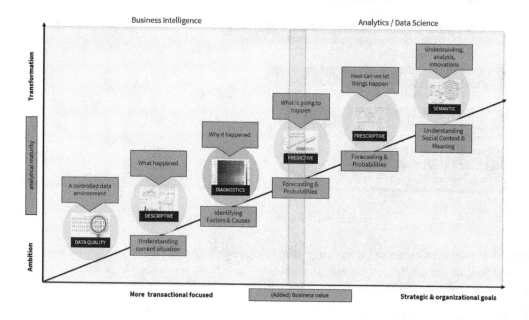

Figure 2.3 – The different phases in the world of data and analytics

In the following paragraphs, we will walk you through the various steps and describe the typical *data analytics* questions that arise during those phases. This way, you'll be able to understand the various types of questions you'd like to answer for your data-driven decision-making processes.

Understanding descriptive analysis

Within organizations (and even within departments or teams), it usually begins with basic questions such as the following:

- What is our debtors' payment behavior (how long is an invoice open)?
- When and how often are medicines registered (or dispensed)?
- How many people are admitted to the **intensive care unit** (**ICU**) and how many to the nursing wards?
- How much did I sell in the last month?
- What is the total number of incidents reported to our service desk?
- How many invoices have we sent in the last month, how much is still owed to our debtors, and what is the total amount owed?

These are simple but valid questions for any organization embarking on its journey into the wonderful world of BI. This step is also known as **descriptive analytics** or **descriptive analyses**, and the central questions are these: *What happened? How did we do in the previous month? Have we sold enough items, or have we converted enough?*

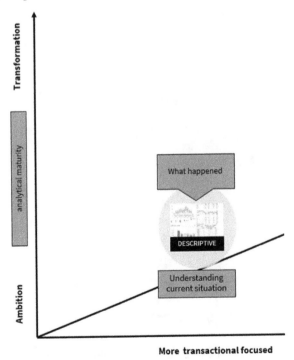

Figure 2.4 – The first step of the data journey: the phase of descriptive analytics

Most organizations begin with simple tools to visualize these fundamental questions, which is entirely legitimate. Although this is the most basic form of BI, now is the time to plan ahead of time, before a maze of reports supported by the most complex macros or coding emerges (and it is eventually no longer manageable).

During this phase, we must master the differences in terms that we will be able to use when analyzing or developing our first insights:

- **Variable**: This is a characteristic number or quantity that can be counted or measured. A characteristic or number is also known as a data item. Some examples are age, gender, business income, expenses, country of birth, class grades, eye color, and vehicle type.

- **Mean**: Also known as the average of all numbers in a given set of numbers.

- **Median**: The median is the midpoint of a sorted list of numbers in a set. If there are a lot of outliers, this median is a better description of the data.

- **Mode**: The mode is the most common number in a set of numbers.

- **Outliers**: An outlier is a number that lies outside of the majority of the other numbers in a set.

- **Aggregations**: Aggregated data is data that has been summarized using a method such as mean, median, mode, sum, and so on. It is the gathering of several things into a group.

When we look at the possible aggregations in a visualization, an important thing to remember here is that we must take care of the aggregations and thoroughly understand them. During the first step of the data journey, we will go over some examples to give you more insight into the most commonly used aggregations.

The first example is displayed in *Figure 2.5*, where we describe the aggregation *average*:

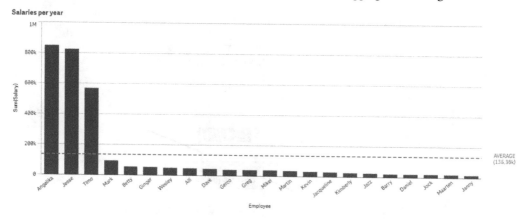

Figure 2.5 – Describing the aggregation: average

When we want to look into a company's annual salaries to see what we could ask if we wanted to work for them, if we want to calculate the **mean** or **average**, we must be aware of the differences with the outliers. In our example, we calculated the average by adding all of the values in our list (including the higher salaries) and dividing it by the number of occurrences. In this case, we had a total of $2.975 million, which we divided by the number of occurrences, 22 in this case, to get an average salary of 135.36K.

That is an excellent salary; we can live with it. However, if we are not aware of the outliers in higher salaries, we may be easily duped. So, we'll go a step further and use another aggregation, the **median**, which is the number in the middle of a sorted list of numbers. In *Figure 2.6*, we display the value of the aggregation median:

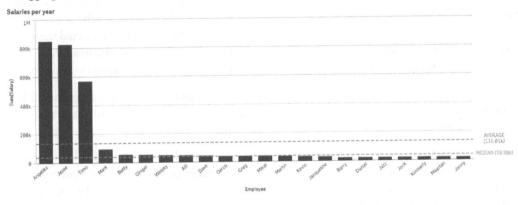

Figure 2.6 – Describing the aggregation: median

When we look at the median salary, we can see that it is set at 39.98K per year, which is way lower than the company's average salary. This is shown in *Figure 2.6*.

The **mode**, or the most common number in a set of numbers, is the third aggregation. In *Figure 2.7*, the third aggregation, mode, is displayed, and in one blink of an eye, we can see the different outcomes of those three types of aggregations:

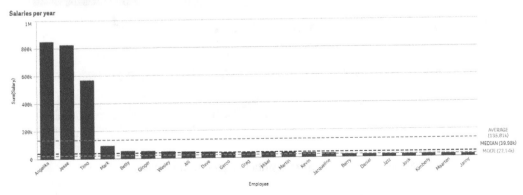

Figure 2.7 – Describing the aggregation: mode

Even the most common year salary is 22.14K, which is a completely different number than the median (the middle) or average (the total sum divided by the number of occurrences).

After showing you those three different aggregations, you will have noticed the variance in outcomes. This is an important lesson—you always have to take care of the type of aggregation that you want to use. The next important element is outliers, which we will discuss in the next section and explain with an example displayed in *Figure 2.8*.

Outliers are individual values that differ significantly from the majority of the other values in a set. Identifying outliers is always one of the first things a person should look for when trying to get a sense of the data. The definition of an outlier is somewhat subjective. Many people define an outlier as any data point that is three standard deviations or more away from the dataset's mean. A standard deviation indicates the degree of dispersion in a certain dataset. It indicates how much the observed values deviate from the mean (or the average). As an example, suppose we have collected the ages of five students. The standard deviation then gives a picture of the age differences between these five students. A small standard deviation indicates that the students come from the same (age) group.

Early identification allows you to understand what they are, investigate why they are outliers, and then decide whether or not to exclude them from the analysis. However, it can also assist you in identifying elements that you can address to solve 80% of your problems (*Pareto analysis*).

Figure 2.8 depicts a debt collection dashboard, where we used a visualization known as a distribution plot. It's simple to spot an outlier with this type of visualization. In our example, a customer has 44 outstanding invoices totaling €2,281,200.00. We can easily find and solve a problem with this debtor if we can find those types of outliers:

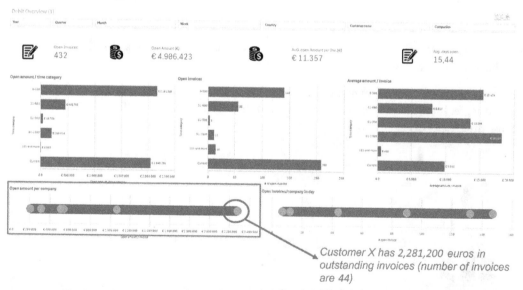

Customer X has 2,281,200 euros in outstanding invoices (number of invoices are 44)

Figure 2.8 – The usage of a distribution plot to find outliers

In this section, we discussed aggregations such as mean, average, median, mode, and outliers. What we've learned from those examples is that we should be aware of the differences in how those values are calculated, as well as how we can easily spot outliers that we can focus on to solve problems or find the cause of those outliers.

Identifying qualitative or quantitative data

Quantitative implies something that is measurable and can be counted in numerical terms (**quantity**—something you can count or measure). Qualitative data cannot be counted or measured, and it is not numerical (**quality**—categorical data that cannot be counted or measured).

In fact, data (or variables) has different types that we must consider; when we begin analyzing, we must be aware of those different data types and how to use them.

Let's have a visualization of how data can be branched into qualitative and quantitative categories and further categorized into nominal, ordinal, interval, and so on:

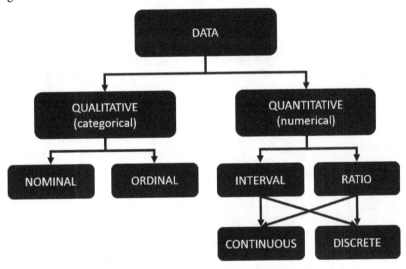

Figure 2.9 – The different forms of data types

Let's go through each category present in the preceding diagram:

- **Qualitative data**: Examples of qualitative data include gender, sales region, marketing channel, and other things that can be classified or divided into groups or categories.

- **Quantitative data**: Examples of quantitative data include height, weight, age, and other numerically measurable items.

- **Nominal data**: This is qualitative data that does not have a sense of sequential order, such as gender, car brands, fruit types, people's names, nationalities, and so on.

- **Ordinal data**: This is qualitative data with a sense of order. A good mnemonic for ordinal data is to remember that ordinal sounds like order, and the order of the variables (or data) is important. Consider the following examples: one to five, from good to best, or small, medium, to large.

- **Interval data**: Interval data is useful and enjoyable because it considers both the order and the difference between your variables. Interval data is quantitative data that has no absolute zero (the lack of absolute point zero makes comparisons of direct magnitudes impossible). You can add and subtract from interval data, but not multiply or divide it—temperatures in °C, for example. 20°C is warmer than 10°C, and the difference is 10 degrees. The angle between 10 and 0 is also 10 degrees.

  To remember the difference between the meanings of interval, consider *interval* as *the space between*. So, you're concerned not only with the order of variables but also with the values in between them.

- **Ratio data**: This is a type of quantitative data that has an absolute zero. You can multiply and divide ratio data, in addition to adding and subtracting. Height, for example, can be measured in centimeters, meters, or inches of feet. There is no such thing as a negative height.

- **Continuous data**: This is quantitative data that is not limited to a single value, as discrete data is. Continuous data can be divided and measured to as many decimal places as desired. A person's height, for example, is classified as continuous data because a person can be 5 feet and 5 inches tall, as can the weight of a car, the temperature, or the speed of an airplane.

- **Discrete data**: Discrete data exists when values in a dataset are countable and can only take certain values—for instance, the number of students in a class, the number of fingers on your right hand, the number of players needed in a team, the number of children you have, and so on.

Along with understanding and using the right data terminology, here's an example showing the importance of using the right data tools.

Intermezzo – Excel as a source can go wrong!

Within the various organizations that we worked for, we unfortunately had to conclude that Excel reports often hides the truth. We saw also that every version of an Excel spreadsheet had its own truth, and that different versions of that "so-called truth" were stored between several departments and teams in several folders. Another situation that we noticed is that organizations create sources (in Excel format) that are used as a foundation for dashboards and reports. It often does not hurt to use these in combination with the original sources, but if Excel is your only source and heavy macros and multiple versions are often used, this could be a huge problem.

For an organization where we were allowed to do a fantastic project to develop and further shape reports, fortunately, we were able to take care of this with a state-of-the-art BI solution. However, what outlined our surprise was that we were (unfortunately) not allowed to link to the original sources but had to link to their own developed (with complex macros) Excel files.

Understandably, the project ultimately went nowhere. If we reported an error, it took days before you could discover what was going on. After all, the error could come from anywhere. But experience also taught us that those types of reports should never contain Excel as a source. Ultimately, all errors reported were caused by the administrator of these Excel spreadsheets. We'd learned an expensive lesson, that's for sure, and we finally threw the towel in the corner (saying no is also a lesson).

Understanding diagnostic analysis

The exciting part of going on that data journey is when your curiosity kicks in and you start asking questions such as *why?* This means you are already one step further along your journey. In his book *Turning Data Into Wisdom*, Kevin Hanegan (coauthor of this book) describes the step for this approach as **exploratory analysis**. All of this implies that you want to find out why things happened.

We can see that curiosity has arisen, and we are eager to learn what has caused the differences in figures and numbers. We begin by asking questions such as the following:

- Why are the numbers the way they are now? Why are sales this month lower (or higher) than last month?

- Why did department X convert the most while department Y lagged?

- Why did we sell fewer products C this month than last month?

- What are the causes of these statistics, and why is there more absenteeism due to illness?

- Why is department X's absenteeism higher than department A's?

- Why are these medications prescribed for these conditions?

- Why is there an increase in visits to the emergency room (or the doctor's office), and what are the underlying causes?

- Why are the numbers of COVID-19 cases higher in certain areas when compared?

When you begin looking for causal factors and the consequences of those factors, your organization or you as an individual are already moving up the data and analytics ladder. This is referred to as **diagnostic analytics** or **diagnostic analysis**.

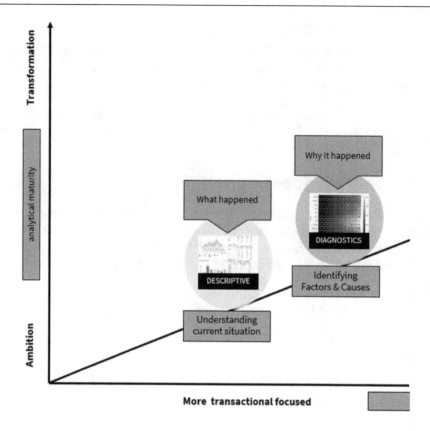

Figure 2.10 – Exploratory analysis: the second step of your data journey – the phase of diagnostic analysis

The first step of descriptive analytics focuses on measures of each variable (sum, count, average, and so on) of data that are independent of one another. Diagnostic analytics has developed the necessary curiosity to examine all of your data and create insights by utilizing your analytics skills to determine all aspects of data and how they relate to one another. While descriptive analysis helps to explain *what happened*, diagnostic analysis allows us to explain *why* it happened.

The presence of ambassadors with statistical and/or analytical skills within an organization drives this step. It is critical that people are guided by the hand during this phase and learn to analyze the results so that they can make better decisions supported by data—as we call it in this book, *data-informed decision-making*. This is a difficult task for many individuals and organizations.

The key components of the diagnostic phase are the ability to visualize your data using various types of visualizations so that you can investigate patterns, anomalies, and, of course, outliers, and determine whether there are any kind of relationships between the variables' outcomes in the visualized data.

Intermezzo – proud!

In a somewhat larger organization, standard reports were initially made for HR, facility services, and the IT department. These three departments made their own reports and had one person per department who was working on those dashboards and reports. What struck us at that time was that the external information provision was actually *state of the art*, but that the internal (staff) information provision still left something to be desired.

The buzz started when we began with a small project to help the staff of several internal service desks find out which servers with all kinds of communicational connections between each other had problems and reported incidents (classified as Critical, High, Medium, or Low) and the service requests. Every incident or service request needed to be registered in the source system and needed to be handled within the agreed **service-level agreement (SLA)** lead time.

All desks needed to report on a monthly basis the number of incidents, the number of service requests, and the lead time to the management team. Every team lead was working as a siloed team, and every team was creating monthly reports on its own and ultimately delivering this report on the 5th day of the new month to the controller of the operations office. They would then combine all separate reports, perform their own analysis, and create a management report. This report was delivered on the 10th day of the new month.

When the manager of the team explained his *strategic objectives* and his bigger vision, to recognize an incident before it occurred, we started out with a measured plan and built the first interactive dashboard for the management team. From this point in time, we were able to have the complete report on the 1st of the new month. A buzz was created and more questions arose.

The next report was a report to manage third-line suppliers. The lead time for those types of dispatched incidents or requests was mostly too long and the department wasn't able to discuss the open cases. With a newly created report, we were not only able to discuss the lead time of our third-line incidents or requests but we were also able to keep our suppliers to the agreed SLA handling times. Identifying "why" questions and being able to actually analyze and answer them, we were able to save more than €150K in only 1 year.

During the first two phases of descriptive and diagnostic analysis, we will discover that a data quality issue is present. Also, organizational definitions of certain calculations or field definitions are lacking.

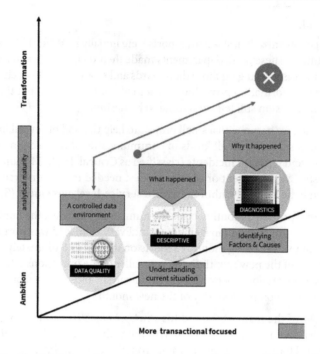

Figure 2.11 – The third step of your data journey: the discovery of data quality issues

Examples here can be how we define and calculate revenue or margins. Fortunately, data management or data governance is increasingly embraced by various types of organizations, just like the role of a **chief data officer** (**CDO**), which we discuss in *Chapter 5, Managing Your Data Environment.*

After all, if we go back to *Chapter 1, The Beginning – The Flow of Data* (*Figure 1.12*), we discussed the different disciplines that should have a place within an organization.

Incidentally, it is a separate field of work. In *Chapter 5, Managing Your Data Environment*, we will discuss the elements of data management and how to take care of data quality.

Nonetheless, it is prudent to consider and manage data management or data quality. From a fundamental standpoint, you can begin by addressing and displaying data quality issues in your initial dashboards and reports.

A good example is the story (*intermezzo*) of one of our projects, the *Data Prewashing Program.*

Intermezzo – the Data Prewashing Program

During various projects within different organizations, unfortunately, we had to conclude that data quality often leaves something to be desired. The frightening fact is that organizations often have not even discovered this themselves. An example is the story of an organization where we had to work on certain visualizations on top of their core business application. The project team set off energetically, and the first results were visible within a short amount of time.

Very quickly, it turned out that more than 75% of the dataset was not complete to enable us to measure the most important business objective (the number of requests compared to a certain target amount): the "reasons" for submitting the request was not filled in the source system. Well, how can you measure then, or how should we visualize this?

The first step was to go back to our customer and ask what they suggested we should do. We agreed to create a gap in time, measure from a certain point in time, and leave out the data before that point in time. Fortunately, that concept gave us better measures, but it turned out that just under 25% of the specific field was not filled.

As a sidestep, a list was made with the people who recorded this data and we also investigated whether this field was "mandatory" or a free field within the registration system. As a project team, we then entered into a discussion with the client and discussed the things we found out. The client's phrase "Oh, it is often the same person who makes a mistake" was a good opening to discuss the first steps for increasing the data quality.

We then indicated that we wanted to use the so-called Data Prewashing Program so that the data entry and storage of elementary fields could be controlled on a daily basis, and in this way, the data quality could be improved.

The Data Prewashing Program is nothing more than a list that you provide daily with missing fields and with which you can control the data entry of certain fields. With current technologies, you are able to completely automate this, although personally managing the data entry and storage of data will always be part of it and is the task of the data owners, team leaders, or managers.

For example, we have already been able to help a number of customers with setting up the Data Prewashing Program, and messages are sent on a daily or hourly basis to people who make a mistake when data is entered in "mandatory fields" of a transactional system.

Data quality must be addressed and managed, but as previously stated, we are able to do so in simple steps. Here are the simplest ways to begin improving your data quality:

1. Discuss the fundamental fields that require *good* data quality for measures/KPIs, and so on.

2. Make a list (table) of those elementary fields and display the bad or empty data fields in this table. Include this list in your solution.

3. Go over the list with your customer and set up a feedback loop through them.

4. Provide a tip... make the field mandatory through their software supplier.

In *Chapter 5*, *Managing Your Data Environment*, we will go over the data management process in detail. After you have taken care of the fundamentals of data quality, your curiosity will grow exponentially, and the world of predictive measuring will be open to you, and your first questions—such as what is likely to happen—will arise.

Understanding predictive analytics

Predictive analytics or **predictive analysis** is the next stage of analytics. This is, in our opinion, one of the most enjoyable and amazing phases of any project on which we have worked.

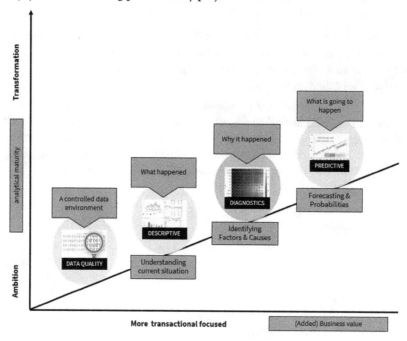

Figure 2.12 – The fourth step of your data journey: the phase of predictive analytics

When a solid foundation for data management has been established, achieving greater governance becomes possible. The next step is to arouse curiosity and cast a glimpse into the future. Predictive analysis is the study of historical data to forecast future behavior. Predictive analysis necessitates the use of various techniques, models, and even behavior. However, when done correctly, it can assist an organization in becoming more proactive. We know from experience that 80% of predictive questions are time-related when we look at predictive use cases (over time, next year, next month, and so on).

The following questions become current:

- What is the expected revenue next year (next quarter, next month)?
- What is the expectation of the number of customers?
- How many products will we sell if we grow by 10%?
- How many patients can we expect (taking into account the population growth or decrease) in the emergency room or GP's surgery?

- What will be the increase in drug use, especially aimed at the modern addiction of opiate use, if we continue on this path?

- Can we stop fraud on the doorstep? In other words, can we identify which applications are a potential risk?

Figure 2.13 depicts an example of a forecast that includes the number of possible requests as well as the expected numbers (note: a prediction is always wrong, as we can't predict with 100% assurance, as there are many factors that influence that number):

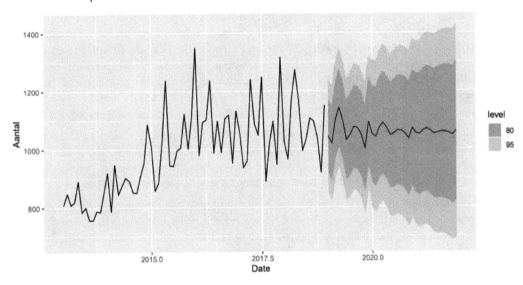

Figure 2.13 – An example of a forecast with the number of possible requests
with the expected numbers (note: a prediction is always wrong)

Many inspiring examples of predictive analytics can be found on our path to wisdom and on the ever-expanding internet. We've selected two of them:

- Sometimes, we are able to find connections in data where you would not expect them. For example, the tax authorities discovered in the past that there was a greater chance that someone committed tax fraud within a certain series of numbers in their social security number. At first, this seemed to be based on nothing, but a thorough analysis revealed that this connection could be explained: the social security numbers were distributed in a specific district in 1975. It turned out that the social security numbers with an increased risk of tax fraud belonged to people who lived in a residential villa area in 1975. This article was found on `https://biplatform.nl/517083/predictive-analytics-vijf-inspirerende-voorbeelden.html` (please use Google translate to read in English).

- Police forces in the United States and the United Kingdom use predictive analytics to predict crimes or generate risk reports. In the United States, all types of sensors (such as cameras) are used, as well as reports of crimes and messages from people suspected of being criminals. All of this data is combined, and the control rooms indicate which risk areas exist in (near) real time. As a result, the police can try to predict where a crime will occur, allowing for more targeted efforts in high-risk neighborhoods.

Intermezzo – adding predictive value to data

Another inspiring example is predicting the number of visitors in emergency care. For a number of healthcare organizations, we did some amazing projects to give some predictive analysis outcomes. Of course, you have to learn from the past in order to predict the future (and again, predictions are always wrong). By combining open data such as data from the **Central Bureau of Statistics**, weather data, football team schedules data, and so on, it was easy to predict how many visitors would come to the emergency post (per coming year, quarterly, month, or week). This input was needed, among other things, for application to the various budgets required.

In addition, we were presented with a number of hypothetical questions, such as: does the number of visits to the emergency post increase when it snows? Or if temperatures are below 0, does the number of visits increase? Another hypothesis was: if football team AZ or AJAX is playing, there are fewer visits or calls to the emergency dispatch center of the GP post.

We first learned about the system based on past results (and luckily, we had enough data to use) and were able to predict 95% accurately what the expected growth or decrease in the number of visitors to the emergency post would be. We were even able to predict the growth or decline per age group. Finally, we were, of course, able to answer the hypothetical questions.

Fortunately, we can share one of the answers: the football matches of AZ or AJAX have absolutely no influence on the visits or calls to the emergency dispatch center of the GP post.

In the end, when you eventually get a call from the clients from those GP posts and you get the comment that the predictions were spot on and the client actually can do something with the insights, then that really is the best compliment you can get!

Understanding prescriptive analytics

Prescriptive analytics is a more advanced level of analytics. During this stage, you will not only predict what will happen in the near future but also what you will need to do to make that future as good as possible. During this phase, organizations attempt to answer the question, *How can we ensure a particular outcome?* This phase goes beyond the realization of predictions and can forecast a number of measures to capitalize on the previous phase's results (forecasting).

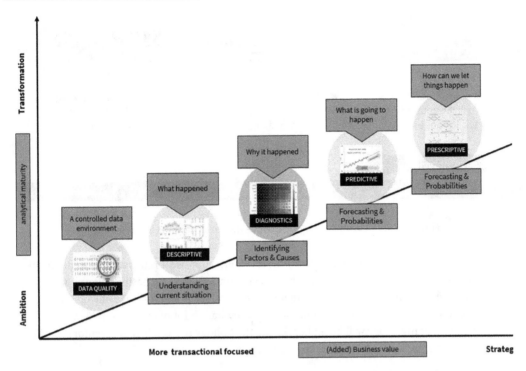

Figure 2.14 – The fifth step of your data journey: the phase of diagnostic analysis

Some nice examples are given here:

- Preventive checking of buildings with an increased risk of fires

- Proactively ordering parts that are likely to break on a machine soon

- The hiring of personnel who must first be trained for a longer period of time; strategic personnel planning

The concept of optimization is central to the phenomenon of "prescriptive analytics" or "prescribed analytics". This simply means that when developing a prescriptive model, every minor detail must be considered. Supply chain, labor costs, employee scheduling, energy costs, potential machine failure—everything that could be a factor should be considered when developing a prescriptive model. *Figure 2.15* shows a model where the decisions, predictions, and effects that should be considered are shown:

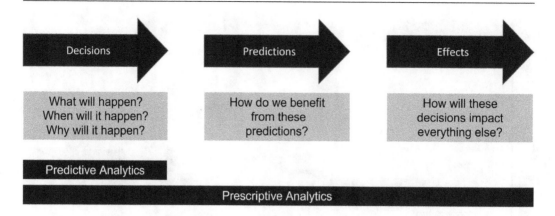

Figure 2.15 – Describing the prescriptive model and things to think of

As an example (from the book *Turning Data into Wisdom*), suppose a retail store uses descriptive (what happened) and diagnostic (why it happened) data to understand purchasing patterns and trends around their products. The store anticipates that sales of product A will increase during the holiday season. The company recognizes that it does not typically have a lot of extra product A inventory, but it anticipates that inventory will be higher during the holiday season. When inventory reaches a critical mass, prescriptive analytics will request a resupply.

Another example is a manufacturing plant that has a variety of machines in operation. Those machines are jam-packed with sensors. All of the data from those sensors is collected, and it must stay within a certain bandwidth. When the threshold is reached, the model can predict when a new part must be ordered, and when that order is placed, an appointment for repairs is automatically scheduled.

Because prescriptive analytics employs sophisticated tools and technologies, it is not suitable for everyone. To understand the necessary steps, models, and techniques to progress to a more complex analysis, it is necessary to have a basic understanding of all phases of the maturity model.

We described the descriptive, diagnostic, predictive, and prescriptive phases. Now, let's have a look at the final phase of the model: AI.

AI

AI is revolutionizing the way we work and is being used in a variety of fields. AI is currently one of the fastest-growing technologies, and many businesses are expected to incorporate AI into their operations. However, AI has many facets and techniques that must be considered. After all, if you're doing it because everyone else is, you're wasting your time!

With *Figure 2.16*, we've come to the last step of the data journey: the phase of semantic or artificial intelligence.

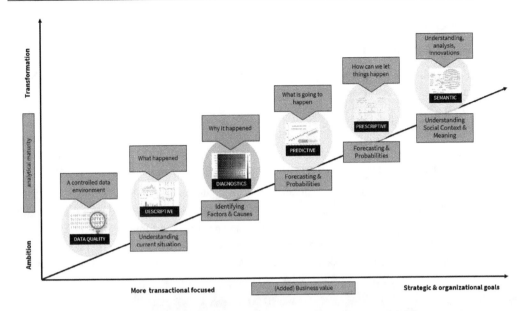

Figure 2.16 – The last step of your data journey: the phase of semantic or artificial intelligence

Otherwise, it will only cost money if the business value is not determined and presented. The techniques used vary and are diverse, and there are numerous examples where **machine learning (ML)**, AutoML, or other forms of this amazing technique are used.

Some inspiring examples include the following:

- *Using object recognition, automatically replenish shelves in a retail facility.* AI can add significant value to retail. You can use object recognition to detect when a shelf is empty or about to run out. A signal can then be sent to the replenishment mechanism, ensuring that the compartment is always filled with articles and the retailer does not lose sales.

- *Complying with construction safety regulations.* Cameras with AI image recognition can be used to improve compliance with construction safety regulations. When the technology detects employees who are not wearing the prescribed protective equipment or who are in dangerous situations, management is notified and action can be taken quickly.

- *Make packaging and labels interactive.* Packaging can be made interactive to increase customer interaction and sales by using digital watermarks, QR codes, and ML. A consumer can scan a package offline or online to earn incentives or learn more about a product.

  Consider the following:

  - Request a demonstration

  - Fill out a form for a chance to win a prize

- Play a video explaining the recipe by a chef

- Ask questions, fill out a questionnaire, and so on

From an e-commerce standpoint, you can collect and report data by scanning (via a mobile app) all events that occur on a phone, or even predict or add prescriptive elements if there is enough data. This frequently yields interesting insights that can be used to improve your customer/consumer relationship.

- Finally, an example from an Amsterdam University of Applied Sciences student group: they completed a minor project for the platform Kids in Data (www.kidsindata.com).

This platform aims to assist children all over the world in working with data and understanding what data literacy is, as well as what types of visualizations are available and when they should be used. They were given the task of developing a scan app, and by combining object recognition and ML, they were able to create a system that recognizes various types of visualizations and provides information to the students. *Figure 2.17* shows a screenshot of this developed app.

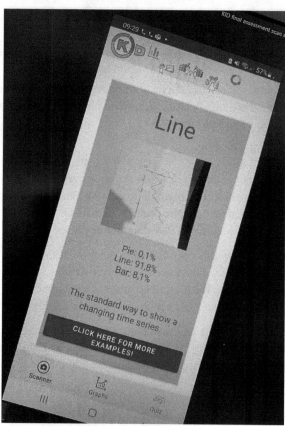

Figure 2.17 – Scan app: Kids in Data

> **Intermezzo – early recognition of illnesses**
>
> A project was carried out to learn to recognize the eye disease **macular degeneration** with AI. For this, ML was used to learn to recognize eye diseases from medical images. You can also implement AI as a self-learning system and treat various diseases on the basis of learning models to detect visual material (send signals).
>
> The technology behind this is that image recognition is getting smarter. When AI eventually misses a disease, this can be indicated by the doctor and the algorithms are adjusted again. The great thing about this project was that not only that macular degeneration could be recognized at an early stage, but also that eventually, more than 30 eye diseases could be recognized and the interface to the healthcare system was realized.
>
> In addition, the AI results are stored in the file and immediately available to the doctor. However, the human aspect is important—the decision should always apply and you should not leave the decisions to the computer or computationally developed algorithms.

Can data save lives? A success story

Each minute counts in emergency healthcare, whether it is to save a life or to ensure the best possible quality of life after treatment. Optimizing the process from emergency calls to medical (angioplasty) procedures saves valuable minutes. Zone of Safety Holland, North accomplished this in collaboration with several hospitals in the area by utilizing the Call to Balloon dashboard.

Martin Smeekes, the director of the safety region, and his team of experts wanted to improve the critical process of Call to Balloon. Ambulance response times in this region of the Netherlands could not be improved further than the current 95% accuracy.

Martin wanted to improve the entire process, from the initial emergency call to the actual treatment (angioplasty). Everyone understood that by working together, they could achieve improvements in the time between the emergency call and the treatment.

This is how we began and worked on the Call to Balloon solution, which provides a general overview of realized times over a given time period. The smallest details of a single emergency call could be examined. The combination of data from various angles, as well as the ability to gain a better understanding on various levels, provides users with insights that would not otherwise be possible or visible.

Displaying the results in a dashboard is one thing, but being able to discuss them, suggest improvements, and have them implemented on all sides (dispatch, ambulance, hospital) is fantastic. This is where data-driven decision-making came into play, and teams from various organizations discussed the outcomes of cases that had passed the target lead time.

These developed dashboards include data from emergency calls and subsequent treatments in the region. This resulted in insights that would not have emerged without this information. These new insights led to improvements in the emergency care chain, saving vital minutes and thus improving patients' quality of life.

The **Call to Balloon** dashboard displayed a process flow to illustrate the various steps in the process, as well as the average and median times. The process schema that is visualized shows the main **Key Performance Indicator** (**KPI**) "Call to Balloon" and the **Performance Indicators** (**PI**) that support the main KPI. In *figure 2.18* the KPI and PI's are described. In *Chapter 6, Aligning with Organizational Goals*, we discuss the methodology of KPIs and have included this success story as well.

Call to Balloon	The total time from the emergency call to the performed treatment, the angioplasty
Response time	The time from the emergency call to the arrival of the ambulance
Call to Door	The time from the emergency call to transfer the hospital personnel
Door to Balloon	The time from transfer by the hospital personnel to angioplasty
ECG to Balloon	The elapsed time between the ECG (by ambulance personnel) to angioplasty

Figure 2.18 – The used definitions for the performance indicators that we used in this project

When we knew those steps, we were able to put them into our visualization solution and design it as a process. *Figure 2.19* is the solution that we came up with:

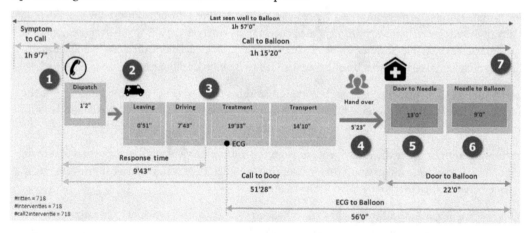

Figure 2.19 – The visualized process schema of Call to Balloon

Figure 2.19 displays all the sequential steps in this process and each has its own definition:

1. The patient develops heart complaints.

2. The patient calls are dispatched and the dispatch team registers the needed data in the source system.

3. The staff of the ambulance is called in and they man the ambulance and leave the station.

4. The ambulance drives off from the station and drives toward the patient.

5. When ECG is performed and angioplasty is needed, the patient is transferred to the hospital.

6. The patient is delivered to the CAD room where the treatment is performed.

7. The vein has been punctured and the stent is placed.

With the dashboard, displayed in *Figure 2.20* with the average times (and median times, if you prefer), the safety region was able to analyze the different steps by using all timestamps of those process steps. Data can be thoroughly examined. There are several options for obtaining information on achieved (standard) times:

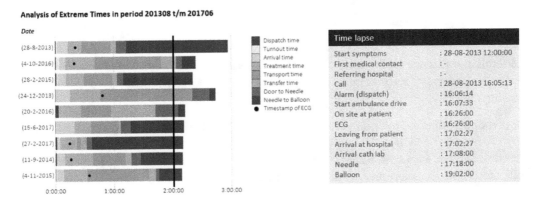

Figure 2.20 – The visualization that the safety region used to analyze the process steps

Figure 2.20 depicts a stacked bar chart that depicts each step of the process. The timer is set to 120 minutes. By visualizing it in this manner, the team was able to discuss and improve on all individual cases. When the specific extreme time chart was analyzed, the users could click on one of the bars, and the program that we built opened an overview automatically with all the detailed information about the specific patient and ride. We call this technique the *Flipping Technique*, which simply means; don't look only at the things that are doing well, flip it and look at the things that need attention.

With the gained knowledge, they were actually able to improve in various process steps, as detailed here:

1. When the team began analyzing the data, they discovered that 95% of the dispatch calls were accurate when ambulances were dispatched to the patient. As a result, Martin and his team decided to change the protocol and send the ambulance straight to the patient's address.

2. While the ambulance was on its way, dispatch would ask the 911 call reporter additional questions, such as whether the patient required medication, when the first symptoms appeared, and so on. These responses were saved in the source systems.

3. When the ECG was performed, the ambulance staff indicated whether angioplasty was required, and the team that was required to perform that treatment was called in directly (the patient was announced), so there was no wasted time. As Martin stated, we know that angioplasty is required, so why waste valuable time waiting for the specialists' team to arrive?

4. The process for delivering a patient to the first aid department has changed. Patients who previously had to wait in the first aid department are now taken directly to the CAD room. The reason for this is that angioplasty must be performed directly, and they already know from the ECG that this treatment is required. So, why waste those life-threatening minutes in the emergency room?

5. Another significant finding was that the CAD room was not always ready for the next patient. As a result, the procedure was altered, and the CAD room is now always ready for the next patient.

As a result, no second is wasted, and the safety region was able to save 20 minutes of potentially life-saving time in the process lead time.

As a result of this remarkable success, Martin Smeekes and his team decided to test the *Call to Needle* (in the event of a stroke) process, as well as a *Call to Knife trial* (in case of emergency lifesaving surgeries).

One of the most difficult problems was keeping track of time in the hospital. Nowadays, a patient is given a wrist sensor, and the time is automatically recorded in the systems whenever a certain point is reached. This was a big wish at the start, and it was eventually implemented for patient care. As a result, the data became more precise, which is necessary for such processes.

Intermezzo – amazing moments!

During this project, there were two moments in time that will never be forgotten. The first moment was the first presentation of the solution to Martin Smeekes and his team. The chairman of the Dutch Society of Cardiologists, a professor, also joined the meeting. The moment he saw the first display of the dashboard and the analytical possibilities, he jumped out of his chair and walked toward the screen. The professor immediately pointed out some elements that could be improved. An amazing moment to feel that vibe that we had interpreted things well.

The second moment was in 2014 when Martin and I discussed the *Call to Balloon* case and I said that I would like the safety region to be the smartest organization in the Netherlands. He agreed to join the competition, and the safety region won the public award and the jury of the Smartest Organization in the Netherlands competition due to the following reasons:

They are 100% focused on continuous improvement based on data-informed decision-making.

They are willing to communicate with all parties and to actually go through the improvement steps with each other and actually implement them.

The data literacy skillset and organizational data literacy are high.

Therefore, they were able to improve the Call to Balloon process and the Call to Needle processes within 20 minutes.

Summary

Finally, data and analytics open up a world of possibilities. However, when it comes to the first questions, you should consider why you want to measure certain things, what your organization stands for, and where you want to go. You then move on to providing information about the mission, vision, and strategy that will be developed.

Everything is built on this foundation! This is required so that an organization can eventually develop into one that can make decisions based on data. The big pitfall is that we start doing things because others are doing them, that we measure everything because we can measure everything, and that we eventually lose sight of the forest for the trees and swerve completely out of control through a fog of data. That can't, and shouldn't, be the goal.

After reading this chapter, we should have a better understanding of the data journey, including which steps to take and how to apply them to our daily lives. We talked about descriptive analysis (what happened), diagnostic analysis (why did it happen), predictive analysis (what is likely to happen), and prescriptive analysis (how can we ensure things happen) in the wonderful world of AI and ML.

We came to a close with a story about the Netherlands' safety region. You've discovered that they became a successful team by relying on data, allowing the insights to speak for themselves, and using the insights to make data-driven decisions.

In the next chapter, we'll go over the four key pillars for establishing a data and analytics environment from an organizational standpoint.

3

Understanding the Four-Pillar Model

Everyone is familiar with and understands the concept of data and dashboards. We observe increased demand and acceptance for data and analytics projects. Due to this increased demand and acceptance for data and analytics projects, we see also a higher demand for data literacy skills.

When we get specific, there are four fundamental pillars in data and analytics that we must address in our businesses: **organizational data literacy**, **data management**, **data and analytics**, and **education**.

To truly grow, we must first understand the facts about data literacy, which is primarily addressed to employees of a company. This is a good thing, but if we approach data literacy solely for personal growth, we will miss out on a lot of opportunities. This is why the **four-pillar model** is an important approach that allows you to consider, plan, and develop your data and analytics strategy and all components involved.

This chapter will assist you in understanding the four critical pillars for a successful approach, which will help you in defining your data and analytics strategy for the entire organization.

The following topics will be covered in this chapter:

- Gaining an understanding of the various aspects of data literacy
- Introducing the four fundamental pillars
- Mixing the pillars

Gaining an understanding of the various aspects of data literacy

As we discussed in *Chapter 1, The Beginning – The Flow of Data*, data literacy is defined as the ability to read, understand, and argue with data. We went a step further and added, "*it means how a person uses data and understands the world around them*".

It's the human aspect that means it's also a matter of behavior—that people can work with data because they want to, not because they have to! We need to be able to criticize the insights we derive from that data mountain, and this includes not only the use of cool software but also the adoption of critical thinking and the adoption to embrace all aspects of data literacy. *Figure 3.1* depicts the skills that are required to grow in this beautiful data and analytics world.

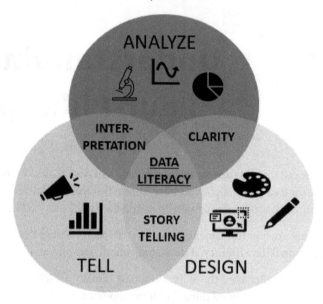

Figure 3.1 – Defining data literacy skills

As shown in *Figure 3.1*, this data literacy Venn diagram addresses specific hard technical skills and soft skills (such as communicating and understanding how people use and see colors in data visualizations, and so on). Mostly, people are familiar with the term *data literacy*, but very few are sure which competencies or skills are related to data literacy, and even fewer people are aware of which of those competencies are relevant to their role. In *Chapter 11, Defining a Data Literacy Competency Framework*, we will help you to identify what data literacy competencies are, and which skills and mindsets are relevant for each competency.

It is also important to note that data literacy is not about expecting to or becoming an expert; rather, it is a journey that must begin somewhere. Why do we believe that data literacy, or the ability to be data literate, is critical for our businesses? As previously stated, making data-informed decisions is more important than ever in this digital transformational era! Why? As we all experienced, due to the COVID-19 pandemic, our digital mindset and ability to embrace the digital revolution advanced by at least 5-7 years within a year! We all learned to work from home and to use data and insights to understand what was going on around us, and businesses realized the value of data-informed decision-making as well. Everywhere we looked, in every country, the most amazing and terrible visualizations appeared to inform us about the pandemic, and we needed to learn to read, argue against, and criticize the information that we were seeing.

Introducing the four fundamental pillars

When a company lacks the necessary soft or hard technical skills, as well as the tools to work with data, the leadership operates in a clouded environment. As a result, they are hampered from making data-informed decisions because they lack the critical and required data vision or insights. Worse, they will fall behind in their businesses, losing their competitive advantage and—ultimately—their customers.

We can all use data-informed decision-making to improve our performance, innovate our work and products, and add more value to our businesses when we have a data-literate workforce. This applies not only to individuals but to your entire organization, from top to bottom, team to individual. This enables your organization to overcome challenges more quickly—or more accurately—more easily, and become able to drive your future plans (your strategic objectives).

When we look back to the first pandemic year, 2020, we see that a rapid digital transformation was required; in 2021, the "race pace" was even faster. What we saw and noticed is that:

- Data is essential for organizations and aids in digital transformation.

- Our services and deliveries must be faster, and we require data-informed decision-making to do so!

- **Software as a Service** (**SaaS**) and no-code/low-code are trends that help us speed up our work because time is money and we need to develop our data environments in a convenient and easy way.

- The cloud works for all of our organizations; customers can quickly get on board; there is no need to set up large technical environments. Instead, it is about selecting the right configuration and getting started quickly with your data and analytics journey at lower costs and with the ability to scale quickly.

- We can see all around us that the transition to the cloud is accelerating at breakneck speed.

- Data management, establishing a solid, future-proof data strategy, is more important than ever!

Figure 3.2 illustrates the four fundamental pillars of data and analytics. These four pillars are critical issues that we must address in our businesses. To truly grow, we must first understand the core facts about data literacy, which is primarily addressed to the people who work within an organization rather than having an "organizational data literacy plan" ready for the entire organization:

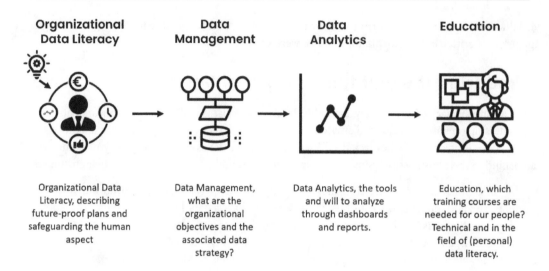

Organizational Data Literacy

Data Management

Data Analytics

Education

Organizational Data Literacy, describing future-proof plans and safeguarding the human aspect

Data Management, what are the organizational objectives and the associated data strategy?

Data Analytics, the tools and will to analyze through dashboards and reports.

Education, which training courses are needed for our people? Technical and in the field of (personal) data literacy.

Figure 3.2 – Describing the four fundamental pillars

In the following paragraphs, we will explain all four pillars, and in the following chapters, we will guide you through the various elements of the four pillars in greater depth.

Becoming acquainted with organizational data literacy

This first crucial pillar emphasizes the significance of the human aspect of data literacy. It enables you to comprehend how data literacy and all related elements influence an organization's future and, more importantly, the business "culture". It is a blueprint that will assist in understanding the various elements of the four pillars and breaking them down into a constructive plan:

Figure 3.3 – The first pillar: organizational data literacy

Because everyone has a different level of experience working with data and we need to address data literacy at all levels within an organization, we must include the human factor in our future plans! As a result, it is critical to promote data literacy through education, the development of a future-proof plan, and a focus on the small victories that people achieve on a daily basis.

Data literacy is something that affects everyone and every organization. The more people who can debate, analyze, work with, and use data in their daily roles, the better data-informed decision-making will be.

The most important aspect is that your organization must be prepared! It must be prepared to embrace data and analytics as well as the amazing world of data literacy. When it comes to embracing that journey for your organizational data literacy, the following are some important points to consider:

- **Leadership**: It is critical that your organization has a champion, an evangelist, and a data leader who can discuss, highlight, inspire, support, and educate on data literacy

- **Data literacy sponsorship**: Financial support for projects, plans, and communication

- **Assessments**: The ability to develop and assess employees' progress in data literacy

- **Aligned objectives**: Are your organizational and data literacy objectives aligned?

To begin, maintaining organizational growth requires taking care of your employees on all levels and ensuring that they are prepared for the future. Data literacy must be addressed from the top down in your organization. It is critical that our leaders demonstrate how they work with, analyze, argue against, discuss, and criticize data insights. What if they don't? If our leaders aren't embracing data-informed decision-making, how can we expect our employees to? Leading by example is an essential component of the data literacy environment in the workplace. When we embrace data literacy, our businesses will be able to measure and improve on their organizational goals, maximizing the value within their organization and having a competitive advantage in all situations that arise. How can you grow during the intermezzo? Here's a synopsis of one of our success stories (the URL to the longer version is in to our referral list).

> **Intermezzo – how can you grow?**
>
> At a previous company, for example, several offices used tooling to create amazing dashboards and reports. Several departments created reports for the internal organization when we first started. Over time, more and more groups requested licenses as well as additional dashboards and reports. It was discovered that all reports and dashboards looked different, that the setup for connecting to data was different, and that there were no coding conventions or cohesion among the staff of those various departments. It wasn't long before the environment became uncontrollable, necessitating the establishment of a competence center.

We began this journey with a plan that described what to do, how to set up, and how to grow in a controlled manner. We started with 4 employees and fewer than 100 users (within an organization of more than 20,000 employees). We had 15 people on our team a few months later, including analysts, testers, dashboard designers, and full-time management. We had over 3,000 users and 140 dashboards that were used throughout the entire internal organization 5 years later.

How did we achieve such rapid growth? We had a centralized strategy that provided better control and data management. As we created more dashboards, we established standard guidelines and coding conventions. As a result of everyone speaking the same "data language", we were able to work faster and across teams. We could even reuse data (we had a centralized metadata repository) and data reports. We assisted the organization in becoming "data literate" and actually using the insights that were created for their data-informed decision-making by providing workshops, communication, newsletters, and so on. So, we were able to convert mountains of data into actual usable information for decision-making at one point.

The importance of data literacy in all its facets is needed—that is what we see and read in various publications. In one of those publications, it is mentioned that throughout all industries, the demand and availability of data for a company's data-informed decision-making process have exploded. But research also pointed out that the available data and insights were not delivered to the hands of people that needed to make and create decisions. Next to that, people needed to just simply understand the insights that were created. In the end, this research also concluded that there is a huge opportunity in working with data but that the skill set for data literacy needs to be more addressed from a corporate point of view as well.

For more information, go to the presentation by Mike Capone, CEO of Qlik—October 2018 at `https://bit.ly/3pdNMqs`.

The conclusion is that there is room for growth, but you must plan ahead of time. We will help you with a framework for understanding change in an organization when it comes to data literacy in *Chapter 4, Implementing Organizational Data Literacy,* so that you can write that plan and be successful. As the second-most important pillar of our framework, we will go over the elements of data management in detail in the following section.

Discussing the significance of data management

Still, from a technical and business standpoint, data management is sometimes set aside, and organizations only begin with setting up their data and analytics environments. Nowadays, we see (fortunately) that due to the growth and complexity of data and the required data environments, a solid data strategy and a shared data vision have never been more important than they are now!

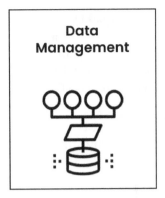

Figure 3.4 – The second pillar: data management

For a few years, we've seen a paradigm shift and the need for a controlled data environment, making data pipelines with a low-code/no-coding technique more important. With that low-coding/no-coding flexibility, you can identify data, secure sensitive data, and provide data analysts with an end-to-end data lineage.

Although tools are important, we will not recommend any in this book. Instead, we'd like to give you a practical approach to consider when starting with data integration, building data pipelines, or data warehouses.

When businesses want to work on their data management processes, improve data quality, or even monitor the data environment, the following five steps must be followed:

1. **Data strategy**: Develop a shared vision, assign data owners, and so on.
2. **Training and coaching**: Train, coach, and mentor your data owners, stewards, and business users.
3. **Processes**: Set up a process to improve data quality, set up continuous improvement, and so on.
4. **Control**: Describe your organization's data principles, create a data management mindset, or even set up a data office and possibly assign a CDO.
5. **IT**: Maintain a data register and dictionary, use data modeling tools, and monitor your data environment and quality.

Data management is an important element of data literacy—this is also stated in publications. The need for data at the correct time, in the correct place, and in the hands of the correct people will definitely help in making data-informed decisions. This is exactly why we think that data management in all its facets is an important pillar of this methodology!

For more information, go to the *TechTarget*, October 2019 at `https://www.techtarget.com/searchdatamanagement/definition/data-management`.

You should keep in mind that when your strategic objectives are clear, it is easier to think about your data strategy. From there, it will be easier to embrace data management and improve your data quality. Consider data literacy training when hiring new employees and assist them in boosting data literacy in this way. You will also increase the flow of data and the value within your organization as a result. We go over the actions and processes in greater detail in *Chapter 5, Managing Your Data Environment*:

Figure 3.5 – The third pillar: data analytics

For more information, visit: `https://towardsdatascience.com/why-visual-literacy-is-essential-to-good-data-visualization-5b9dffb5aa6f`.

Defining a data and analytics approach

Employees will need the appropriate analytical tools to build and analyze tables, graphs, and other visualizations, in addition to the skill set to work efficiently with data. We look at data and analytics in various ways, as we described in *Chapter 2, Unfolding Your Data Journey*, and we've described all steps of the amazing journey that you can go on. But also, we see that the majority of organizations will remain within the descriptive and diagnostic stages. This is not a bad or weird situation—those types of organizations are just not ready yet to grow toward predictive or prescriptive analytics. They might not even have the desire to have predictions or even **machine learning** (**ML**) activities in the future.

Within the data and analytics pillar, we have a few important elements that we will discuss in more detail, including the growth of data, the right data and analytics tools, **artificial intelligence** (**AI**) and ML, cloud solutions, and how data literacy itself fits into this pillar too.

The rapid growth of our data world

We know that data and analytics continue to evolve beyond our imagination. As mentioned in *Chapter 2, Unfolding your Data Journey*, the world will generate more than 180 zettabytes of digital data by 2025. It's therefore good to see that organizations embrace new technologies to help them transform and grow in their data-informed decision-making. This digital transformation helps to identify efficiency and grow their competitive advantages. In the last years, and especially during the pandemic, we learned that data and analytics became important for organizations.

The COVID-19 pandemic was an accelerator in this case. The digital race was accelerated due to the lack of data that we needed for even the simplest decisions in our daily lives. As an example: *Do we have enough beds in the hospital? How many tests are done? How many people are sick?* and so on. The most common consideration during that time was "if we just had that data", regarding the pandemic in 2020 and the explosion of the number of coronavirus cases. The data was incomplete and only indicative! In 2021, that was certainly the case with the information about vaccines. When we look back at this period, one thing is clear: the pace of digital transformation has accelerated tremendously. According to the experts, in 2 years, we have certainly raced 5-7 years ahead in this transformation. To give you an idea of the struggle during the COVID pandemic, we have an intermezzo that illustrates how we coped with the lack of data or the lack of correct data.

Intermezzo – Dare to decide

In August 2020, after a brief vacation, we discussed a COVID dashboard that had been developed (as many data junkies did). But we had been struggling with the data and the continuous changes that had been made in the datasets. The insights that were created were good, and we were able to build a score-carding perspective from them. But after many discussions about the data, the changes in data, and the lack of data, we decided to "not publish" the developed dashboard. In *Figure 3.6*, there is a small glimpse of this dashboard displayed:

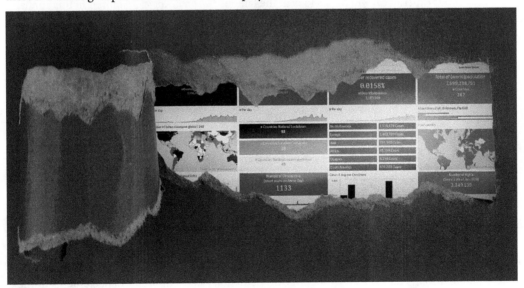

Figure 3.6 – Dare to decide

Up until today, we still hold fast to the decision not to publish the dashboard. The numbers are totally off, as we did not collect data from the start and simply because a lot of people were not tested, or not registered. From that point on, we decided to actually look at the pandemic from a different perspective.

We found datasets from clinical trials (`www.clinicaltrials.gov`) and commercial flights from all over the world via *Flightradar 24* (`https://www.flightradar24.com/data/statistics`). In this way (with some other combinations), we could have a better look at the effects that the pandemic had on our world, not by just using the data from Johns Hopkins University but by using data that was from a more reliable source and data that could actually tell a story of the pandemic's effects.

The full story can be found at `https://www.linkedin.com/pulse/torn-between-two-angelika-klidas/`.

The rise of data and insights is one notable result, but also the rapid transition to digital for companies was amazing. To actually work with data and utilize it in dashboards and reports, you need tools. In the next section, we will give you some information to guide your choices in buying the correct software.

Tools

In today's world, data tools need to support decision-making. We often get questions such as *How do you select a tool? Which tool should we use?* and so on. The responsible persons within an organization usually (that is our experience) will have a look at the famous *Gartner Magic Quadrant*. In this annual report, Gartner compares various kinds of tools, based on 12 critical capabilities:

- **Security**: To ensure that the platform is secure.

- **Governance**: Being able to track and manage the usage of the platform.

- **Cloud-enabled analytics**: The usage of analytics in the cloud, on-prem, and across a multi-cloud deployment.

- **Data source connectivity**: Enabling users to connect and use data from a variety of storage platforms.

- **Data preparation**: Drag and drop functionality, creating measures, groups and hierarchies, and so on.

- **Catalog**: A way to find and digest and consume data in an easy manner. The catalog needs to be searchable and datasets need to be easy to locate and consume.

- **Automated insights**: Augmented analytics at the core of the platform, using ML to help users generate insights on the spot by identifying elementary and important data elements in the data model.

- **Data visualization**: The creation of interactive dashboards and the availability of a great number of visualizations.

- **Natural language query**: Help the users to search through the data by using a search engine (such as Google) to type or ask questions about a specific dataset.

- **Data storytelling**: This is about generating a data story, and needs to be combined with various possibilities to add text, headlines, visualizations, and so on.

- **Natural language generation**: Creating automatic linguistic descriptions of insights found in a dataset.

- **Reporting**: Creating pixel-perfect reports that can be scheduled and sent to a larger user community.

The complete report can be found on Gartner's website (`https://www.gartner.com/doc/reprints?id=1-292LEME3&ct=220209&st=sb`). Also, reports from Forrester (`www.forrester.com`) and BARC (`https://barc-research.com/research/bi-trend-monitor/`) can help to make the choice that best suits your organization.

The development of tools and the usage of ML or AI are more and more common. There are tools in the market that use those techniques, and even **natural language processing** (**NLP**) is a commodity nowadays. In the next section, we will briefly describe the role of ML and AI in data and analytics.

The rise of ML and AI

The tools that we use are shifting more toward conversational analytics with the inclusion of NLP and even ML. We've even seen tools that advise you what to display, what to do, what to choose, or even which type of visualization is the most suitable. This is actually one of the best developments that we've seen! Just by asking (by typing or speaking) a question to the dataset, it gives a result back and even some visualization suggestions.

The rise of ML and AI creates a lower threshold to work with data and support our data-informed decision-making. After all, when we do have data and are willing to use any tool, data becomes "information" and we need to action those outcomes. In this way, we are able to create a mindset in which we can work with the insights that are created. From there, we are actually gaining the knowledge to grow on our data-informed decision-making journey.

Moving to the cloud

Along with ML and AI, the role of the cloud is also key in an effective approach to data and analytics. At the beginning of our own personal journeys, we started out with solid on-prem solutions. We had to buy servers and software, create connections (which took quite some time to implement), and so on. During the last few years, we've seen an enormous shift to the cloud where scalability and the release speed of new features are growing rapidly. We've also noticed that the shift to the cloud, or even installing a hybrid environment, was definitely shaped during the pandemic. Additionally, we've noticed that organizations needed to operate in a more efficient and cost-effective way, even using AI to find answers to challenges in a simpler way. The cloud strategy is continuing to grow, and the rapid development of improvements in those cloud environments is amazing.

There are reports available from Gartner that state that half of IT spending will be shifted to the cloud by 2025 (`https://www.gartner.com/en/newsroom/press-releases/2022-02-09-gartner-says-more-than-half-of-enterprise-it-spending#:~:text=Accelerating%20Shift%20to%20the%20Cloud,%2C%20according%20to%20Gartner%2C%20Inc`).

Data literacy is a key aspect of data and analytics

"*Most of us need to listen to the music to understand how beautiful it is*," Hans Rosling (RIP—February 7, 2017) once said. But that's how we often present statistics: we show the notes but don't play the music. When we are able to play the music, we tell the story of how amazing things will happen!

It has been stated numerous times that we must keep the data visualizations we provide interpretable, interesting, exciting, and accessible to all. We can accomplish this by using carefully selected charts and adding context to our visualizations. In this way, we can assist our clients in understanding their business questions and delivering actionable insights to our organizations.

However, there is more to visualizing data and how to present good data visualizations. Many books, publications, and articles are written by talented specialists! Reading those articles, we see that there is a difference in understanding the data that you are using for your visualizations and the visual approach that you are using for your reports and dashboards. Some of us call this "visual literacy". In fact, if we compare it with the statement of Hans Rosling, visual literacy could be the music, in connecting the strategic goals and forming them into a chorus: a melody.

After all, when we have the foundation in place for our data strategy, that aligns with our strategic goals (see *Chapter 5, Managing Your Data Environment*, and *Chapter 6, Aligning with Organizational Goals*). From there on, we are learning and developing our analytic mindset to learn to ask questions (*Chapter 8, Questioning the Data*). And at the end, we most likely start learning to work with more advanced visualizations and asking hypothetical or *what-if* questions. From there, we are about to understand what correlations and other data analytics components are and how we can use those kinds of visualizations in our data-informed decision-making journey.

Creating visualizations based on your data is an excellent way to simplify data and create engaging analysis. You can also make it more engaging for your audience by visualizing the data. Learning from experts and authors, such as Alberto Cairo (`www.albertocairo.com`) and Stephen Few (`www.visualperceptual.com`), you can understand how to properly visualize data by using the appropriate charts and colors.

Alberto Cairo once said during a session:

> "*You should not sacrifice clarity for the sake of variety!*"

This sentence emphasizes the importance of keeping things simple and clear; after all, we all want the audience (of our visualizations) to understand what they are looking at! As mentioned in the first section of this chapter, data literacy is a buzzword that was coined by MIT and other larger analytical organizations. As we (the authors) say, it may be a buzzword, but we are now better equipped to explain the data and analytics story. The four basic data literacy aspects are depicted in *Figure 3.7* to help you understand them better:

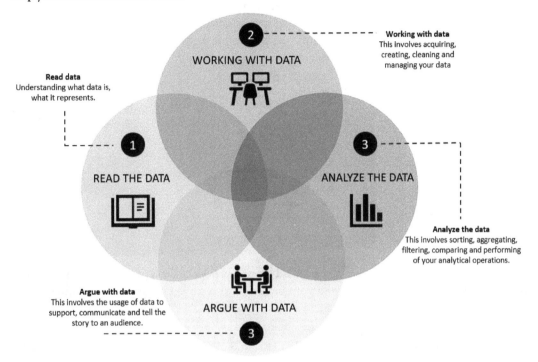

Figure 3.7 – The four primary elements of data literacy

This diagram will help you understand what the four elements are. We will discuss elements such as these in more depth in various chapters of this book. All of these elements are part of the "data and analytics pillar" from a behavioral standpoint.

To conclude this section, we've discussed several topics that fall under the third pillar, data and analytics. We need to ensure that our tools are scalable and accessible; we see the need for speed when it comes to the economic crisis and the effects of the coronavirus pandemic. But also, we have to choose a tool that suits the organization. We have several ways to make our choices. When your business does have helpful tools available, don't discard them as your sunk costs will be terribly high. Make your choice wisely. But also remember that it is not a bad thing to have more than one tool, as long as you know what you'll be creating with it!

We ended the section with a brief discussion about visualizing data and how data literacy fits in this pillar as well. In the next section, we will discuss the fourth pillar: education.

Understanding the education pillar

The fourth and final pillar is education. This pillar includes not only internal resources and technical software training, but also data literacy workshops, idea sharing and reward, and external sources. You should also think about different learning methods, such as self-service learning, role-based learning, peer mentoring, or a combination of different types of learning programs:

Figure 3.8 – The fourth pillar: education

Find a data-literate evangelist to assist you and lead by example! Make them your winners! Allow the evangelist to teach, preach, and assist your data and analytics team in evolving and educating your organization. Data literacy must be ingrained in your company's DNA!

Intermezzo – learn to analyze!

For a project, we needed to assist in the transition of the organization to a **data-informed decision-making** (**DID**) organization (we refuse to say *data-driven organization* because you can't be driven by data, only by insights or information). This project was designed to help with the transition to a new way of working in new data and analytics environments by establishing a solid data environment. This organization needed to consider not only the right, future-proof tools but also a team with specific skills to better support and assist the business. Technical skills were required for this team, but communication, analytical, questioning, and problem-solving abilities were also evaluated.

There was a variety of training planned, and we assisted the team in developing its data literacy skill set simply by spending some time learning how to analyze within your data and analytics environment. We have a tendency to use simple analysis methods such as filtering (by organizational department, year, month, products, and so on), but there is more to analyzing than this. There were many ohs and ahs just from spending a few hours learning to analyze and discussing the next question. We knew we had a foundation for spreading information within the organization by assisting the data and analytics team in learning to analyze.

In addition, we assisted the team in asking the right questions to the business when they had questions about reports or dashboards. They were able to deliver actionable insights rather than flat reporting overviews in this manner. One example of these newly acquired skills is the ability to question requests they receive by simply asking *Why do you want to know this?* and *How are you going to use it?* Only by answering these and other questions will you be able to get a complete picture of the data needed and deliver a targeted solution with insights that the business can act on right away.

There are some excellent data literacy training and assessment resources available online. The blended method is the most successful training combination. It's a good idea to start with the basics of data literacy and how it can help, and explain that we're all data literate in some way (see *Chapter 1, The Beginning – The Flow of Data*). Start by learning to analyze with the tools that your organization is using, and then teach your employees how to use the tools to their full potential.

Consider the available data literacy courses as the next step. Following those fundamental steps, broaden the learning path by incorporating real-world examples, organizing hackathons or datathons, and participating in data challenges. In this way, you add a competitive element to data use and design for the general public. Of course, assist your staff in learning which questions to ask of the data so that they can actually improve their work and gain more efficiency or effectiveness.

Here are a few pointers to help you boost this pillar and develop data literacy in your organization and your personal life:

- Ensure that employees understand and learn how to ask appropriate questions. In this case, the most important question is *WHY*. More on this topic can be found in *Chapter 8, Questioning the Data*.

- Ensure that employees understand which data is required, how to analyze it, and how to test its relevance and validity.

- Can your staff interpret the data so that the results are accurate and useful? Are they fully prepared, and do they understand which use cases are addressed (please see *Intermezzo – it's not controlling, it's assisting*).

- Show your employees how to use A/B tests to determine which options and types of visualizations work best for your organization or departments.

- Investigate the advantages of creating simple visualizations so that the results are accessible to leaders with varying levels of data expertise. People tend to focus not only on the visualizations that they require but also on those that they can read! You don't need to be a data scientist to work with insights!

- Show how to tell a data story to help decision-makers see the big picture and act on the findings of their analysis. More information on data storytelling can be found in *Chapter 10, Turning Insights into Decisions*.

- Maintaining healthy organizational growth begins with a focus on every employee in your organization, to foster a desire to be assured, confident, and intrigued by data. Your business will grow as each person advances in their personal data literacy journey!

Intermezzo – it's not controlling, it's assisting

A decade ago, in larger organizations, we had a centralized **Center of Excellence (CoE)** for data and analytics. We were working with a variety of standards and guidelines within this CoE. The first step in our projects was to conduct a project intake (you can find this project intake form in *Chapter 14, Appendix A – Templates*). During this project intake, we discussed not only the desired functionality but also some **non-functional requirements (NFRs)**. These questions are shown in *Figure 3.9*.

By answering those questions, we were able to not only manage the licenses but also manage and track the usage of our developed dashboards and reports, with dashboards that answered questions such as *How many business users are there? When and who uses which dashboard? Which graphs work and which do not? When is the busiest time of day? How many sessions are available? Which licenses are used? How are licenses managed?* (how many users are logged in at the same time), and so on.

Despite the fact that our customers were internal, we managed their success and were able to plot the questions from the project intake against actual usage. When we noticed that the dashboards were not being used frequently or that only one sheet (the dashboard) was being used, we visited our customers on a monthly basis. When we saw that usage was falling short of expectations, we always asked, *How can we help?* or *Should we set up a workshop so that we can help you train the staff?*

We were able to deliver some new workshops on numerous occasions (despite the fact that we always did a workshop during our implementation phase). We were able to assist the staff in understanding the dashboards, reports, and analyzing techniques in this manner. But the most important thing is that they understood the use cases that we addressed!

In addition to those workshops, we had a monthly workshop on **business intelligence (BI)** and how it could help us grow, gain efficiency, improve processes, and so on. The most important point we wanted to emphasize was that "action" was required; do not take the measures for granted, but instead, analyze what is behind the measure and take action to actually improve. This is why we believe in education and assisting your staff with targeted education and measuring what you need to know in order to grow.

Let's go through the NFR project intake:

Non-Functional Requirements	
Number of expected users	<10 | 10-50 | 50-100 | 100-250 | >250
Expected frequency of use	ad-hoc | daily | weekly | monthly | quarterly | yearly
Expected mode of use	Standard reporting | Search interactively
Up-to-datedness of the data (Refresh rate)	ad-hoc | daily | weekly | monthly | quarterly | yearly
Application availability	
Addition and or explanation	

Figure 3.9 – NFR project intake

Mixing the pillars

We have frequently observed that organizations have implemented data and analytics in a variety of ways, most of which began with the idea "we need a tool" to create management information. In fact, static reports were created in the systems we've worked with all the time in the past. People were running around with static lists, trying to figure out when a file, product, or whatever was finished. We used to believe that big data environments were unnecessary because we could manage things perfectly with some kind of data visualization solution. In fact, we still see it around us: organizations begin by visualizing information for decision-making but neglect the organization that needs to embrace data-informed decision-making.

Figure 3.9 illustrates the different ways in which everything can go in various directions. In fact, looking back to 2007/2008, we thought a data management environment was unnecessary and visualized everything we could with the tools available at the time. This strategy was used until a few years ago. At that time, we saw the importance of data management rise, and new solutions entered the market, putting data management and data quality back on the strategic agenda:

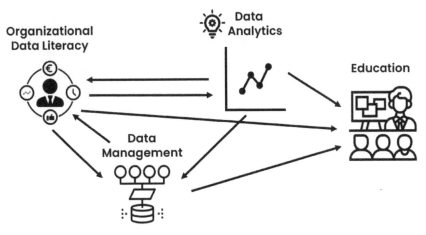

Figure 3.10 – There are various ways to use the pillars

The idea is that the organizational data literacy and education pillars must be addressed, while the data and analytics and data management pillars are dependent on the maturity of the organization and may be addressed in stages.

Summary

After reading this chapter, we have a better understanding of the four-pillar approach and how we can use it to be successful in our organizations' use of data and analytics. It assists us in deciding what to consider when we want to professionalize our data and analytics environment or data and analytics teams.

In the following section, we discussed a brief overview of organizational data literacy and the steps you must take. The following section provided a brief overview of data management and why it is critical to implement this in your organization. This topic is covered in greater depth in *Chapter 5, Managing Your Data Environment*.

The following section concerned data and analytics, and it was not only about purchasing a tool that you wanted to use, but also about learning how to work with it and creating visualizations that people could actually read. The final component is education, which is required for all staff members within your organization; leading by example is essential for your organization to embrace data and analytics. Data and analytics should be in your company's DNA! The educational component of the four-pillar model includes all chapters that embrace some form of learning.

We discussed how to approach projects and help your organization grow during its data literacy journey by using work experience stories as examples in our intermezzos.

In the following chapter, we will discuss organizational data literacy and how our framework can help you determine which steps you should take to become a successful data-literate organization.

4

Implementing Organizational Data Literacy

Is your organization a data-literate organization? Does it leverage insights to make decisions? Does it tie any analytics projects and initiatives to strategic goals? Does it blend data with multiple human factors, such as a motivation to ask questions or an openness to new ideas and perspectives? Is it able to be agile and scale to all employees when a new decision needs to be made leveraging data? If you cannot answer yes to all these questions, you are not alone. However, you may strive to be able to answer yes to all these at some point in the future. When you can answer yes to all of these, your organization systematically and systemically utilizes data and analytics to make the best possible decisions across all levels.

Much of this book is devoted to individual data literacy, but for organizations to be data literate, the skills and behaviors of employees are just one dimension. In addition, they need to have the right tools and technology, the right organizational strategy and processes, and the right culture to foster data literacy.

In this chapter, we will discuss all of these dimensions as well as the framework for rolling out an organization-wide data literacy program. We will cover the following main topics:

- Implementing organizational data literacy
- Planning the data literacy vision
- Communicating the data literacy vision
- Developing a data-literate culture
- Creating a data literacy educational program
- Measuring success
- Celebrating successes

By the end of the chapter, you will have a good idea of what organizational data literacy is and what are the various components that are required to achieve it. You will also learn tips and strategies for how you can roll out data literacy initiatives within your organization.

Implementing organizational data literacy

Many organizations desire to become more data literate; however, they do not know how and where to start or what to focus on. While organizations may all be at different stages of data literacy, all organizations should leverage a consistent framework that provides steps and best practices to maximize their data literacy maturity.

Figure 4.1 shows such a framework for implementing organizational data literacy:

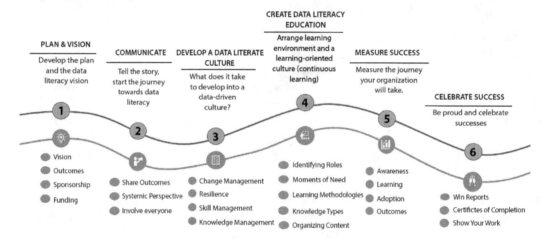

Figure 4.1 – Implementing organizational data literacy

Organizations must have a plan and vision for data literacy, which they then communicate to all employees. They will need to develop and foster a culture that embraces data literacy and data-informed decisions. They will need to provide employees with access to various learning content specific to data literacy. Along their journey, they will need to make sure they benchmark and measure progress toward their vision and celebrate successes along the way. The remainder of this chapter is focused on explaining these six dimensions of the framework in much more detail.

Planning the data literacy vision

Before starting an organizational transformation to become data literate, you need to first establish an overall data literacy strategy and vision for the organization. That strategy and vision need to align with the employee culture. From there, you need to establish specific objectives that start at the top of an organization and cascade down. For example, an objective could be to back all decisions with data, or another one could be to be able to trust the organization's data. After your objectives are established, you need to identify specific activities that will drive you toward attaining the vision and objectives.

To help you start thinking about what your organizational data literacy vision should be, the following list identifies a few common traits of data-literate organizations:

- **Data and data-informed decision-making are part of an organizational strategy**

  Leveraging data to make informed decisions is part of an organization's strategy. This typically includes organizations seeing data as an organizational asset, having specific data literacy objectives at the organizational level, and having executive sponsorship and leadership support.

- **Promote and employ a data-literate culture**

  A data-literate culture allows all employees to obtain trusted and actionable insights that they can use to make decisions. This is done by implementing the right governance and processes with data, implementing the right tools and technology, enabling employees to find and access relevant data and insights in a self-service manner, and empowering employees to use data and insights to make decisions. These all have to be wrapped by a culture that supports this. We will discuss specific aspects of a data-literate culture later on in this chapter, in the *Developing a data-literate culture* section.

- **Leaders believe in the value of data literacy**

  Leaders should evangelize data as a strategic and long-term asset, leveraged across all parts of the business. They should also lead by example. If your leaders are not working with discovered insights, and don't ask critical questions of them and the underlying data, then they can't and won't ask the same from their employees.

- **Data is both trustworthy and trusted**

  Data is centralized, and a corporate-wide data strategy is in place, but departments have data ownership to manage the data quality. Data is seen as a strategic asset, and the organization considers data quality as a strategic initiative. This means it is discussed on a regular basis at the executive level.

- **Democratization of data**

  Making better decisions with data requires everyone in the organization that needs to have access to the data to have access, as well as the right tools and skills to properly use it. This does not mean everyone has access to all data. Individuals should only have access to the data relevant to their needs.

- **Data is embedded in every decision, interaction, and process**

  A key principle of a data-literate culture is that organizations do not use data to justify a decision they have already made; rather, they use it to gain new insights. Using data analytics by itself is not going to move the needle. The desired outcome is to use analytics to find insights to make better decisions. Everyone is expected to make decisions informed by data.

- **Invest in data literacy training for everyone**

  Data literacy education should be provided and even mandated for all employees within the organization. It is important to allow employees dedicated time during work to take data literacy training. The training cannot just be self-paced, one-size-fits-all generic data courses either. It should include mixed and blended learning, including videos, classroom training, self-study, and much more. This topic is discussed in greater detail later on in this chapter in the *Creating a data literacy educational program* section.

- **Invest and roll out the right tools and technology to support data**

  After the organizational strategy and processes that support data literacy are established, organizations should select the right tools and technologies to meet the needs of everyone working with data. This could include data storage, data integration, data mining, data cataloging, analytics, and advanced analytics tools and technologies.

- **Support a test-and-learn environment for continuous improvement**

  An organization that embraces a growth mindset will see failure as a learning opportunity. After all, the sooner you learn about what is *not* working, the sooner you learn about what *is* working. Organizations need to embrace this style and culture and create a space for employees to have the freedom to fail as long as they learn something from it.

Once you have defined your strategy and objectives and identified traits, as in the preceding examples, you will need to turn some of these into **key performance indicators (KPIs)**, with targets to allow you to measure success. Here are a couple of example targets we have seen implemented at various organizations:

- Over 85% of the organization attends at least level 1 awareness training on data literacy in 1 year

- The organization delivers at least 8 data literacy workshops to its employees in 1 year (2 per quarter)

- 95% of all employees have data literacy and data-informed decision-making skills listed in their individual development plan

- The organization will have two specific companywide meetings in 1 year, with the sole focus on giving updates specific to data, analytics, and data literacy projects

- The organization communicates win reports to all employees per quarter on success related to data literacy

In this section, we have discussed the importance of having a solid data literacy vision. Even if your organization is just starting out on its data literacy journey, it is important to have a vision of where you want to end up with data literacy. Now that you have planned the rollout and established the vision and success criteria, it is time to communicate this to the entire organization via an internal marketing initiative.

Communicating the data literacy vision

In this section, we will focus on how you can internally market and communicate the data literacy vision to the entire organization. The keys to effective internal marketing are focusing on desired outcomes, adopting a systemic perspective, and getting all employees involved in the whole process.

Focusing on desired outcomes

During the planning stage, you have identified what you want the organization to do at a strategic level. Now, you need to go one level deeper and communicate the specific problems you are trying to solve. For example, if the organization tends to make instinct-based decisions, partly because either the data team does not provide the data or the decision makers do not trust the data, then those are the problems that you should communicate you are trying to address. We discuss how to properly question and ensure that you are asking the right questions in detail later, in *Chapter 10, Turning Insights into Decisions!*.

Adopting a systemic perspective

When implementing a data-literate organization, it is imperative to think systemically and understand how the different parts of the organization work across the data literacy journey. Thinking systemically means being able to understand the bigger picture of everything related to your decision. Let's consider a simple, non-business example. If you were to bring a new pet home or are considering having another child, thinking systemically means you understand those scenarios do not just affect you but also many other people, including partners, children, other pets, and so on. Not only do you understand that it will affect others, but you understand how it will affect others, including various possible unintended consequences.

In business, a team, an entire organization, or even beyond the organization, an entire supply chain can be considered a system. When discussing decisions that may affect one part of those, thinking systemically will require you to think about how they may affect all parts of those systems.

Back to data literacy, we believe data literacy is a team sport, and this means that decisions and strategies need to be thought of and understood for all groups (all parts of the system). Some organizations will invest lots of time and resources in the creators of analytics, but then completely ignore investing in the consumers of insights generated by the creators.

Getting everyone involved in the whole process

Earlier in the planning stage, we talked about the importance of the democratization of data and ensuring that data is embedded in every decision. To support that, you need to ensure every single employee is both enabled and empowered to use data. To truly enable employees, they first need to understand the value of insights obtained from data and how they can help them achieve their goals. Everyone in the organization needs to think critically about the potential use cases and applications specific to them. Getting everyone involved in the whole process will greatly aid the effectiveness of your internal marketing campaign to communicate the organization's intent and usage of data literacy. It will also lead to better decisions, as it allows more people to safely access data to analyze, interpret, and apply their perspectives.

This can be accomplished by sharing win reports and other assets that highlight the outcomes and value provided by data to the organization. Introductory workshops and lunch and learn events should be provided for all employees to learn about the benefits of data and how data literacy is the key to unlocking the value within the data for the entire organization. You can highlight how the data helped inform your decision, and potentially even discuss what has happened previously in similar situations when data was not used to make a decision.

Developing a data-literate culture

Technology and data are evolving faster than organizations can evolve their culture to leverage them. While a portion of organizational data literacy is about having the right tools and technologies, those tools and technologies will not have the desired impact unless the organization has the right culture. The heart and soul of a data-literate organization is its culture as it relates to the way it integrates data, insights, decisions, and actions. Many organizations understand the importance of this but have been challenged in transforming their culture to one that supports data literacy and the use of data to make decisions. In this section, we will discuss three required areas to support a data literacy culture: change management, driving resilience, and skill and knowledge management.

Managing change

The biggest obstacles and adoption barriers that organizations face when they try to become data-literate organizations are managerial and cultural. Both of these require strong change management, and that change management requires the organization to continuously adapt its structure, culture, and management capabilities. It also requires the organization to provide the right environment and learning content to properly help employees learn any new skills required for the change to be successful.

For organizations to maximize the value they receive from data, they must drive a change. There are many change management frameworks available that can be used. One we have seen succeed as a method for driving organizational change to support data literacy is the eight-step model created by Harvard Business School professor John Kotter, as depicted in *Figure 4.2*:

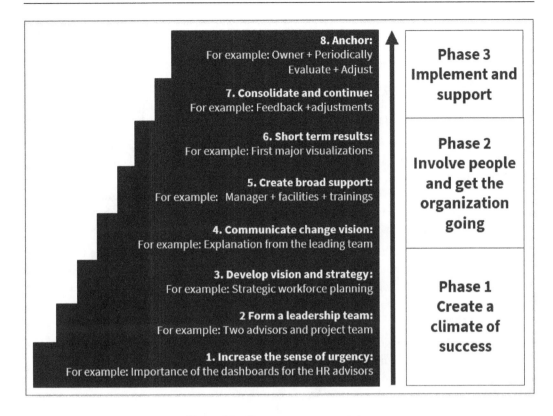

Figure 4.2 – Change management step

Kotter is a leading expert in the field of change management and introduced this eight-step process in his book, *Leading Change*. Let's have a look at the process in more detail:

1. Create a sense of urgency for the organization. The intent is not to scare employees about what happens if we do not change, but rather to show an open and honest approach to ensuring all employees are aware and involved in the change. This will help build support for the change.

2. Form a guiding coalition that garners leadership and visible support from influential individuals. This will help mobilize more stakeholders. Influence may come from positional or informal aspects. Harnessing the power of social influence is a great method to help increase change acceptance. As more people accept the change, this creates a positive spillover effect, which in turn provides more influence on others to accept the change.

3. Create a clear vision to ensure that people can understand the purpose of the change and the desired outcomes of the change. It makes the change more palatable and helps reduce the anxiety that emerges naturally from a change process. This should include information such as what got the organization to this point, what is the decision to be made, how important it is, what the time frame is, and what the success criteria are.

4. Select the right data and visualizations to communicate, and craft a narrative that helps the audience understand the vision. Ensure your communication reinforces how the vision is directly tied to the purpose of the organization.

5. Remove any change barriers. A change will encounter barriers, which could be in the form of policies, procedures, silos within the organization, or a lack of the right skills. You should identify each barrier and then work on a plan to overcome each one.

6. Create quick wins. Early success helps minimize change fatigue while reinforcing momentum at the same time. Wins should be frequently and publicly communicated. Quick wins prove that change can happen, no matter how small. This not only reinforces you are on the right track but also helps keep people motivated for the longer change process ahead. People may not stick around till the end to see if it was successful, but they will be more likely to if they get feedback and celebrate wins early and often in the process.

7. Build on the change. When sufficient momentum is built and early successes are visible, be relentless with the remaining aspects of the change until the vision is a reality. When people see quick yet incremental progress in their work or their team's work and that work gets celebrated as wins, they will feel motivated, be more engaged, and, ultimately, more likely to continue with the change.

8. Institutionalize the change. The change is not a single event—it's an ongoing process that needs to be sustainable. It is common for organizations to put a lot of emphasis on a change, and then when the action goes live, move on. In many cases, that will result in everyone going back to their old ways of doing things before the change.

Make sure everything related to the change is updated to be sustainable and ongoing. This includes defining the right performance indicators, as discussed in *Chapter 6, Aligning with Organizational Goals,* and institutionalizing those into the dashboards and measurement frameworks that are used to run the business.

Driving resilience

Research highlights that about 70% of organizational change initiatives fail. Given the impact of change load on individuals and organizations, and the fact constant change is here to stay, an important organizational strategy should be to not rely on change management alone, but also focus on building and driving a resilient organization. Building resilience will help people be proactively ready for future changes that we know will come.

Resilience refers to our ability to adapt to stress brought on by change and adversity. Not only does resilience allow us to adapt, but it also acts to help us grow and improve as a result of the situation.

Resilience is really hard for us as humans. The human brain developed in a way that it was designed to be attentive to threats. As a result, negative stimuli get more attention and processing. This is true still today. This narrows our minds and promotes less-than-ideal reactions and responses when faced with change. This ends up making us feel overwhelmed, and we resist the change.

In fact, not only do we feel overwhelmed and resist the change, but a few other things happen as a result as well. This is called **threat reactivity**. Our brain tricks us into overestimating threats, underestimating opportunities, and underestimating resources for dealing with threats and fulfilling opportunities. These are situations that are highly likely to occur during a change.

The good news is that resilience can be learned and increased with specific practice. One common approach to increasing your resiliency is to be very deliberate in identifying your thoughts and behaviors and intentionally trying to modify them. The more we do this, the more practice we get, and our brains will actually adjust to help us reinforce the skill.

Let's take a look at an example of resilience at both an organizational and an individual level, as seen through the COVID-19 pandemic. This example is also highlighted in *Figure 4.3*:

Organizational Resilience   **Individual Resilience**

Flexibility & Adaptability	Changing business model. New work environment. New work tasks.
Work-life boundaries	New work times
Connect	Leaned on work groups, family, friends, and social groups
Hope	The pandemic will end eventually, and we will get through this

Figure 4.3 – Resilience during COVID-19

A resilient organization during COVID-19 needed to support flexibility and adaptability in a changing environment. Consider all the restaurants that had to close their dining rooms to guests during the pandemic. They needed to be both flexible and adaptable to a new business model thrust upon them without any prior notice. Resilient organizations needed to set and model healthy work-life boundaries, including new work times and time off required by employees to support children and family members who were either sick or being homeschooled as a result of the pandemic.

Individual resilience through COVID-19 also required flexibility and adaptability. For example, employees at the restaurants we just mentioned would also need to be flexible and adaptable to their work environment, their work tasks, and their work hours changing as a result of the pandemic.

Individual resilience is increased by the number and quality of connections and healthy relationships. Individuals leaned on their connections, whether they be family or friends or even pets, as well as work groups and social groups, during the pandemic. Finally, individual resilience is increased by having a positive outlook. Having hope that the pandemic would eventually end, and that you would be able to manage through it, helped many individuals throughout that tough time, and others.

Managing the organization's skills and knowledge

A key component of a data-literate organization is its ability to properly manage the organization's skills and knowledge. This sounds pretty straightforward, but it is actually an evolution of how organizations typically focus on their employees. Let's go back to the early 1990s when the field of talent management first emerged. The focus was on managing employees through what was called the employee journey, or employee life cycle, which started from recruiting and onboarding to performance management, through to ongoing learning and development. In most cases, these departments based their programs on job descriptions, roles, and hierarchies within an organization.

That has worked in the past, but now, with all the technological advancements we are seeing, jobs are evolving fast, and many employees will need reskilling shortly after they are hired to learn the latest skills. Data-literate organizations should shift their focus from job descriptions and academic qualifications to skills and competencies. We discuss skills and competencies in greater detail in *Chapter 11, Defining a Data Literacy Competency Framework*, but an example would be to focus less on specific job titles and levels, such as data analyst, and focus more on specific skills, such as proficiency in the skill of data mining.

In the past, with a focus on jobs, organizational strategies thought of employees as interchangeable parts of the supply chain. If someone leaves, you need to hire someone else for the same job description. In the new world, data-literate organizations organize their strategies around the idea of skills and competencies to be cultivated. This lends itself to organizational structures that are less siloed where employees can contribute to many parts of the organization, based on the skills and competencies they possess. As an aside, this not only helps foster a data-literate organization, but it also helps with employee engagement and retention, as it puts the employees and their skills and competencies at the center of work, rather than a specific job.

The organizational process of managing skills and competencies focuses on acquiring, training, and utilizing those skills and competencies to build the best data-literate organization. This process involves determining the right skills and competencies required and then evaluating employees against the desired performance levels. We will discuss the specific skills and competencies required across an organization to foster data literacy later on in *Chapter 11, Defining a Data Literacy Competency Framework*.

Now that we have discussed the importance of data-literate organizations focusing on managing skills and competencies, we can focus on the second part of this strategy, which is how to document and share employees' knowledge. With every decision that an organization makes, people are leveraging data, along with their experience in the business. This allows them to go from data to information to knowledge and eventually wisdom, commonly referred to as the DIKW pyramid, as shown in *Figure 4.4*:

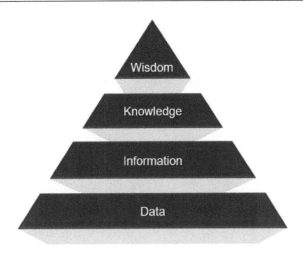

Figure 4.4 – DIKW pyramid

While organizations invest a lot of time and money in strategies and processes for handling their data, they typically do not invest enough time or money in strategies and processes for handling their information and knowledge. In many organizations, those levels are left with the specific individuals who have them and are not stored, codified, or documented, making it incredibly hard for others within the organization to make use of them. This severely impacts the ability of an organization to be fully data literate.

Data-literate organizations need to have a deliberate strategy and set of processes for capturing these higher-order elements such as actionable insights and relevant information and knowledge so that employees can access and use them whenever they need to. The data-informed decision-making process is at the heart of data-literate organizations and is built into their DNA.

Creating a data literacy educational program

In the previous section, we talked about the importance of managing skills and competencies. One key element of this framework is the ability to upskill your employees on these skills and competencies. The specific skills and competencies are discussed later on in *Chapter 11, Defining a Data Literacy Competency Framework*, but for now, it is important to know that these are a combination of hard skills and soft skills. When most organizations invest in data literacy education and data literacy maturity models, they tend to focus on hard skills. They often talk about capabilities in terms of technology and tools, but they often leave out the necessary soft skills to become fully data literate.

An organization may build many dashboards and reports, but then just hope that the business can use them appropriately. Other times, organizations will put data literacy training in place for their employees, but they make it one size to fit all. Data literacy training needs to be role-based and specific to the organization, its culture, and its processes. In addition, organizations tend to use learning solutions that teach the same level of proficiency, using the same learning approach. Data literacy training needs to be thought of as a journey rather than a single event. You need to learn how to crawl and walk before you can run and master specific competencies. In addition, traditional educational approaches that use formal learning are becoming less and less effective in today's world. Organizations need to embrace a new approach to learning delivery that meets the needs of today's employees.

In this section, we will cover eight dimensions to factor in when creating a data literacy educational program:

- Employee roles
- Learning levels
- Moments of need
- Learning methodologies
- Knowledge types
- Learning elements
- Organizing content
- Searching for content

These categories are visually depicted in *Figure 4.5*:

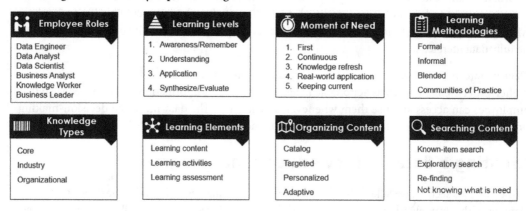

Figure 4.5 – Data literacy educational program dimensions

Let's take a detailed look at these categories.

Identifying employee roles

Data literacy is not achieved by mastering a uniform set of competencies that applies to everyone. Those that are relevant to each individual can vary significantly depending on how they interact with data and which part of the data process they are involved in. For example, the skills relevant to someone responsible for cleaning and preparing data for analysis are different from those relevant to someone responsible for interpreting the results of the analysis.

Also, remember that data literacy is not just a set of technical skills. There is an equal need and weight for soft skills and business skills. This can be misleading for some technical resources within an organization, as those technical resources may believe they are data literate by default as they are data architects or data analysts. They have the existing technical skills, but maybe they do not have any deep proficiencies in other skills such as communicating with data, challenging assumptions, and mitigating bias, or perhaps they do not have an open mindset to be open to different perspectives.

We segment the roles into six separate roles:

- Business leader
- Knowledge worker
- Business analyst
- Data engineer
- Data analyst
- Data scientist

Every organization may have variations of this, and individuals may do the job of more than one role, but the purpose here is to show the differences at a high level and ensure that your organization provides the right training specific to its roles. The following list describes, at a high level, each of the six roles:

- **Business leader**: Business leaders are not the ones who will do any data mining or data science work. They are ultimately the ones responsible for any decisions made with data, including the decision itself, communication of the decision, and the change management process that will drive the decision.

- **Knowledge worker**: Knowledge workers include anyone who has their own insights relevant to their own needs. As you learned in Chapter 1, *The Beginning–The Flow of Data* everyone works with and analyzes data. Everyone will come up with their own insights, even if it is just for them—for example, analyzing their own performance or where to go on vacation.

- **Business analyst**: Business analysts interpret the insights they receive from a data analyst or data scientist, applying their domain knowledge to ultimately make a data-informed decision or a business recommendation.

- **Data engineer**: Data engineers design, develop, and maintain any architecture or device that stores, prepares, and analyzes large amounts of data. Many times, their job involves data modeling and integration tasks, and tasks related to improving data quality. Typically, the output from a data engineer is quality, clean, analytics-ready data that other parts of the organization can analyze.

- **Data analyst**: Data analysts access, manipulate, and analyze the data made available by the data engineer. They will use analytic techniques to answer analytical questions asked by the business, enabling organizations to make data-informed decisions.

- **Data scientist**: Data scientists perform various tasks, including data mining, **machine learning (ML)**, and probability and predictive modeling, to find and extract insights from data. Whereas data analysts will look to find answers to existing analytic questions, data scientists look to find patterns in data without existing questions.

Another way to approach this is to look at the phases of the data journey that a person is involved in, regardless of what role they play. We will discuss the various phases in much more detail later on in *Chapter 10, Turning Insights into Decisions*, but here is a quick overview:

1. Identifying decisions to be made
2. Understanding, acquiring, and preparing relevant data
3. Turning data into insights
4. Validating the insights
5. Transforming insights into decisions
6. Communicating decisions
7. Evaluating outcomes of decisions

In *Chapter 11, Defining a Data Literacy Competency Framework*, we will identify the various skills that are relevant to each of these phases.

Learning levels

When designing a data literacy educational program, it is important to include multiple learning levels within it. You can label them with sequential terms, such as basic, intermediate, and advanced, or you can use more descriptive terms based on the outputs, such as awareness, understanding, application, and expert. This is important for two reasons. First, employees cannot expect to jump from knowing nothing to being experts all at once. It is a journey. As such, there are various skill levels that could be achieved at each level. For example, a basic skill level for an employee who needs to interpret analytic results would include the ability to understand simple statistical terminology, such as mean, median, and mode, and various aggregations, such as average and sum. An intermediate level for that same employee would include wider and more advanced skills to be able to know whether interpretations can be derived from results. An advanced level for that same employee would include having a deep understanding of statistical terminology and the ability to recognize statements and interpretations and evaluate them against the data and other facts. The second reason is that not all roles will require the same level for each skill.

For example, a leader who is reviewing proposals may only need to achieve an understanding of a skill, whereas an employee doing the specific work will need to achieve an expert level. In another example, people who are responsible for making decisions from insights provided will need to be able to interpret the results of a given statistical or analytic test. They don't need to know how to actually implement those tests, though, only just interpret the results. Someone else within the organization requires more advanced levels of the same skill so that they can apply and implement those statistics or analytics. We will dive deeper into the learning levels for each skill in a later chapter when we discuss a data literacy competency framework.

Covering all moments of need

Organizations tend to think of data literacy training as a single point in time when someone starts not data literate, and they become data literate after completing the training. However, neither learning nor user adoption works like this. Data literacy education programs need to take into account the five moments of need for an employee: learning for the first time, continuous learning, knowledge refresh, real-world application, and keeping current, as shown in *Figure 4.6*:

Figure 4.6 – The five moments of need of an employee

The "first" experience

The learning of a brand-new subject is most often delivered all at once, during the course of several days straight. This is done in an attempt to take in a mountain of information in a short period of time. But ideally, the first experience should be a manageable serving size that whets the appetite and lays the foundation for the continuous experience to follow.

For example, when launching new data and analytic tools and technologies, don't provide an intensive multi-day crash course on every feature and function. Start with a specific task that this tool will help the employee achieve that they could not before, and teach them that. This will make them aware of the technology, in a manageable serving size, and they will then want to continue to learn more.

The "continuous" experience

Studies show that information learned over time is remembered more than the same amount of information learned all at once. This approach encourages a cycle of learning and application, learning and application, and so on, and with each return to the learning phase of the cycle, employees are armed with more experience and real-world understanding regarding how they will apply what they are learning.

Rather than teaching data literacy as a finite multi-day event, think of it as a process. Similar to how universities offer continuing education programs to postgraduates, your data literacy education should follow this. This blended style allows employees to learn specific topics followed up by a chance to practice them in real-life scenarios. Then, they continue on to the next topic, potentially the next week.

The "knowledge refresh" experience

Employees will never remember everything that they learn related to data literacy (or any topic, for that matter). It is very common that employees may be working on a project and remember specific data literacy principles that they learned previously, but they fail to remember the specific details of how to apply them. To help with this situation, the learning program should allow employees the ability to jump back to that point in their learning experience and easily review it again. Employees should not have to retake the entire training course or module just to obtain those specific details of how to apply something; they should be able to quickly refresh something they have already learned.

In one of the training classes offered, your organization may discuss a specific topic that needs to be refreshed later. For example, an employee may be working within a dashboard and needs to remember how to do comparative analytics within a specific tool. They do not want to have to sit through the entire training they already took. They want to be able to go to a learning management system or similar and look up a job aid or a clip of the training as a video specific to this request.

The "real-world" experience

Remembering information does not automatically translate to being able to apply the information. The learning experience is often built upon simple examples that can be understood by a broad range of employees and roles. Because the examples are engineered for educational purposes, they frequently follow a happy path without encountering errors or exceptions to the intended workflow or process. In the real world, the application of what you have learned does not always go quite so smoothly. This is where a data literacy educational program needs to provide employees with the ability to get advice from others on a real-world application. Common examples of this range from moderated discussion forums to mentors and coaches.

The "keep current" experience

Things change all the time, and employees must continuously learn new information. There are always new tools and technologies being leveraged, and organizational processes are always evolving as well. Learning content needs to be governed to ensure that all the information it provides stays current. For content developers, it may require nearly as much effort to maintain this content as it did to initially create it. However, without this ongoing effort to keep the content current, users will quickly lose confidence in the content if they discover information that is, at best, out of date or, worse yet, incorrect. Similar to knowledge refreshes discussed earlier, employees should easily be able to identify new content without having to sit through an entire learning course or module where only a portion is new content.

Typical examples of this within an organization may be as simple as release notes for changes in a process, to specific learning modules on what has changed in the ecosystem.

Learning methodologies

Data literacy programs should ideally blend formal learning with informal learning opportunities.

Formal learning is structured learning with specific learning objectives. This is commonly accomplished in organizations via either face-to-face classroom or virtual online training sessions with an instructor. **Informal learning** involves employees learning from daily experiences doing their job, outside of a classroom. It can include things ranging from immersive experiences and simulations to conversations with mentors and coaches and other colleagues, reading social media posts, listening to podcasts, webinars, book clubs, and other communities of practice.

In addition to providing both formal and informal learning opportunities, employees will benefit from creating shared experiences to learn with and from other employees. This is typically accomplished through **blended learning**, which includes a blend of self-paced learning modules and activities, with weekly live sessions with peers and an instructor.

Organizations aspiring to be data-literate organizations should also build a *community of practice* specific to data literacy. Communities of practice are groups of people who share a common desire and passion for a particular task or skill or subject. Employees will deepen their knowledge and expertise by leveraging communities of practice as this provides them opportunities to interact with peers on an ongoing basis, specific to the topic. In communities of practice, there is no hierarchy or instructor. All members can provide knowledge to other members and influence via social and collaborative communication and sharing of ideas.

Including all knowledge types

A world-class data literacy educational framework cannot just include core data literacy knowledge and skills. There need to be some aspects of the knowledge and learning that are specific to their business, industry, and organization. This is why subscriptions to third-party learning platforms that offer various off-the-shelf courses on data literacy topics are useful, but cannot be the complete solution.

The learning needs to be augmented with knowledge specific to the organization, industry, and business domain, as shown in *Figure 4.7*:

Core Knowledge & Skills	Industry & Role Knowledge	Organizational Knowledge
Generally applicable technical and business skills	Knowledge, information, and skills specific to an industry, or specific to a given role	Knowledge and information specific to the organization
For example, interpreting basic data visualizations	For example, specific calculations and visualizations commonly used in finance, or in the energy industry	For example, specific processes that the organization uses

Figure 4.7 – Three types of content to include in your data literacy education

Let's go through these domains in the following list:

- **Core knowledge and skills**: Core knowledge and skills relates to training and knowledge content that helps employees with foundational knowledge and skills, regardless of which role or industry they are in. For example, everyone in a data-literate organization should have the knowledge and skills to be able to interpret a basic data visualization.

- **Industry and Role knowledge**: Data literacy can be useful across any industry that leverages data. However, if the goal is to make better decisions with data, it is important that employees tasked with making those decisions understand the industry and business knowledge specific to the decision to be made. For example, if a software company is trying to make a data-informed decision as to how to decrease the number of software bugs they have, people analyzing the data and making decisions would need to know about the software development industry, what is defined as a bug, what are appropriate industry benchmarks for how many bugs are acceptable, and various things like that. If analysts or decision-makers do not understand the data and how it is applied in the specific business context, they will not be able to make the best decisions. Training and knowledge programs should ensure that employees receive the right industry and business knowledge as part of the data literacy educational framework.

- **Organizational knowledge**: Organizational knowledge is related to how your organization works. This includes knowledge about the people, processes, strategy, and culture. Every organization is different. Just having core skills and industry skills is not sufficient. Learning offerings need to also include knowledge that is unique to how the organization works. This could include the process of how your organization makes tactical decisions, or it could include which organization owns specific data structures you may require in your analysis.

Learning elements

Educational programs are more than just the sum of all the learning videos or modules or courses. Those are absolutely critical for employees to achieve the desired learning objectives, but the ability to practice what you are learning, as well as the ability to assess whether you have obtained the desired learning objectives, is critical as well. **Learning activities** allow employees with safe opportunities and environments to reflect on and practice what they have learned. These can be labs, exercises, and other activities that require employees to practice what they have learned. If the learning is specific to a tool or technology, organizations should set up a sandbox environment to allow a safe place for employees to practice. **Learning assessments** are used to validate that a user has met the desired learning objectives and is ready to add to their existing knowledge.

Organizing content

One of the most important considerations for setting up a data literacy educational program is how the knowledge and learning content is organized and displayed. Employees expect useful experiences, tailored to their interests, their job, and their needs. While your organization may have an abundance of learning content, it is imperative to make sure employees do not waste time trying to find relevant content.

The challenge is determining the best way to organize and deliver just the right information to the right employee at the right time. This includes how to combine relevant content with insights about the employee's current needs. There are four types of content organization:

- Catalog
- Targeted
- Personalized
- Adaptive

These types are illustrated in *Figure 4.8*:

Push and Pull	As Close to Point of Need as Possible		Context-Specific
Catalog	**Targeted**	**Personalized**	**Adaptive**
Everything listed	Role-based	Rules-based	Data Driven
Searchable	Product-based	Decision Tree	Impoves overtime
	Experience-based		
	Geography-based		

Figure 4.8 – Ways to organize data literacy educational content

Let's go through each of the content organization types:

- With a **catalog** search, all the content is listed, but not in any organized manner. This is good for employees who may want to search and find relevant content, but not good for an employee who does not know what they don't know. A catalog can be useful for data literacy educational programs, but it should be only used by experienced employees who are already at a specific level and who are looking to find other learning tasks for professional development.

- With **targeted** content organization, content is organized and presented based on a targeted audience. This can include what role the targeted segments have. It can also include the level of experience of the employee. For example, there could be a pathway of curated learning specific to business leaders who want to achieve a basic level of competence in interpreting data visualizations.

- **Personalized** content organization is similar to targeted, but it becomes truly individualized. Because every employee is different, they may need slightly different and individualized content. This could be accomplished by asking the employee to identify relevant needs and content, and then displaying the personalized content for them. This is commonly accomplished based on a wizard-like approach that leverages rules and a decision tree behind the scenes to determine what to display. In more mature organizations, they have already defined the specific mappings of what sort of learning an individual needs, so the relevant learning can be displayed as soon as the employee logs in. Later on, in *Chapter 12*, *Assessing Your Data Literacy Maturity*, we discuss the levels that can be achieved for each competency. All of the learning should be displayed using these levels, such as beginner, intermediate, and advanced, as an example.

- Finally, with an **adaptive** organization of content, the content that is displayed to the employee evolves over time, based on data and by leveraging ML. A common example of this would be recommendations of knowledge base articles, podcasts, and other learning content based on data of what similar employees consumed.

Searching for content

The user experience that is implemented for your data literacy educational program should take into account various ways that employees will want to search for relevant content. There are commonly four ways that your employees will want to search for content, based on factors such as their role, their level, and their moment of need, as shown in *Figure 4.9*:

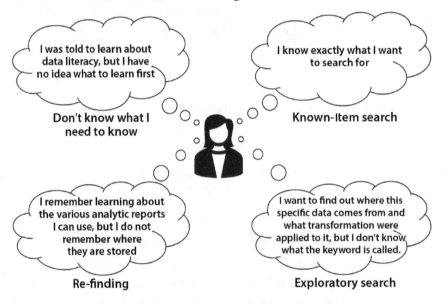

Figure 4.9 – How employees search for data literacy education

Known-item search

In some situations, employees know what they want to search for, and they know which words they can use to describe it. They may be looking for training on a particular tool, or they may be looking for a specific organizational process for cleaning data. In those cases, the key for the employee is they want to find the right information quickly. This can be implemented by leveraging a search across all knowledge and learning assets. Other approaches include a list of quick navigational links based on key or popular topics.

Exploratory search

In other situations, employees may have some idea of what they need to know, but they may not know how to articulate it and may not know the right terms or keywords that are used to find it. This is especially true with software training. They may know what they want to accomplish, but they may not know what that is called within the software. Employees in this situation also do not really know where to start to look, although they are able to recognize when they have found the right answer. Searches are not really useful with this type of exploratory seeking of learning content as employees are not able to articulate what they are looking for. Common solutions to this include good navigational structures within the environment, including a site map so that employees can browse it and explore or discover as they go, similar to a site map within a grocery store. You may not know exactly what you are looking for, but you know enough to know if it is a spice, a vegetable, or a protein, for example.

Re-finding

We mentioned earlier in the section how important it is to allow employees to easily find content that they have already consumed. A lot of time is typically spent by employees trying to re-find useful information and learning. Typical solutions for this use case include adding the ability for employees to bookmark content or create their own playlists of content.

Don't know what I need to know

The most common use case for employees just starting out with learning a topic, such as data literacy, is that they do not know exactly what they need to know. In these cases, it is the task of the organization to show them what they need to know. The ideal solution for this is to have a prescriptive pathway of content that the user should consume based on their current skills and gaps specific to their role.

To conclude this section, it is important to remember that data literacy is not one size fits all, so the educational program should not be either. This was a lot of information to share, covering various categories and dimensions that organizations should consider for their data literacy programs, but you should start by selecting the ones that make the most sense for your organization and where you are in the journey.

Organizations just starting out should not attempt to tackle all these various categories and use cases at once. Pick the ones that are most important to your organization to get started, such as prescriptive learning pathways for various roles within the organization. Then, continue to add and evolve for additional use cases, such as continuous learning, over time.

What ends up being challenging for mature organizations is that support for one specific category does not work for another one. For example, support that works for onboarding new employees does not work for employees who are already onboarded, and who want to continuously learn. Ideally, your systems would allow employees to either self-select or automatically select support based on where they are in the journey. For example, the system identifies any employee who has started in the past 3 months as a new employee and directs them to the support for onboarding.

Measuring success

Measuring the effectiveness of your organizational data literacy initiative is an essential step in the process. It will help you understand where your gaps are so that you can then prioritize and improve in those areas. It also enables you to communicate to the organization where they are in the journey and encourage further adoption.

In this section, we will talk about various strategies to evaluate and measure the success of an organization's data literacy initiative. This section will not cover how to assess organizational or individual data literacy maturity. Those topics are covered later on in the book in *Chapter 12, Assessing Your Data Literacy Maturity*.

Measuring the success of an organizational data literacy initiative can be shown at four different levels, as depicted in *Figure 4.10*:

Figure 4.10 – Four levels of measurement of data literacy initiatives

Let's now look at each level in greater detail:

- **Awareness**: Awareness measures who is aware of the data literacy initiative and its goals and objectives. This can be measured in a variety of methods, ranging from less accurate to more accurate. It can be measured by how many people received communications about the initiative by providing surveys to understand how many people are aware of the initiative. Change is a process, so it is important to measure awareness so that we can identify where we are in the journey. Not everyone is going to have learned the required skills and processes right away, so focus on driving awareness first.

- **Learning**: Learning measures which employees have taken training on various skills, as well as whether they acquired knowledge from the courses. This can be accomplished by providing assessments or evaluations at the end of each learning course.

- **Adoption**: Adoption measures two separate components of the data literacy initiative. One level measures the adoption of tools and technology. This can be evaluated based on the usage statistics for the relevant tools. Another level measures how data literacy is applied in meetings and in making decisions. This can be evaluated with surveys or evaluations to understand how many decisions are leveraging the organization's decision-making with data processes and whether there are any barriers to employees leveraging them (such as a lack of manager support).

- **Outcomes**: Outcomes measure where the organization is compared to the intended goals and outcomes for the data literacy initiative. Earlier in this chapter, we looked at how, during the planning phase, organizations develop their goals for how they will use data literacy within the organization. You will have also decided on key metrics to evaluate those goals. Now, you can monitor those key metrics to measure the goals to see where you are in terms of your desired outcomes.

  Outcomes are typically longer-term measures, and when an organization is just starting out with its data literacy journey, it needs to show shorter-term progress. This is where the other measures come into play.

Now that we have learned about how to measure an organization's data literacy, we will move on to discussing how to best celebrate successes within your data literacy initiative.

Celebrating successes

We have previously mentioned that becoming a data-literate organization is a journey over time. This journey requires a proper change management process. One of the key elements of this approach, to help reinforce the change, is to celebrate successes when they happen. This will not only increase morale overall, but more importantly, it will help build support for those employees who have not embraced or adopted the change to data literacy because they want to see it to believe it. These successes do not have to be large wins; even small wins, such as people completing a training course, will boost engagement. Here are a few tips on how you can celebrate your data literacy successes early and often:

- Provide win reports to the entire organization. Do not just focus on large wins; even small wins help show progress and boost engagement. These can be things such as monthly newsletters that highlight employees who have completed a specific data literacy learning pathway, or the rollout of a new technology to aid in the process of making better decisions with data.

- Provide certificates of completion and digital badges for employees who complete specific data literacy learning pathways, and share the badges on internal forums, the intranet, and even on external social media sites.

- Spend 5 minutes at the beginning or end of meetings to provide wins or recognition to individuals or groups. This can include, for example, how a group of employees worked collaboratively to uncover a mistake in one of the insights due to assumptions or bias.

- Show your work. Set up lunch and learn and other opportunities for employees to show what they have done specifically to data literacy. This gives them recognition in front of their peers, and it also allows everyone to obtain some new information and knowledge through this informal knowledge-sharing approach.

Summary

In this chapter, we have learned what it takes to be considered a data-literate organization. This does not just involve training individuals on data literacy skills—it also requires the organization to have a data literacy strategy that aligns with the organization's strategy. It requires tools and technologies and a culture that supports and empowers employees on their data journey.

We also discussed the steps you should follow if you want to launch a data literacy initiative within your organization, starting with planning the vision, and then moving on to communicating the vision, developing a data-literate culture, creating learning environments, and then finishing up with measuring and celebrating successes. You should now be able to go back and identify where you are in your data literacy journey and then identify steps to take it to the next level.

Now that we have learned about the first pillar, organizational data literacy, and how to implement it, we will move on to the second pillar, data management, in the next chapter.

Further reading

Please go through the following resource for further reading:

- *Kotter, J.P. (2012), Leading Change, Harvard Business Review Press.*

5
Managing Your Data Environment

The data elements that we capture in our transactional systems every day have enormous potential! We can generate interesting information to see whether we are still on track with our strategic objectives, how our business is doing, or how successful we are at what we do. With this gathered information and data we are able to take a variety of actions to improve our services, products, business operations, and so on. As described in *Chapter 2, Unfolding Your Data Journey*, we see issues with data quality and the need for data management in some form in order to advance in our data and analytics maturity.

Remember that the power of (big) data is not in the data itself but in how you use it!

Data management is the process of managing, maintaining, operationalizing, and securing your data environment. Data's importance has grown significantly in recent decades; where we once thought data registers, metadata, or even data management were unnecessary, it now appears that data is an asset on company profit, loss, and balance sheets. As a result, as previously stated, data has enormous potential and value. This makes sense given the rapidly increasing amount of data. When working with qualitative dashboards and reports, we must consider our data environment.

To be honest, there are numerous books, methods, articles, and websites that discuss or describe data management, master data management, data governance, data quality, and other related topics. We'd like to share our hands-on approach to data management with you in this chapter. This way, regardless of how large or small your organization is, you will be able to address data management and take care of that important step in your data and analytics maturity and solve data quality issues from the start of your journey.

In this chapter, we will discuss the following topics:

- Introducing data management
- Understanding your data quality
- Delivering a data management future
- Taking care of your data strategy

Introducing data management

As previously stated (*Chapter 2, Unfolding Your Data Journey*), when we create information for our organization using data from our transactional systems, we encounter a variety of issues such as poor data quality, missing data, varying definitions of elementary data fields, and so on. Although **business intelligence (BI)** is not the cause of this problem, its use makes it painfully clear.

One of the primary reasons we should address and work on data quality issues is to save money! According to Thomas Redman's book *Getting in Front on Data*, poor data quality accounts for 50% of an average organization's operational costs. He also claims that organizations can cut 80% of their operational costs by improving data quality.

Another reason is to improve process quality and thus service quality. Customers appreciate it when a process runs smoothly the first time, and we will have happy customers. Good data is required to keep processes running smoothly and to achieve the goals that they must handle. Working on data quality is thus an important aspect not only for process improvement and progress toward *error-free* processes but also for a good reputation. Lower costs and satisfied customers are not the only reasons. Data is an important part of company strategy today, and thus an important asset for the company. It is possible to achieve efficiency and effectiveness in business operations by generating insights from the available data environment. Poor data quality stymies the efficient and successful implementation of data-centric business strategies, ultimately costing a company a lot of money!

Figure 5.1 describes the five fundamental points that explain the true potential of data and how to fully utilize it:

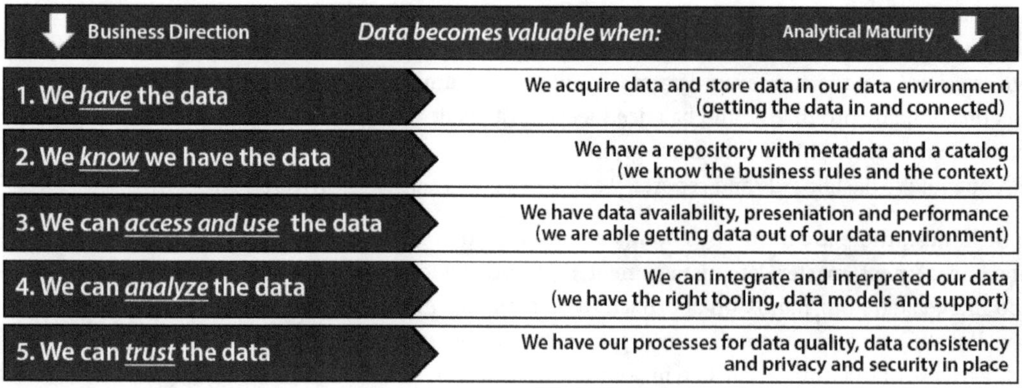

Business Direction	Data becomes valuable when:	Analytical Maturity
1. We *have* the data		We acquire data and store data in our data environment (getting the data in and connected)
2. We *know* we have the data		We have a repository with metadata and a catalog (we know the business rules and the context)
3. We can *access and use* the data		We have data availability, preseniation and performance (we are able getting data out of our data environment)
4. We can *analyze* the data		We can integrate and interpreted our data (we have the right tooling, data models and support)
5. We can *trust* the data		We have our processes for data quality, data consistency and privacy and security in place

Figure 5.1 – Chart showing when data becomes valuable

By determining a data strategy that is stored, described, and accessible in order to use the data to analyze in a trustworthy manner, we must have processes in place for data quality, data consistency, privacy, and security.

Understanding your data quality

Our systems are overflowing with data to support both primary and secondary processes. This information is stored in the underlying databases of our transactional systems. We do this to support the steps in our processes and to create a large history of data in our databases. When we start extracting data, some complicated issues can occur: think of different formatting data elements, working with various platforms, or the frequency at which we can capture data. We need to take care that the extraction of data remains clean, consistent, and flowing. Unfortunately, data is not easily extracted from systems and converted into information. According to author Thomas Redman, a *data element* goes through two basic stages in its life:

- The moment when you first save the data element within the transactional systems

- The moment you use the data element

When we examine data thoroughly, we discover that the majority of our registered data is never used again after it is stored in our systems. When the data is of high quality, we can use it for data-informed decision-making, planning, and business processes.

The quality of data becomes apparent only when it is used to generate dashboards and reports. As previously stated, we frequently see data quality issues arise when an organization begins extracting and visualizing data, and it becomes painfully clear that we must address the elements of data management and data quality in our data and analytics processes.

By talking to business users, you are able to determine whether or not a data element is relevant for dashboards and reports. You can do this with the following types of questions:

- Is the data up to date enough for you as a business user, and can you easily access it if you need it for decision-making?

- Can you make sound decisions based on the information that is currently available?

- Is your data complete, or is there data missing that you require to complete your work?

- Is your data qualitatively correct, do you trust your data, or does the quality of your data vary?

- Is the data at your disposal relevant enough, and do you understand it?

- Can you interpret the data correctly?

Improving data quality is only possible if you look for the causes of bad data. There are three factors that influence the quality of data:

- Errors can occur when observing and recording data.

- The accessibility of data files to users at the desired location and time.

- A data element has no meaning on its own. Based on what they assume or know, business users assign meaning to data elements. The less freedom you have to interpret the meaning of a data element as you see fit, the more likely it will be correctly interpreted, understood, and applied.

Intermezzo – Starting to improve data quality in a small-scaled healthcare environment

We were able to do a project with various health care organizations a few years ago. This was a fun project because health care is a subject close to our hearts. We began with projects to truly understand what needed to be reported to authorities, as well as what needed to be improved in processes, and so on.

We began with some visualizations and reports. We discovered a data quality issue with some of the analyzed data fields from the initial visualizations and reports. To figure out what to look for, we talked with the product owner about which fields we were primary and which fields were secondary. To concentrate on the fundamentals, we identified several tables that needed to be addressed and discussed on a daily basis. For example, if you want to register a patient in the system, you'll need their date of birth, address, urgency of the visit, gender, and so on.

These fundamental elements are required for classification and reporting to internal and external organizations. However, the accuracy of register time, dates, and so on is also important. Because data quality was not mentioned previously, we proposed adding a section to the dashboard with several *elementary* tables that had inconsistencies in registration quality. *Figure 5.2* shows an example:

Figure 5.2 – Example of a data quality report

By including those reports, organizations were able to discuss data quality in a productive manner, and as we discovered, the data quality of those elementary fields was not only discussed but also corrected every morning! As a result, they noticed that the quality of their registrations, visualizations, and reporting was improving.

One of the most amazing moments during those times was when one of our customers told us that they were proud to see the data quality improving and that the beginning of the day was the ideal time to discuss the actions to improve.

Delivering a data management future

Many organizations want to get more returns from data and grow to a higher maturity level after delivering a solid data infrastructure and the first reports based on that new infrastructure. In practice, we see that *data-informed decision-making* does not succeed or even begin without the support of management and the entire organization.

Embracing data literacy will help you develop your decision-making skills, and people will learn to ask the right questions, interpret the findings, and take appropriate action. It is critical to give data management a prominent place within the data and analytics team or within your organization to ensure a steady supply of information. But keep in mind that data management is more than just buying a tool. It is, once again, a process that must be thoroughly set up in our data and analytics world. *Figure 5.3* depicts the five steps in the framework that we use in our projects and the project approach. The data management framework will be described in detail in the following sections:

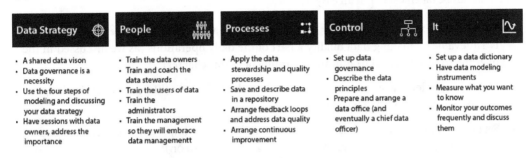

Data Strategy	People	Processes	Control	It
• A shared data vison • Data governance is a necessity • Use the four steps of modeling and discussing your data strategy • Have sessions with data owners, address the importance	• Train the data owners • Train and coach the data stewards • Train the users of data • Train the administrators • Train the management so they will embrace data managementt	• Apply the data stewardship and quality processes • Save and describe data in a repository • Arrange feedback loops and address data quality • Arrange continuous improvement	• Set up data governance • Describe the data principles • Prepare and arrange a data office (and eventually a chief data officer)	• Set up a data dictionary • Have data modeling instruments • Measure what you want to know • Monitor your outcomes frequently and discuss them

Figure 5.3 – The five-step approach of data management

When you are able to define and work on the displayed steps, you can actually begin (no matter how small the step) improving your data quality in a practical sense. Starting with the fundamental fields and adding them to your dashboards, you have the option of working to improve your data quality. Of course, the data quality reports must be discussed and actions taken; this is the human factor that is required to actually improve!

In the following section, we will go over the five steps in more detail.

Data strategy

Wanting everything is the same as wanting nothing at all. A data intake provides information on the most important technical and functional properties of a data element. By determining which data is required to measure organizational goals, you will only collect the information that is required for data-informed decision-making. This is the crucial part of creating and having a data strategy.

To be more specific, establishing a data strategy that is driven by the business strategy of an organization will help to guide all data management activities. A solid data strategy should also include people, processes, and technology to ensure that data as an asset is managed by the organization. To get attention and buy-in from the whole organization, the following steps could be considered:

1. Distribute an internal questionnaire to elicit feedback, address the importance internally, and build support within your organization.

2. Gather the results and set up interviews with the key players.

3. Develop an approach plan and describe the actions that must be taken.

4. Determine the data owners, data stewards, data architects, and the data engineers, then list them centrally.

5. Discuss the norm of the levels of data quality; the system could be 95% full, but the quality is another figure that must be mentioned as well.

Getting buy-in within an organization can be arranged in several ways. We have three main points for you that can be taken care of in an easy manner:

- Provide context and explain why data management and data quality are important. This is achievable by making data quality a part of the daily operations (as we discussed in the intermezzo about a small healthcare environment in this chapter).

- Identify a challenger or an evangelist to address the issue(s) within your organization; this helps to create that needed buy-in.

- Set up communication channels to spread the word about the importance of data management and data quality (newsletters, monitoring, workshops, and so on).

Taking care of your data strategy

According to Bernard Marr's book, *Data Strategy*:

> *To be truly useful in a business sense, data must address a specific business need that will help the organization reach its strategic goals or generate real value.*

As we discussed earlier in this chapter, it is no longer about the data we have at this point—it is more about your company and what you want to achieve with it. When you understand how data can assist you in activating your strategic objectives, you will be able to move forward.

Obtaining all of your data is not the way to proceed on your data journey. There are various types of data fields, and that is what you should consider before deciding what you want to use and how you want to use it. In *Figure 5.4*, we depict an information pyramid to illustrate how different data or information needs exist at each level of an organization. In *Figure 5.4*, the information and data streams are divided into three categories: **Strategic**, **Tactical**, and **Operational**.

Those levels have their own informational, and therefore data need. Decision-making is actually one of the three levels but varies in the level of detail, the number of targets, and so on. The bottom level is the **Operational** level where we will find fewer strategic decision-making reports but also more detailed information on what to do today, what my personal scores are, and so on. When we move up to the **Tactical** and **Strategic** levels, less aggregated data is required. Although the management needs to be able to ask their supporting teams for analyzing the values and target, detailed information is needed in the analysis section. But the management team needs to be able to see in one glance of an eye how the organization, department, or team is performing:

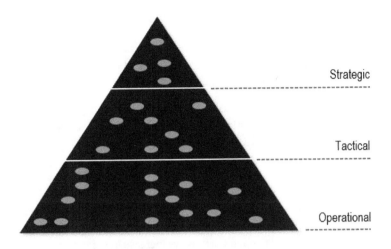

Figure 5.4 – The information pyramid

Creating a data vision

A data vision describes a set of decisions and choices made by an organization in order to map out high-level actions to achieve high-level objectives. To develop a solid data vision, we must first understand what we require in terms of data usage, including where it is stored, collected, maintained, shared, and used. To actually succeed in meeting your data and analytics goals, we need common methods and formalized primary and secondary processes. These methods and formalized processes are essential for establishing your data vision and therefore support your data strategy. We can use some common steps to achieve this, such as identifying your data, where your data is stored, how you can get your data, and if you are able to combine and enrich your data. In the following section, we will go over the steps to determining your data strategy.

Identifying your data

This crucial step, we believe, should be included in your measurement plan (functional design). When you describe the organizational goals, you should be able to locate the data you need to create visualizations or reports.

It is critical to determine what you require, how, and if you can use it. You will need to understand where it is stored, what is required to retrieve the data, what the descriptions are (the metadata), and, perhaps, if your organization is larger, you will also find data stewards and data owners.

As a general rule, if your organization truly views data as an asset and wishes to use it, your data strategy must ensure that the data can be identified, described, and used.

Discovering where your data is stored

Saving your data in a secure manner is critical for your organization and your data and analytics environment. In practice, we see data stored in small extrapolated data marts (created by any tool), such as relational schemas, star schemas, and so on.

When developing a solid data strategy, we must consider the fact that data must be accessible and shareable. When we have it in a secure location that is described and accessible, there is no need to copy the data and perform our technical magic on it over and over again.

Retrieving your data

We need to be able to retrieve data from a single point of truth, as we explain to our students and customers. Why should we rebuild connections or transformations over and over again when they have no value? The only thing that will happen is a massive increase in the number of dashboards and reports that contain various calculations that are not centrally designed or registered.

We also see a shift in which data is reused in more systems that support management decision support or business processes.

Combining and enriching data

Data integration (**DI**) solutions and so-called data pipelines are now commonly used to combine and enrich data. We can store structured data from our transactional systems as well as unstructured data collected primarily from external environments in our data environments.

We see in our projects that DI is not defined as a specific role within some organizations, so there is no cohesion between teams for collaboration (everybody is focused on their own bit of information or specific data integration projects). As a result, the work is mostly dispersed throughout the organization. This is a risk that we should be aware of; as organizations grow in size, you will most likely require a dedicated person to oversee the data teams. This will be covered further in our *People* section.

We discussed four steps to define the way we think about the data strategy and where we should focus our efforts. Keep in mind that sharing data in the form of pulling data from a data warehouse or other data storage and other types of environments is required. We should always approach it from a business necessity rather than a technical or IT necessity. For extracting, integrating, and transforming data, the needs and desires of the business must always come first.

The good news is that we've seen some fantastic data integration solutions where we can go data shopping. We can select datasets from a data environment in a webstore-like environment using those tools.

When we can work with data and integrate it into our environments, we can discuss data quality and even justify targets for our data quality levels from a governance standpoint.

Setting the standard

Only when the standard is known can data quality be measured. What are the content expectations, and is it absolutely necessary? Is 80% sufficient? Remember that while the systems may be completely filled, the quality of the data is unaffected. We can determine the desired business rules and standards through a series of structured workshops/interviews or questionnaires. As a small example, data entry is done by operations, and that data is stored in our databases. When we have 100 fields that need to be filled by our operations, we could expect a data filling or storage rate of 90%. But data entry and storage is one thing—that could be 90%—but the quality is often much lower—as low as 60%.

Determining the standard is a decision that must be made by management (support) in order to place data management on the strategic management agenda.

The end result will be that we will have a solid data strategy and will be able to measure our organizational goals. However, the human factor in this case is the next necessity that we must address, in order to identify why data is required, who is interested, and so on. As a result, we must consider that there are various types of roles within an organization, which are described in the following section.

People

People are required within an organization; they collaborate with transactional systems to support our primary and secondary processes, and all of them could (and should) be interested in data and contribute to improving data quality. This is determined by the person's position within the organization and the type of work they perform. In this section, we will discuss the various types of roles that can be addressed if you want to improve data quality in your organization. Taking care of those roles, or implementing those depends totally on an organization. From our perspective, a bigger organization could obtain all those roles, but a smaller organization could have less roles, or combined roles.

Who has an interest in improving data quality depends on their position within an organization:

- When registering data in an organization's transactional systems, an **employee** wants as little administrative burden as possible. They may wish to perform their duties with greater pleasure and less stress. In fact, it should be as simple as possible.

- **Managers** (at all levels) appreciate good reports that are based on good data quality (after all, dirty data in is dirty data out), and they would like to benefit from fewer repetitions, checks, or errors in data recording while performing data-informed decision-making.

- The **data owner** is in charge of the data in a specific data domain. A data owner is responsible for ensuring that information within their domain is properly managed across multiple systems and business activities.

- The **data steward** is a broad-minded **data specialist** who serves as a liaison between IT and the business within an organization. The data steward ensures that the data is correct, complete, and of high quality. They accomplish this with the assistance of the data owner, to whom they report.

- **Data Architects** should meet with the management teams and help to determine the method to gather the data that is required and how to organize it. The Data Architect reviews and analyzes the data environment of an organization, taking care of the planning of future data bases and help to investigate and implement technical solutions to manage data for their organization and its data users.

- A **Data Engineer** is someone who works in a variety of tasks from building systems to collecting and managing data, creating data models that convert raw data into usable information that others (Business Analysts, Data Visualization Specialists, and so on) within the organization can use. A Data Engineer works closely with the **Database Administrators** (**DBA**) and the Data Architect.

When an organization hires a **chief data officer** (**CDO**) (usually in larger organizations), the CDO is ultimately in charge of the entire organization and is a member of the management team. They assist organizations in transitioning to a digital, but most importantly, information-driven way of working.

In the following section, we will go into greater detail about the roles of the data owner, data steward, and CDO, as we see a growing need for more organizations to professionalize their data strategy and the need for those typical data office roles.

Data owner

The data owner is responsible for the data within a specific data domain, such as a data owner for HR data or facility management data. A data owner is responsible for ensuring that the information in their domain is properly managed across multiple systems and business activities.

As a result, the data owner must understand who the company is, what it wants, and how it is structured. The data owner understands the systems, which systems are used, who is responsible, and that data quality is critical in order to provide consistent and correct information to your end customers across your various channels.

Data steward

The data steward is a broad-minded data specialist who acts as a liaison between IT and the business within the organization. A data steward's responsibilities include ensuring the data's correctness, completeness, integrity, and quality. In addition to the data owner, they play a specific role in discussing data quality topics with the employees of that specific department.

On the one hand, the data steward is a source of information for all types of data-related questions. On the other hand, with the available data sources, they are constantly searching for (new) possibilities.

They understand the meaning and reliability of data, as well as its applications. The data steward is familiar with the company's processes, data sources, and the organization and its customers. They maintain the connection between customers and the organization by analyzing and presenting data in the best possible way.

Chief Data Officer (CDO)

The CDO is ultimately responsible for an organization's digital transformation, but most importantly, for an information-driven way of working. Aside from being a data-focused manager, they are also a *data evangelist* who double-checks the figures and numbers on the dashboards and inspires the organization to work from the standpoint of data-informed decision-making. The CDO must ensure that data is managed correctly and oversees data management activities.

If this position is filled with sufficient mandate and decisiveness, the CDO will be able to quickly demonstrate their value to the organization. In short, the CDO is the driving force behind an intelligent and data-informed organization.

By telling the story over and over, you build support and spread the importance of good data. Make certain that everyone in the organization understands why you should work on data quality, which obstacles to expect, and where opportunities for improvement exist.

You are able to achieve this by doing the following:

- Providing information on data quality (high-over and showing trends)
- Maintaining conversations with key players in your organization
- Planning and delivering workshops on the importance of data quality (showing the numbers, discussing the trends, and so on)
- Planning and delivering workshops on the proper registration of data elements (and explaining the importance of good registration, and so on)

Processes

A BI environment requires information that is consistent, integrity, trustworthy, and meaningful. As a result, the data quality process aims to achieve and maintain high data quality, ensuring better information for your business.

If you want to start improving your data quality, we can categorize the data quality forces as follows: data discovery, profiling, rules, monitoring, correction, and quality reporting.

In *Figure 5.5*, we see the six-step model in more detail:

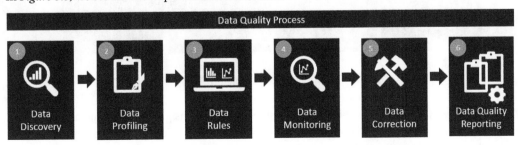

Figure 5.5 – The data quality process

Data discovery

When you begin gathering requirements for mapping out the required information, there are ways to design what is important for your organization based on your organization's objectives (see *Chapter 6, Aligning with Organizational Goals*).

The next step is to identify the basic data fields for each process. What is important is that decisions must be made about whether or not to address data quality (for example, you tackle an elementary field, a less important field—perhaps because it is not used for decision-making, for example). See, for example, the story of pre-washing in *Chapter 2, Unfolding Your Data Journey*.

Data profiling

Data profiling is a method for data analysis that can give a quick insight into the value, structure, and quality of data. In *Figure 5.6*, we introduce you to several techniques that are involved in data profiling:

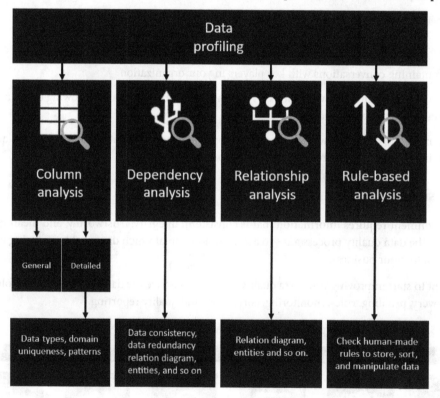

Figure 5.6 – Data profiling

With the different techniques described, it is possible to generate insight to determine how far data deviates from the norm. Data can also be examined for quality issues. These signals define the scope of the following step: improving data quality!

In today's data world, it is also possible to use algorithms to visualize data quality. This can be a fairly simple algorithm that depicts outliers in the data—for example, detecting peaks and troughs of customers based on the first few digits of the postal codes. Peaks and dips in the collected, stored data can indicate a data quality problem.

Or, from a data science perspective, a **neural network** (**NN**) that predicts the value of an attribute based on other data elements, such as an algorithm that predicts a salary based on the age of a person, how many hours per week the person works, and the job title. The next step is then to compare the predicted salary with the registered salary.

It is also possible to easily detect another example of duplicate customers with an algorithm or, for example, place names, province names—Province of North Holland, Prov Noord-Holland, Province of NH, and so on. When you are able to detect anomalies, you will be able to identify and correct them in a sufficient way. When an algorithm such as this is trained well, it is possible to filter out a big amount of errors in no time; in this way, **machine learning** (**ML**) can make a radical difference. Data fields that should in any case be checked include the following elements so that a valid statement can be made with regard to data quality:

- Technical name
- Functional name
- Minimum value
- Maximum value
- The number of duplicates
- The number of numeric fields
- The number of NULL fields
- The number of rows
- The number of unique fields

Which fields must be checked or are fundamental for your data-informed decision-making must be determined per process, source, dashboard, or report so that we can focus on the correct data quality aspects. Aside from the previously mentioned elements, the following controlling aspects must be considered:

- Individuality (for example, a customer number may only appear once, or a social security number belongs to one person)
- Completion (postal code 999999 or 9999XX; this, of course, differs per country)
- Integrity (data that is referenced, for example, when entering an order for a customer; first, check whether the entered customer number exists)
- Reliability (date of birth of a person in system A does not match the date of birth of system B)

- Date logic (for example, `20220101/01JAN22/01-JAN-2022`).

- General logic (house numbers should never begin with 0)

- Business or industry logic (for example, does a broker sell 100,000 houses per day?)

- Discontinuity (is the data still important for our data-informed decision-making or do we have to set a break from a certain period in time?)

- Meaning (Has logic that is not directly traceable been applied? Is there a mutual agreement? For example, an asterisk after the customer's name indicates that the customer relationship has ended. This must be communicated to your data and analytics department.)

- Incomplete data (data not yet registered)

- Misusage of data fields; the data field is used for a purpose for which it was not designed and obtained, and so on

A method for conducting your research could be as follows: Determine what the quality issues are using data research. Investigate the data by performing a fault cluster analysis, for example (based on eliminating possibilities that could cause a fault to occur). Alternatively, conduct an event analysis (studies when the data is used and where errors can occur).

Then, determine the impact on the organization (what is fundamental and what is not).

Data rules

Applying data rules can be done from two types of perspectives: a technical point of view and a business perspective.

From a technical perspective:

- Using business rules in the data environment's transformation layer (data warehouse, for example)

- Identifying *errors* and taking the necessary corrective actions

- Determining *warnings* and, if applicable, taking the necessary actions

- Creating automated feedback loops (for example, checking fields and linking this directly back to the business user via—for example—mailing)

From a business perspective:

- Beginning feedback loops (so that they can return to the agenda on a daily/weekly basis, or visual performance management—making data quality visible on monitors, for example)

- Reporting and correction (for example, by sending e-mails, making reports, and putting issues on the agenda)

- Configuring actions at the software vendor (making fields mandatory)

- Implementing data entry training to eliminate errors during registration

Intermezzo – a data quality issue causes problems

We created an amazing ServiceDesk application some time ago (back in 2008). We were able to analyze the data, from incident to machine, to see the software that was implemented on that machine and which provider we had to address the question to after working on the project, which was amazing! The management was completely unfamiliar with the transition from high aggregations to such a detailed level. Not having to wait 15 days for reports from our administration office, but having direct insight and more proactive actionability on the first of the month saved a lot of money at the time (and yes, a very positive business case!).

So, at the time, we were mostly walking around with a laptop, and we could easily show the facts displayed on the dashboard. However, if we wanted to know which machines had issues, we had to have the **configuration ID (CI)** of that machine, but if the CI was not a required field, you can imagine what happened during that time. However, by shortening the feedback loop, displaying the results, and preaching about the importance of data quality, we were able to help everyone understand why we needed to fill that CI. At the very least, data quality was on the team's mind.

We ended up with a 99% qualitative CI filling in our system and were able to improve the machines that were causing problems.

Data monitoring

Monitoring allows for insight into the developments and trends of data storage and data quality. It is possible to detect an increase or decrease in the number of fields to be registered by monitoring the storage of those fields that are leading, or elementary, for example. We have an example displayed in *Figure 5.7*, with a suggestion on how to track the data storage within the transactional systems. This enables structural issues to be addressed directly at their source. These measurements must be repeated on a regular basis, not only during management meetings but also in regular discussions with business users:

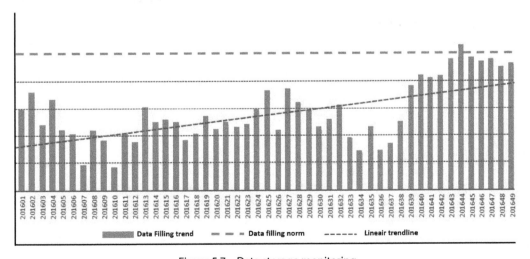

Figure 5.7 – Data storage monitoring

Data correction

Data correction is the step of cleaning, organizing, and migrating data so that it is properly protected and serves its intended purpose. It is a misconception that data correction means deleting business data that is no longer needed.

With regard to data that does not meet the standard, it is necessary to discuss whether the data should be cleaned, enriched, duplicated, and/or standardized. Addressing these issues can be done partly with the help of automated conversion rules and partly manually. Nevertheless, it should also be discussed with the data owners so that they are able to address data issues with their teams. This also forms the basis for the design of the data warehouse and data quality reports, which we will cover next.

New solutions are on the rise; with those new techniques, you will be able to show the data in—for example—a table, highlight the data, and give the opportunity to your dashboard and reports to correct the data on the fly! The new technology helps to see, correct, and restore the data back again in the original source systems. This technique is called *write-back*. *Figure 5.8* shows an example of correcting budget figures:

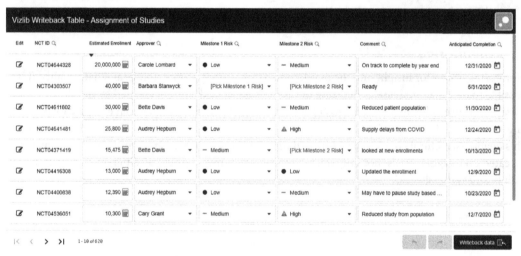

Figure 5.8 – Using a write-back functionality

With this new technology, we are able to address, discuss, and correct data quality even better, and all of this from a pragmatic point of view.

Data quality reporting

Tracking, reporting, visualizing data, creating data flows, and monitoring data quality are all critical steps in monitoring data quality. This step requires determining which items can be converted automatically and which should be corrected by business users. *Figure 5.9* is a standard data warehouse environment design with some steps (5) that can be added in a more simple and accessible manner:

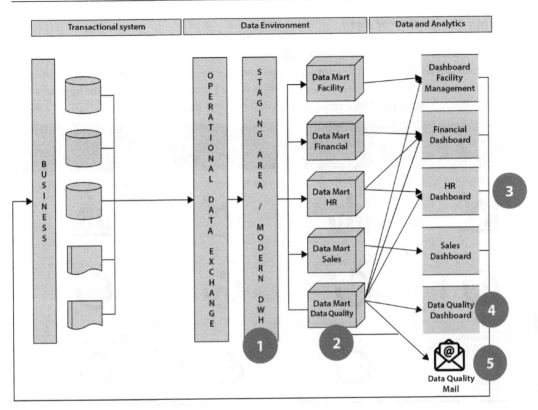

Figure 5.9 – Standard data warehouse setup with quality checks

In this example, we have included five points that can be addressed to improve the quality of your data:

1. In the first step, errors and warnings can be set in the data environment, followed by transformations, corrections, or cleansing activities (business rules).

2. Errors and warnings can be collected in a separate data mart (dataset for one specific process) and reported separately to the business and management.

3. Reports on data quality can be included in operational dashboards. These can then be discussed from the standpoint of visual performance during stand-ups or startup meetings.

4. A separate dashboard on data quality will be created, with elements such as data growth, error growth, and so on.

5. Some tools allow you to send automated emails requesting that data fields in the source systems be changed.

You can easily start setting up the processes one by one by organizing your data environment in such a way that data management has a place and a prominent role within your data and analytics team(s).

Improving the quality of data

Monitoring, continuous improvement, and visualization in a data quality dashboard provide insights into the organization's data quality development and trends. Any structural issues can be dealt with directly at the source. *Figure 5.10* shows elements that we can track when our data environment is properly configured, as well as data elements for monitoring our data environment:

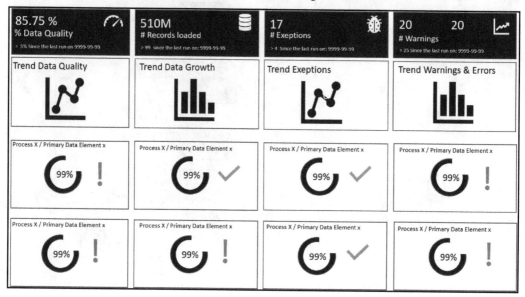

Figure 5.10 – Data quality dashboard

This screenshot contains elements that we have discussed in this chapter. These metrics will need to be discussed on a regular basis, not only during management meetings but also during regular discussions with business users. Only in this manner can we address data quality while also improving it.

Control

Control typically refers to an organization's integrated and controlled processing of data on both a strategic tactical and operational level in order to achieve the desired quality and availability. The process of organizing, cataloging, locating, storing, retrieving, and maintaining data are the subjects of data management.

Control measures can be set up in various ways that mostly depend on the type of organization:

- Operational management or through the CDO (first line)
- An advisory function that assists line management in risk management, compliance, and planning and control (often the second line)

- A possible third line that oversees the first and second lines

- Consult with the organization's controller about where hard and soft measures can best fit in

Data office

A data office is simply the team responsible for ensuring that the data within an organization best supports the organization's objectives. At the highest level, the data office ensures that a comprehensive data vision and strategy are in place and being implemented. A data strategy is made up of three distinct topics:

- **Data governance**

    - What are the critical data points for the organization? The data office ensures that these are visualized, described, and taken care of in accordance with the data governance principle.

    - The data office creates a data policy and manages data quality and masters (the organization's critical data elements).

- **Transformative**: It seems a bit strange to address the importance of a CDO being transformative. To clarify this is not that hard. Companies such as Amazon, Booking.com, Airbnb, and others are digital in their origin and use data and analytics beyond our imagination. Transforming from a traditional to a digital and data-focused organization is a radical process and causes significant organizational and cultural change. This is exactly why a CDO cannot be missed in this type of transformation within an organization. Some factors for that digital transformation include the following:

    - It is vital that the business strategy and the data strategy are linked; the CDO and the data office will be responsible for this.

    - Examining and prioritizing which data is critical for measuring business strategy and ensuring that processes and datasets are consistent.

    - Measuring and monitoring storage, quality, and so on. Furthermore, this must be discussed at (strategic) management team meetings.

    - Implementing, supporting, and monitoring the organization's most critical data roles (data owners and stewards).

- **Data empowerment**. Because data does nothing on its own, organizational data literacy must be about people. Data means working with business users to get them excited about data and to help them develop their skills. In practice, this translates to the following:

    - Implementing a data literacy framework, creating a plan, and securing high-level sponsors

    - Ensuring continuous (self-)development and motivating business users

- Assisting business users in working with data and insights so that they develop the right mindset to *want* to work with data and insights (instead of having to)

- Collaborating with HR to create or purchase training materials and courses

IT

This section contains several technical options for organizations. We decided to highlight some critical topics that organizations should address in order to advance in their data management or data quality processes.

Data dictionary

To be able to register metadata (the glue that holds everything together) and thus speak a universal data language, data definitions must be recorded centrally. A data definition clarifies the meaning and naming of data, such as by storing (and using) table and attribute names and describing their meaning. A universal data language is analogous to two people (or systems) communicating; they understand each other better because they use common data definitions.

An important basis in data architecture is the recording of metadata in a metadata repository. This repository contains definitions of systems, datasets, concepts, data models, and data flows (data lineage) together. It is powered by the dictionary and a data modeling tool. The data architecture ensures that systems can exchange meaningful data and that systems, reports, and analyses build on good data.

Standardizing concepts and definitions

It is important to address and understand what is going on during the first data and analytics projects. It is important to speak the same data language and understand the definition of a data field, but also how the net revenue is calculated. We have seen many times in our projects that profit or revenue is calculated in several ways, therefore it is necessary to focus on standard descriptions and definitions. The resulting concepts should be recorded in a dictionary, which can simply be a list of concepts or a thesaurus that also includes how the global interrelationships between the concepts are described.

A data dictionary or company thesaurus can be completed in a variety of ways, including software solutions, Excel overviews, and solutions within data and analytics solutions. To explain it a little more in detail, we will tell you the story of one of our projects in the next intermezzo.

Intermezzo – data definitions are necessary!

We were working on a project a while back to create a new informational stream between two source systems. Those two source systems were created using different technologies. We were supposed to construct a direct message transport from the source system where the notification was received to the second source system. It was necessary to plan a visit and pass by someone to check and discuss some things from this second source system.

However, the addresses in the two systems did not match because they were interpreted and programmed differently in both systems. So, occasionally, a person passing by the client went to the wrong address, and the client was fined for not being home.

There was a connection between the governmental systems (where people in a municipality lived) in this source system, but a person could be officially registered somewhere but be living at another address.

In this case, we advised the project members and client to return to the drawing board and discuss the data fields that needed to be transported correctly from one system to the other.

Data modeling instruments

A data modeling tool is required from an IT standpoint not only to keep track of the data pipelines but also to serve the right information areas with the help of a created data environment. We will not recommend any software because this book is not about tools and is completely agnostic. The tools out there in the world are amazing, and usable for all organizations. What you choose is determined by the type of organization and the tools that are already in place. To be honest, there is no such thing as a bad tool in the world; choose wisely and remember that it is fine to have more than one tool—it is just important to understand where each tool is used and what is built with it! You can then grow beyond your wildest dreams.

Summary

Recognizing that poor data quality or a lack of data management can lead to a number of issues. In addition, if you do not have a data vision or data strategy that supports your organizational objectives, your organization is likely to focus on the wrong (non-relevant) objectives. Having a data strategy and a clear vision of where you want to go with your data and analytics plans can help an organization advance in its data and analytics maturity.

We now have a better understanding of data, data management, and data quality after reading this chapter. We have provided you with a five-step framework that includes data strategy, data people, data processes, data control, and data IT steps.

The data quality process is divided into five steps: discovering what data you need, profiling, rules (cleansing, correcting, and so on), monitoring the filling data elements in your source systems, and, finally, the amazing part where we see that you can actually measure your data quality. We concluded with the last section of this crucial chapter, in which we discussed IT. Remember—if your data foundation and data quality aren't correct, your reports will never be!

In the following chapter, we will discuss organizational goals and how important it is to design, measure, and display them in such a way that an organization can track its strategic objectives.

Part 2: Understanding How to Measure the Why, What, and How

In this section, we will discuss some important topics, such as strategy and organizational goals, and help you to understand how to handle them. We will provide you with information around the topic of questions, including analyzing and asking critical questions about the insights created from data, and help you to understand that ethically handling data is important.

This section comprises the following chapters:

- *Chapter 6, Aligning with Organizational Goals*
- *Chapter 7, Designing Dashboards and Reports*
- *Chapter 8, Questioning the Data*
- *Chapter 9, Handling Data Responsibly*

6

Aligning with Organizational Goals

While the focus on data literacy so far has been on understanding how to use data to find insights that lead to decisions and actions, this chapter takes a step back to highlight that it is important not only how you go about finding insights but also to ensure that those insights are actionable and provide value to the organization. For this reason, data literacy is closely connected with an organization's strategy and goals.

Before starting any transformation, organizations need to first establish an overall strategy and vision for the organization. From there, they need to establish specific objectives that start at the top of an organization and cascade down. These objectives focus on employee activities to attain that vision. Then, organizations need to align their strategy and objectives with the employees' culture. Organizational alignment only occurs when strategic business goals and cultural values and behaviors are mutually supportive. In this chapter, we're going to cover the following main topics:

- Understanding the types of indicators
- Identifying key performance indicators
- Reviewing for unintended consequences
- Defining what to track

Understanding the types of indicators

In *Chapter 1, The Beginning – The Flow of Data*, we discussed the organizational data flow and how there is so much data available to organizations. What data should be used for understanding whether an organization is achieving its organizational goals? If the organization is not achieving its goals, what data should be used to understand why it is not?

Organizations should not wait till it is too late to understand whether they will achieve their goals. They should leverage an early warning system to help them drive toward those goals and understand when they are falling off track. In this sense, not all data is created equal. Some data is more important at the strategic level. Other data is relevant at the operational level to monitor the business that is driving toward the outcomes.

Before we get into a business example, let's look at a personal example that we can all relate to: *personal health*. In this example, let's assume someone's strategic goal for their health is that they want to live long enough to see their great-grandkids. Everyone may have different strategic goals, and even each person may have different goals at different stages of their life. We need "indicators" that can help us quantify whether we are on track to achieve our goals. We can't wait till we are older when our great-grandkids are born to see whether we achieved this. We need to understand what will help us achieve our goals and then drive and monitor those indicators.

We will discuss strategies for selecting the appropriate indicators for your organization or department later on in this chapter, but for this example, let's assume one of the indicators chosen that we feel needs to be achieved in order for us to hit our strategic goal is heart disease risk. Let's say there is a calculation that is used to calculate the risk of heart disease and that score ranges from 0 – 5. Based on external benchmarks from experts in the field, the target should be to have a score of 2 (or lower) and that becomes what is called a **key performance indicator**.

You may then start to track this indicator on a regular basis. This is great, but you don't want to see one month that you are below target. You ideally want to know what will influence the indicator and proactively work on those. This will also help you identify the root cause of why you did not achieve the target. Based on advice from doctors, it is determined that blood pressure and cholesterol can impact the heart disease score. The doctor may set a target for both of these. This process continues iteratively to then determine and track what will influence blood pressure and cholesterol. The doctor may say that exercising for 150 minutes a week, keeping your weight below a certain level, and keeping calorie intake to certain levels will help reduce blood pressure and cholesterol. This process continues to iterate down till all the drivers have been documented and given a target. In addition, throughout this process, other data is stored and analyzed to help with the complete picture. For example, the doctor will store things such as the number of visits, whether or not the patient is a smoker, their age, and their height. This data does not have a target applied to them, just the data is stored for later use and analysis.

In this example, there are lots of different types of data. There are direct measures, such as weight and calorie intake. There are aggregations, such as average blood pressure, and there are ratios, such as the cholesterol ratio. Then, there are indicators, things that are not direct measures but are rather used to describe how something is performing, such as the heart disease risk score.

The indicators that are determined, via strategic planning, to be critical for driving toward a strategic objective are called **key performance indicators (KPIs)**. Actions that are influencing and driving the heart disease risk score, such as the cholesterol level and average blood pressure, are called **performance indicators**. They are still required as a way to drive toward the goals and are important in helping diagnose why a KPI happens to be below target. For example, if someone's heart disease risk score is above the target, the doctor will look at the performance indicators influencing it to help determine why it's above target. It could be due to the fact the patient has a cholesterol ratio above target. Finally, the data that is stored and analyzed but does not have a target associated with it, such as weight and age, is commonly called a **metric**. *Figure 6.1* depicts the metrics, performance indicators, and KPIs related to a personal strategic health goal.

Figure 6.1 – Example performance indicators for personal health

Let's now pivot and look at a business example.

Assume an organization defines a goal to increase its revenue this year by 25% compared to last year. Each department within the organization then strategizes on its goals to support the organizational goal. Once the goals are determined, each goal will be assigned performance indicators. For example, the sales department may have a goal to close 15 deals each month, and one of their performance indicators could be their conversion rate (how many opportunities end up in a sale). The marketing department may have a goal to bring in 25 new qualified opportunities each month, and one of their performance indicators could be the number of event attendees. The customer success department may have a goal to keep customer retention at 95% or higher each month, and one of their performance indicators could be the average customer health score (a score that takes into account many factors to determine how likely a customer is to leave). Each of these performance indicators is assigned a target.

Each department may have more than one goal and each goal may have more than one performance indicator. For example, for the sales goal, they may also have a performance indicator measuring the length of the sales cycle. The marketing goal may also have a performance indicator related to the number of unique visitors to the website each month. *Figure 6.2* depicts the performance indicators for this business example.

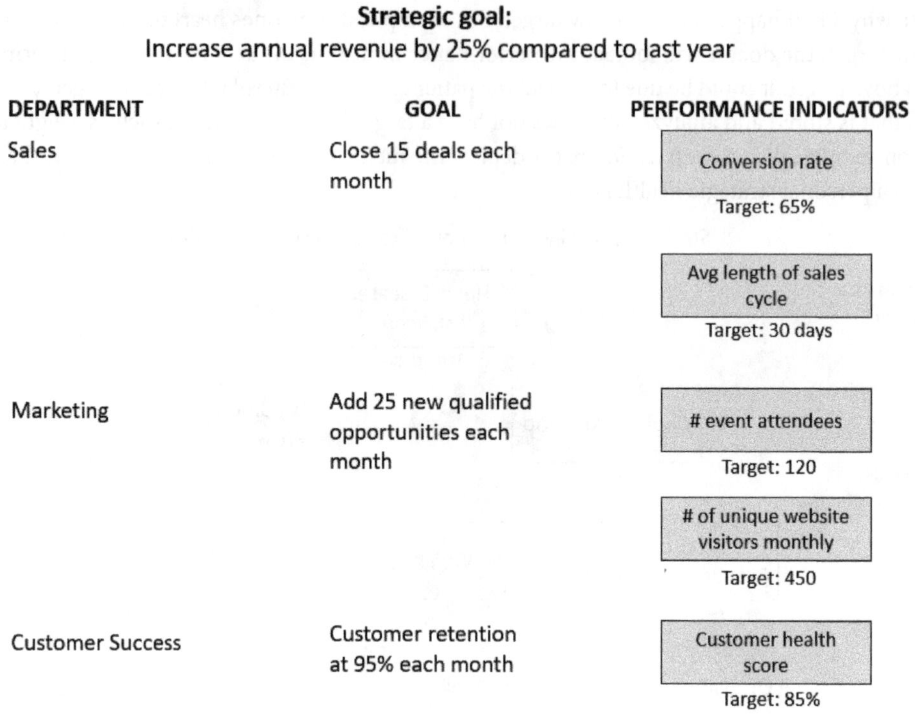

Strategic goal:
Increase annual revenue by 25% compared to last year

DEPARTMENT	GOAL	PERFORMANCE INDICATORS
Sales	Close 15 deals each month	Conversion rate Target: 65%
		Avg length of sales cycle Target: 30 days
Marketing	Add 25 new qualified opportunities each month	# event attendees Target: 120
		# of unique website visitors monthly Target: 450
Customer Success	Customer retention at 95% each month	Customer health score Target: 85%

Figure 6.2 – Example performance indicators for an organization

The organization then reviews each performance indicator and determines which ones are the most critical to measure whether the organizational goal is achieved or not. The top level of an organization cannot have hundreds of KPIs. We will discuss this later on in this chapter, but a general rule of thumb is 5 KPIs at the organizational level. Those selected become the KPIs, and the other indicators that drive toward those outcomes become supporting performance indicators.

Let's look at one more example. Earlier in the book, we introduced the story of a safety region in Holland that was trying to reduce the time it took for patients to get treatment in the hospital when they needed emergency cardiac care. They have a KPI called **Call to Balloon**, which tracks the time it takes from when the hospital ambulance is first dispatched to when they are treated. In addition, they have a series of supporting performance indicators, each with its own targets given as follows:

- **Response time** – The time after an ambulance is dispatched to when it arrives at the patient

- **Call to Door** – The time after an ambulance is dispatched to when the patient arrives at the emergency room

- **ECG to Balloon** – The time after the patient is first treated with an ECG in the ambulance to when they are treated in the emergency room

- **Door to Balloon** – The time between when the patient arrives in the emergency room to when they are treated

In addition, there is a series of metrics to support the various performance indicators. As these are metrics, they do not have targets assigned to them.

- Number of ambulance rides

- Number of interventions

- Time from a patient call to emergency services and the time the ambulance arrives

A visual representation of the performance indicators in this example is shown in *Figure 6.3*.

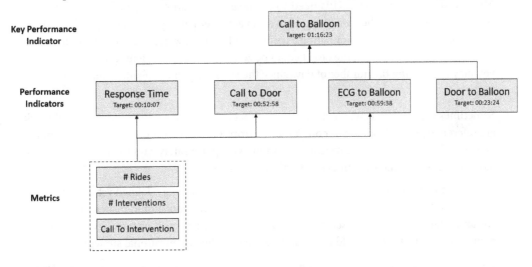

Figure 6.3 – Example performance indicators for a safety region

Now that we understand the various types of indicators, let's move on to learn how we can identify which indicators should be KPIs.

Identifying KPIs

Identifying the right KPIs is critically important for data-informed organizations because they help keep objectives and organizational goals as key drivers of decision making. Having the wrong KPIs can waste a lot of time and effort working toward the wrong outcomes as well as have serious unintended consequences. Unintended consequences are discussed in more detail in the next section of this chapter. This section will help us first identify key characteristics of KPIs, and then how to identify the two types of KPIs: **leading** and **lagging**.

Characteristics of KPIs

Organizations always have some level of KPIs they are driving toward, but there are many times that those KPIs have a flaw in them. These flaws can lead to organizations that are striving to achieve their KPIs, but even if they do, they do not improve on the desired goals and outcomes. The following 10 characteristics will help you identify and define proper KPIs:

- **Ties to strategic objectives**: KPIs should be used to inform your organization's strategic decision making. So, it is only natural that your KPIs need to tie to strategic objectives. Otherwise, you may be spending a lot of effort trying to hit a target on your KPI when it does not in fact align with the direction the organization is heading.

- **Measured against targets**: KPIs need to be measured against targets. There needs to be accountability; it could be something such as an achievement against the target. Sometimes, when you're talking about eliminating expenses and costs in waste, it could be a reduction to meet the target. Sometimes, the target could be zero. For example, if you're in manufacturing, you may be tracking the number of days since the last injury in the plant. In that example, the target is 0.

  Sometimes organizations will leverage external benchmarks to set their targets. Benchmarks are reference points from other companies or from industry best practices. For example, a benchmark can be that the governing board on workplace safety says the best practice is to have one or fewer employee injuries every 6 months.

  There are some situations when a company may not have a strategy defined yet. In those cases, it is hard to have a target for your KPI. In these situations, you should just capture the KPI, without a target, as a way to set the baseline. Then, after a month or two, have a discussion around where the target should be set and tie them to the organizational strategy.

- **Ranges and levels**: The KPIs are going to have ranges of performance, such as "above target," "on target," or "below target." In some situations, those ranges can be expanded more, with the "below target" classification being split into "slightly below target" if you are within 10% of the target, and then "below target" if you are more than 10% below target.

- **Encodings**: Ranges can have different levels of encodings. Encodings are graphical cues to aid in the interpretation of the range. Maybe the most common example is a traffic light visualization. For example, if you are on target, it is green. If you are within 10% of the target, it is yellow. If you are more than 10% off of the target, it is red. Those would be the encodings. They may not be full visualizations, such as a traffic light visualization, but they may just be little icons within the visualization, such as a green arrow pointing up or a red arrow pointing down.

- **Timeframes**: Timeframes explain the unit of time relevant to the KPI. For example, if you are tracking your sales revenue, are you looking at it aggregated daily, weekly, or quarterly? Or, if your target is to have 0 accidents within your office for 90 days, then 90 days is the timeframe.

- **Actionable**: KPIs need to be actionable. As we have discussed earlier in this chapter, finding insights that are not actionable does not help the organization and just wastes time.

- **Owned**: All KPIs need to have a listed owner who is responsible for them. If there are KPIs that are shared across multiple teams and departments, it becomes really hard to drive accountability with them.

- **Balanced**: The aggregate of your KPIs needs to be balanced across the entire system. You should not only have lagging indicators, but for each lagging indicator, you should balance it with at least one or two leading indicators. Leading and lagging indicators are discussed in more detail later in this chapter.

- **Aligned**: All KPIs should be aligned. Alignment ensures that the KPIs are aligned at various levels. This means department-level KPIs should relate to the organizational-level KPIs. The process starts at the organizational level, and then is cascaded down and aligned. Department-level KPIs are created that relate and support the organizational-level ones.

- **Sparse**: In general, less is more when it comes to KPIs. Some people believe having more KPIs is ideal as it will give a better perspective into the state of the business. However, having too many KPIs will lead to overload. None of them will be prioritized over the others, and no one will have time to look at all of them. Many experts believe the right number of KPIs is around 5.

Now that we have identified the main characteristics of KPIs, let's take a look at a couple of examples.

Figure 6.4 provides examples of different ways you can visualize your KPIs. The one on the left is a text visual that shows the **% Orders In Stock** KPI. The value is shown in the middle (**40%**), with a comparison to whether this is up or down from the previous week. The comparison is using color and arrows to visually show whether it is up or down. The bottom of the visual is showing **Target (48%)** as well as the timeframe (**YTD – Year to Date**).

The KPI on the right is the **Avg % Discount** on sales transactions in Q3. The value is shown in the gauge (**7.1%**), and using ranges and encodings, we can see this is below the target.

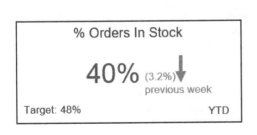

Figure 6.4 – Example 1 of KPI visualizations

The KPI shown in *Figure 6.5* is utilizing a bullet chart to show two KPIs, **Revenue** and **Staff occupation**, as well as how they are doing against their respective targets.

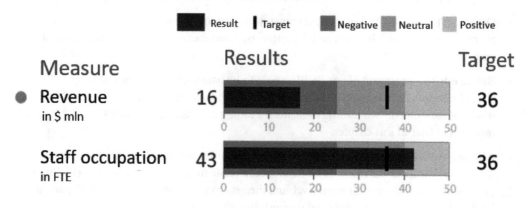

Figure 6.5 – Example 2 of KPI visualizations

You will learn more about choosing the right visualizations for KPIs, as well as for other analytics, in *Chapter 8, Questioning the Data*. Now that we have seen a few visual examples of KPIs, let's move on to go a little bit deeper and understand the two types of KPIs: **leading** and **lagging**.

Leading and lagging indicators

Not all KPIs are designed to do the same thing. There are KPIs that are measuring the outcomes (lagging indicators) and there are KPIs that are measuring parts of the system that are supposed to be driving toward those outcomes (lagging indicators). Sometimes, they're called drivers and outcomes.

Lagging indicators are outcome indicators. For each lagging indicator, organizations should define a few leading indicators, which help drive toward those outcomes.

The outcome is something that's already happened. It's almost too late at that point to change, for example, our quarterly sales revenue. If the revenue that came in that quarter was below the target, it is too late to do anything about it as the quarter is already over. What organizations really need is kind of like an early warning system, which allows them to spot not only that the outcome is in jeopardy, but also why it is in jeopardy. This can give them a chance to adjust during the quarter and work toward achieving the target.

Not only are we looking at those lagging outcomes, but we're also holding people accountable and we're measuring what are called leading indicators, which are drivers, that help those outcomes.

For example, if sales revenue is your outcome-based lagging indicator, you should brainstorm to think about what will help drive sales revenue. Two indicators could be the number of clients you have and the amount of revenue invoiced for each client. This process continues as you then brainstorm what will help drive both the number of clients and the amount of revenue invoiced for each client.

For example, the number of visits to your online store and the number of those visits that lead to a sale (conversion percentage) are both indicators to drive the number of clients. The number of products on each invoice and the average price of the products are both indicators to drive the amount of revenue invoiced for each client.

This process continues down till you have a list of indicators for all parts of the organization, as shown in *Figure 6.6*.

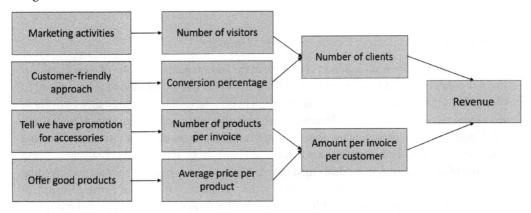

Figure 6.6 – Example leading and lagging indicators

In another example, think about an organization that provides an online video streaming subscription. One of their lagging indicators, which ties to their organizational strategy, is customer retention. Brainstorming on how to impact and drive customer retention, the organization believes that the customer's engagement impacts their retention. A customer that is engaging more, potentially purchasing multiple add-on services, will be more likely to stay than leave. So, tracking customer engagement becomes a leading indicator. If the engagement scores go below target, it is an early warning that there is a good chance the outcome of achieving the sales revenue target will be missed as well.

The question you might be asking at this point is how do you determine the leading indicators? We will answer that later in this chapter. Before moving on to that, we will now learn how to review our planned KPIs for unintended consequences.

Reviewing for unintended consequences

While KPIs are hard to directly influence, they are easily susceptible to causing unintended consequences and driving the wrong behaviors. Revisiting the health example from earlier in the chapter, there are lots of diets out there that recommend some crazy things, such as never eating fat, or only eating fat, and everything in between. Maybe those diets will temporarily lower your weight on a short-term basis, but doing that also potentially has some unintended consequences on your body. Maybe you are vitamin or mineral deficient as a result. Someone that runs every day to stay in shape can potentially have the unintended consequence of directly causing damage to their knees or back.

The key to KPIs is balance and alignment. You don't want to over-rotate one part of a system as you will then deplete another part of it. It is incredibly important to review your planned KPIs against those qualities. Failure to do so will end up in KPIs that may look like they are working and driving outcomes on the surface, but chances are they are negatively impacting another aspect of the business.

Applying Goodhart's law to KPIs

British economist Charles Goodhart once said:

"When a measure becomes a target, it ceases to be a good measure."

This has since become known as Goodhart's law. One of the most famous examples of Goodhart's law is related to a cobra bounty. A long time ago in India, there was an overpopulation of cobra snakes. To try to decrease the number of cobra snakes, the government decided to offer a snake bounty. Individuals received a monetary reward for each cobra snake turned in to government offices. Sounds logical and rational. If people turn in cobra snakes, then they are removing them from the city and decreasing the population. Initially, the bounty appeared successful with large amounts of cobra snakes being turned in. But after some time, individuals managed to manipulate the bounty. They started breeding cobras, and then when they got to a certain maturity, they would turn them over to the government to receive the bounties. This perfectly highlights what Goodhart was referring to in his famous quote.

Let's look at another example, one that's more business oriented. Many organizations will set sales targets to increase what they call the productivity of the salespeople. Assume you work for a car dealer. The car salesman might need to sell 20 cars per month to receive a bonus payment. At the end of the month, they'll make a lot of phone calls, and what ends up happening is they could potentially create a lot of discounts just to get the cars off of their inventory and to sell them. Maybe it's not a bad thing – maybe discounting is good – but let's just assume that in this case, the discounting to reach the target is not a good thing for the business. It could in fact be detrimental to the business and it could reduce profit. Profit is one of their key strategic objectives, so they should consider changing the metric that they're assigning for that, or potentially adding more rigor to the type of KPI. So, they should add some boundaries and some thresholds. Maybe it's not just selling the number of cars, but it's the number of cars with a certain amount of profit.

Let's look at another example of a call center within an organization. Assume that this organization sets an average time per call in, for their employees, as a KPI to track. They could track and see which call center staff take longer for their calls to be completed. The unintended consequences could be that the call center staff may end up giving a customer a quick answer, or a very high-level reply that does not solve the problem, just to get them off the call to reduce the average time. If that organization's strategy includes keeping customers happy and customer retention, then setting call targets without any quantifications on the quality to balance it would not be a good idea.

Now that you have gone through the process of creating lagging KPIs that are tied to your desired outcomes and then some leading KPIs that drive toward those outcomes, a review should be done to ensure there are no unintended consequences. Two common strategies to help review KPIs for unintended consequences are thinking systemically and applying human discretion.

Thinking systemically

Applying a system thinking perspective to how you look at your KPIs will help you look at what is really driving the outcomes. If you are selecting leading indicators that are not actually driving the outcomes, your system will not be balanced, and you will have unintended consequences. Revisiting the health example from earlier in the chapter, if you just focus on your weight but don't focus on the correct diet, you could still eat foods that technically make you lose weight but may not be healthy for you. Over time, that will impact you and your system in a negative way. Think about everything you're doing systemically and if you're driving one behavior, is that going to have a negative impact on another behavior that you don't want? Systems thinking is covered in greater detail in both *Chapter 8, Questioning the Data* and *Chapter 11, Defining a Data Literacy Competency Framework.*

Applying human discretion

One simple way to review KPIs for unintended consequences is simply to apply human discretion. Ask questions that ensure the indicators relate to the ultimate goal. Challenge your assumptions and apply cynicism to them. If it looks wrong, and it feels wrong, there's a chance you should drill down and maybe there's a reason you're feeling that. Don't just look at the potential solution and go with it. Use some human discretion to be critical and curious, and ask questions. This topic is the focus of the next chapter. Now that we have learned about unintended consequences, let's see how we can apply this knowledge to some example KPIs.

Example #1

Assume an organization has a KPI to track the number of meetings each sales rep has with potential customers, the intention being that the more meetings you have, the more sales you will end up having. That could be true, but then you could have the alternative fact of scheduling meetings with people who are unlikely to become customers. They take meetings that are a waste of time, but they are hitting their target KPIs. Reflecting on what we learned in this chapter, if our overall objective is for more customers to buy our offerings, we will want to make sure that the meetings scheduled are with qualified potential customers. Qualified potential customers are prospects who have been evaluated to fit the profile of an ideal customer for the organization who have the intent to buy. Maybe the indicator becomes the number of meetings with qualified customers, and there is a very specific definition of what a qualified customer is.

Example #2

Assume an organization has a KPI to track employee retention, with a target of 95%.

To keep the organization, or a department within the organization, in line with this target, leaders may end up keeping bad employees, and not letting them go, just so they can hit their targets, especially if they have monetary incentives to hit these targets. Reflecting on what we learned in this chapter, a potential solution is to split up retention into voluntary and involuntary, and the targets are specific to voluntary attrition only. This would minimize leaders keeping employees who would have otherwise been exited.

Example #3

One of the most famous examples of an unbalanced KPI comes from a nail manufacturer. Assume the nail manufacturer has a KPI to track time to production. The time to production is the time from when a process for creating an item is started to when the process is completed and the item is ready to sell. If you measure people on that KPI, they could potentially be taking shortcuts just to hit the target. In this example, since the KPI is only focusing on the time to production, and there are no balancing KPIs to specify the quality or condition of the nail, resources ended up making a ton of very small nails.

Reflecting on what we learned in this chapter, we should add criteria and conditions to the target. For example, the height of the nail, the width of the nail, and the quality aspect of what is being produced should all be quantitatively measured and given targets within balanced KPIs.

Now that we understand the difference between measurements, metrics, and KPIs, we have an understanding that KPIs can be leading or lagging, and we also know how to balance KPIs to avoid unintended consequences, we are going to discuss how to determine what the right KPIs are.

Defining what to track

The process starts with determining the outcomes, using lagging KPIs, and then working backward to determine the leading KPIs that will drive toward those outcomes. Determining the right lagging indicators is somewhat straightforward, as they are directly tied to organizational goals. However, determining what indicators help drive those lagging indicators can take a lot of trial and error, and patience.

There are a variety of techniques to determine appropriate KPIs. The three that we want to introduce in this book are activity system maps, logic models, and balanced scorecards. Across all three of these techniques, the high-level process is the same:

- Start with the desired outcome and work backward.

- Throughout the process, we will be making assumptions. Challenge these assumptions.

- As you learn more, revisit the process and tweak the indicators. This is an ongoing process versus a one-time event.

These three techniques will be discussed in greater detail in the following sections.

Activity system maps

Activity system maps, introduced by corporate strategy guru Michael Porter, are a tool to help organizations visualize and plan their business goals. This process makes it easier to identify proper KPIs as well as they will be based on the activities on the map that drive the desired outcomes.

There are three high-level steps in the process of creating an activity system map:

1. The process begins by identifying key elements of the value proposition of your strategy. A value proposition is an innovation, capability, or service that an organization believes will make it attractive to customers. Place these key elements on a whiteboard, a piece of paper, or a PowerPoint slide as colored circles.

2. Identify a list of activities that help drive your value proposition. Add these activities to the visual started in *step 1* as non-colored circles.

3. For each activity, draw lines between it and another activity where the activities affect or depend on each other. Also, draw lines between it and any key element from *step 1*.

Figure 6.7 shows an example activity system map for Southwest Airlines, which Porter used in an article for the Harvard Business Review. Southwest Airlines is a discount airline in the United States and was one of the first discount airlines, and they came up with a different business model to support it.

Porter described Southwest's goal as connecting "people to what's important in their lives through friendly, reliable, and low-cost air travel." He also highlighted Southwest's key value propositions:

- Limited passenger services and amenities
- Short-haul, point-to-point routes between midsize cities and secondary airports
- Very low-ticket prices
- High aircraft utilization
- Lean, highly productive ground and gate crews
- Frequent, reliable departures

Southwest then strategized on activities that could drive those key components; please go through the *references* section to know more.

For example, for limited passenger services and amenities, they identified having no meals, no baggage transfers, no connections with other airlines, limited use of travel agents, 15-minute gate turnarounds, and no seat assignments. These activities all helped support and balance the system to allow them to have very low-ticket prices. To drive a lean, highly productive ground and gate crew, they offered a high level of employee stock ownership, flexible union contracts, and high compensation.

They came up with a strategy, aligned inputs and outputs, and reviewed everything to ensure it was balanced and one set of activities did not negatively impact another set.

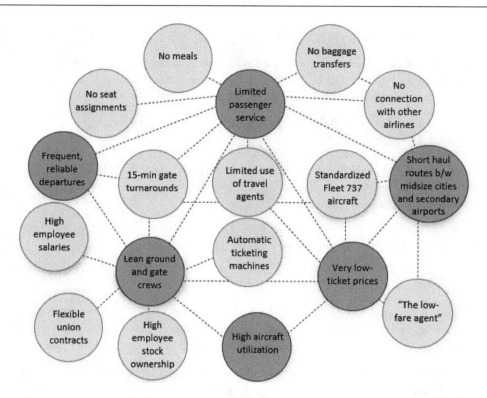

Source: Michael E. Porter, "What is Strategy," *Harvard Business Review*, Nov— Dec, 1996, 61-78.

Figure 6.7 – Southwest Airlines activity systems map

While some of these activities do not lend themselves to metrics, many of them do. These then became the basis for the leading and lagging KPIs. For example, they would have to track aircraft utilization and on-time departures. Those could be seen as lagging indicators, and some of the activities driving those as leading indicators could be the quality and duration it takes to clean the planes in between routes or the number of services that required out-of-stock parts.

What was the end result? Southwest was able to create new opportunities that did not follow traditional rules. What were the results? By the 1990s, Southwest was consistently profitable when many other airlines were losing money and even filing for bankruptcy. By 2011, Southwest had flown the most passengers annually within the United States.

Southwest more recently showed how their ability to be agile and update their strategy using this same approach when COVID-19 hit. In early 2020, Southwest Airlines traffic had already dropped 97% from 2019 due to the pandemic. Showing that strategy needs to adjust at the right time, and agility is key, rather than cutting back on everything during the pandemic, Southwest reassessed their goals and used activity system maps to turn the pandemic into an opportunity. Realizing that most of the travel coming up was going to be vacation and adventure travel, not business travel, they adjusted their routes accordingly.

Logic models

One of the most popular tools for strategic planning is a logic model. It is really useful when trying to develop a new strategic initiative and understand what activities you should be working on. The W.K. Kellogg Foundation has driven the logic model into popular use. The foundation describes a logic model as:

"A picture of how your organization does its work – the theory and assumptions underlying the program. A program logic model links outcomes (both short- and long-term) with program activities/processes and the theoretical assumptions/principles of the program." (p. III, 2004)

A logic model typically can be used in the beginning phase to design and plan for a new program or strategic initiative, and it can also be used to evaluate the quality and effectiveness of the program or initiative after it is launched. It can be very useful in determining good KPIs. A logic model typically defines six things: resources and inputs, activities and processes, outputs, short-term outcomes, intermediate outcomes, and long-term impact (see *Figure 6.8*).

Program Design and Planning

Resources / Inputs	Activities / Processes	Outputs	Short-Term Outcomes	Intermediate Outcomes	Long-Term Impact
What do we need to achieve our goals?	What activities and processes need to be performed?	What assets/info should be created /used to support the intended outcomes?	What do we think the participants will know, feel, or be able to do due to the program?	How do we think the participants will behave or act differently due to the program?	What kind of impact can result if the program is successful?
People Time Money Materials Equipment Technology	Processes Meetings Projects		Awareness Knowledge Attitudes Skills Aspirations	Behavior Practice Decisions Policies Social Action	Social Economic Civic Environmental
			LEARNING	**ACTIONS**	**IMPACT**

Program Evaluation / Measuring Impact

Figure 6.8 – Logic model template

Resources and inputs

Resources and inputs identify the resources available to the program. Resources include human resources, financial resources, technological resources, and any other inputs that are going to be used to support the program's activities and processes.

Activities and processes

Activities and processes describe the actions that are needed to implement the program to reach the desired outcomes. These include designing processes, implementing projects, and developing and providing services.

Outputs

Outputs quantify the direct results from the activities and processes. If one of the activities is providing an educational course to your stakeholders, then the output is the number of classes delivered. If one of your activities is to develop and provide services to your stakeholders, then possible outputs are the number of customers served, or the number of hours of service provided. If your activity is around gathering feedback from stakeholders via focus groups, then a possible output is the number of focus groups held or the number of attendees of the focus groups.

One key point about outputs is they do not talk about the quality of the activities. It is just the quantities at this point. Quality is covered when the logic model is used as an evaluation tool.

Outcomes

Outcomes describe the results that are expected when the program is implemented as planned. They describe changes, not actions. Outputs are the actions, as they are the direct and quantifiable outputs from the program's activities and processes. Outcomes are the results and the impact that the program's activities and processes make on the stakeholders. Sounds very similar to lagging and leading indicators, right?

Logic models split outcomes into three stages, as changes do not happen at the same time. There is a causal chain of outcomes as some need to happen first to drive the longer-term outcomes. Short-term outcomes describe changes you expect immediately or in the near future, intermediate outcomes describe what changes you expect after that (say in 1-2 years), and long-term outcomes, also called impact, describe changes that will occur over time (beyond 2 years).

Rather than identifying outcomes in terms of duration, it may be easier to identify outcomes based on what is being changed as follows:

- Short-term outcomes focus on changes in awareness, opinions, knowledge and skills, and attitudes and mindsets.

- Intermediate outcomes focus on changes in behaviors or actions that result from the new awareness, opinions, and so on, from the short-term outcomes. These include not only changes in behaviors, but also various actions such as contributions, decision making, and policies.

- Finally, long-term outcomes focus on changes in condition or status that result from the intermediate outcomes. These include changes to social, environmental, civic, and economic conditions.

If you are building out a logic model upfront as part of the planning of a program, it is easier to start at the end and identify long-term outcomes and then work backward to identify intermediate outcomes needed to drive the long-term outcomes. The process continues backward when you finish by identifying inputs and resources.

Once completed, you have a robust and balanced list of leading and lagging indicators that can be used for your KPIs.

Now that we understand what a logic model is, let's look at an example (see *Figure 6.9*). Let's assume we are implementing a logic model to plan out our strategy as a new coffee retailer. Their strategy and goal are to make the most consistent and highest-quality coffee around. In the following table, we describe the various components specific to this example.

 🏪	Outcomes		Starting at the end, the outcomes for the new coffee retailer are an avid customer fan base, repeat customers, and increases in sales revenue.
←	Output		Next, the coffee retailer needs to determine what will help drive those outcomes. In their case, they see the number of coffees brewed and the number of coffees sold as measurable outputs.
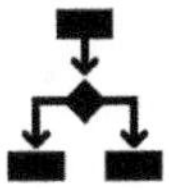 ⛓	Processes		The coffee retailer would like customers to be able to come whenever they want and receive the same, consistent cup of coffee. They would also want to keep the process as efficient as possible to keep costs down.
 →	Inputs		The resources for the coffee retailer include things such as the coffee beans, water, workers, and the time invested. The activities include the entire coffee-making process.

Figure 6.9 – Logic model for a coffee retailer

There are also a few additional components to a logic model that allow us to identify additional performance indicators. These indicators are not leading or lagging, but are rather tied to various business questions that may be asked:

- One is a project measure, which is a measure of projects that are implemented to support the overall program. Let's say we do a branding campaign to sell our coffee. We could track the quality of that campaign.

- Another one is a performance measure. Let's say each department wants to align with these organizational indicators and implement its department-level KPIs. Each location of the coffee retailer could have indicators for the performance objectives of the individual workers. For example, via assessment or inspection, they could measure how good each worker is at following the coffee brewing process that is outlined at the organizational level. In this case, each location could have an indicator for their average score for the efficiency and consistency of the brewing process. This also helps balance the indicators out, as you can have the best process in the world and the best ingredients, but if you do not have the right capacity or the workers are not properly trained or motivated, and they do not always follow the process, then it will negatively impact the organization's desired outcomes.

- Finally, there are risk measures. Risk measures seek to identify potential sources of risk in the logic model activities. In this example, the retailer's coffee beans are sourced from an outside vendor. What if something happens with that vendor, maybe the economy changes, and the prices drastically increase? Maybe the vendor gets the coffee beans from a country where there is a political or environmental disaster, which disrupts the ability of the retailer to receive the coffee beans. These external factors need to be considered and identified as risks in a logic model, and you can create indicators to ensure you are monitoring them. It may be hard to create leading indicators for all these risks, but you can create indicators that highlight what will change if any of these situations occur. In this example, if there is a natural disaster or so, the supply chain may be delayed, or the cost of our resources (the coffee beans) may go up. Having indicators to track the on-time delivery of the resources and the costs of those resources would be a good idea.

The entire end-to-end visual of the coffee retailer's logic model is shown in *Figure 6.10*.

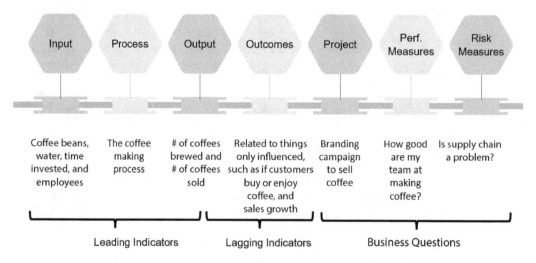

Figure 6.10 – Example logic model for a coffee retailer

Balanced scorecard

One other tool that is used frequently to determine and manage KPIs is a balanced scorecard. A balanced scorecard is an approach for looking at performance measures at different levels within a business. It aims to link an organization's strategy to operational tactics. The scorecard looks at the business from four perspectives:

1. The first is the financial perspective, which tracks financial performance. This is what the executives, shareholders, and board of directors would typically look at.

2. Then, you have the customer perspective, which tracks things related to customers, such as what is the current market share, or what is the customer's current satisfaction. This shows how customers perceive the business.

3. Then, you have the internal process perspective, which tracks operational processes and goals needed to meet the customer objectives. This highlights what the business must do well internally to achieve its goals.

4. Finally, you have the innovation perspective, which tracks things such as training, human capital, and systems. This looks at how the business can continue to evolve and improve.

Each perspective could have a few goals and metrics. *Figure 6.11* displays an example balanced scorecard for a software company.

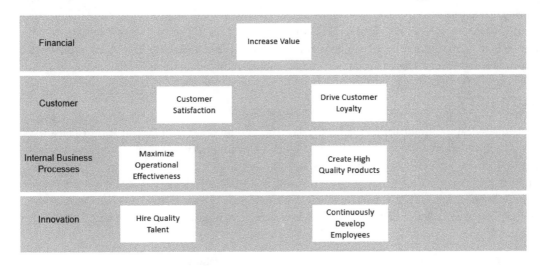

Figure 6.11 – Sample balanced scorecard

The goal of this company is to increase value to its shareholders. One measure for that is to track their sales revenue. The customer perspective includes driving customer satisfaction and loyalty. One measure for customer satisfaction is **Net Promoter Scores** (**NPS**) from a survey and loyalty can be measured by calculating net retention.

The internal business processes perspective includes maximizing operational effectiveness and creating high-quality products. These can be measured by things such as tracking cost savings on an annual basis and tracking net new purchases of products.

The innovation perspective includes hiring quality talent and continuously developing employees. These can be measured by looking at involuntary attrition numbers, and the number of training courses or hours provided to each employee, as an example. Remember, you still need to go through the process to balance everything and to avoid unintended consequences, so reviewing a metric such as the number of training courses provided would need to be balanced to ensure that courses are not just built without any value, just to achieve the target. Potentially, that metric would evolve to tracking something such as the number of internal promotions.

This is a very simplified balance scorecard; usually, they include many more goals and measures at each row. But this is sufficient to show you the approach and how you can use this to determine the right indicators to track. The financial metrics and customer satisfaction and loyalty could become the lagging indicators, and the others could be the leading indicators.

Once the goals and critical success factors are established, the organization needs to then assign performance indicators with targets for each one. For example, related to the customer loyalty goal, the goal could be to retain 95% of their current customers. One performance indicator related to that could be the results from customer satisfaction surveys. Based on historical data analysis, the organization recognizes that any score under 4 (on a 1-10 scale) has a high chance of a customer leaving, so they set the targets accordingly for that performance indicator. Keep in mind that we are sharing a few examples of how to align KPIs with strategic goals. If you are just starting out, do not bite off more than you can chew. No organization can do this all at once. Prioritize and discuss which elements are most important and start with measuring and assigning targets for those.

Summary

Individuals deal with information load every day. The amount of noise that exists within a business really hampers everyone's ability to make data-informed decisions. In this chapter, you have learned how to focus on key performance indicators, or KPIs, that align with an organization's goals. This is important so that you do not waste time measuring and analyzing elements that are not actionable to improve the business. You also learned how to balance and align these key performance indicators so that they work collectively together toward the same outcomes, as opposed to competing with one another.

Now that we have learned how important it is to align with organizational goals, we will focus in the next chapter on how we can critically review and inspect the data and insights coming from these indicators.

References

- "Overcoming the 'Cobra Effect' in Your Business," Continuous Business Planning, accessed June 21, 2022:

  `https://www.continuousbusinessplanning.com/blog/02082019123204-overcoming-the--cobra-effect--in-your-business/`

- Porter, M. From Competitive Advantage to Corporate Strategy. Harvard Business Review. 1987.

- E. Mazareanu, "Enplaned Passengers on Domestic Flights – Airlines in U.S. 2011–2019," Statista.com, April 1, 2020.

- W.K. Kellogg Foundation. *W.K. Kellogg Foundation Logic Model Development Guide*. Battle Creek: W.K. Kellogg Foundation. 1998.

7
Designing Dashboards and Reports

Everyone has probably heard the phrase *a picture is worth a thousand words*. But what if you can't interpret that picture? What if you don't know what you're looking at? We were all exposed to charts, infographics, and other visual aids, particularly during the COVID-19 pandemic, and we've all seen how crucial data has become. We all witnessed visualizations that were made, some of which were even worse than before. Nobody benefits from poor visualizations or visuals that are difficult to interpret.

Charts can deceive us, and charts can lie in a variety of ways, such as giving us wrong or insufficient numbers, weird patterns, and so on. We recently witnessed a politician exhibit a single line graph on a piece of paper and remark, "Well, it goes up, so don't bother; the line is moving up." Without a single word of explanation, no specific facts to examine, it was simply stated, "The line is going up, so it's good".

We do not claim to be master data visualization gurus, but we have learned a lot in our time working in this field. In this chapter, we'll go through the fundamentals of data visualization. In this chapter, we'll go through the fundamentals of data visualization. By the end, you'll have a better understanding of the importance of proper color usage in visualizations (because the color is important), how to design a dashboard using the **Dashboard, Analysis, Reporting (DAR)** approach, and when and why to use specific data visualizations. We will do so by using instances from the COVID-19 pandemic, as well as experiences from our own professional lives.

In this chapter, we will cover the following topics:

- The importance of visualizing data
- Deceiving with bad visualizations
- Using our eyes and the usage of colors
- Introducing the DAR(S) principle
- Defining your dashboard
- Choosing the right visualizations

- Understanding some basic visualizations
- Presenting some advanced visualizations

The importance of visualizing data

As one of our leading examples (thank you, *Alberto Cairo*) once stated, *any chart, no matter how brilliantly made, will lead us astray if we don't pay attention to it!*

It has never been more vital than now to be able to interpret graphs, tables, and infographics as we have all learned how to deal with data and produce fascinating and wonderful representations for our viewers. However, if it is poorly built and we are unable to recognize defects in the graphs, we may make incorrect conclusions.

Going back in time, we began many years ago by making visualizations. Hundreds of drawings of our forefathers might be found in the Altamira caves in Spain. And it's difficult to believe that these drawings are around 15,000 years old, making them the oldest in the world. *Figure 7.1* depicts one of Altamira's incredible cave artworks:

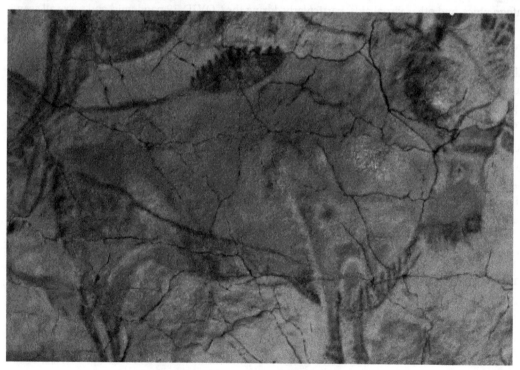

Figure 7.1 – A rock painting in Altamira, Spain

Note

The source of the image can be found at `https://www.spain.info/en/places-of-interest/caves-altamira/`.

These incredible rock paintings are about 15,000 years old! If we go back further in time, the Egyptians could also tell fantastic stories with their hieroglyphs. So, historically speaking, our forefathers first learned to understand and communicate through visuals, followed by scripts and writing. As a result, we are better equipped to comprehend images. We use these facts and discoveries to create understandable pictures through design and color usage.

William Playfair (1759 to 1823), one of the founding fathers of data visualization, developed some excellent visualizations back in the day. *Figure 7.2* shows *Playfair's Atlas*, which was created in 1786!

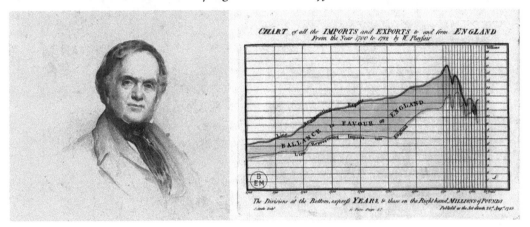

Figure 7.2 – Playfair's Atlas

Note

The source of the image can be found at `https://www.christies.com/en/lot/lot-5388575`.

Playfair reasoned that if longitude and latitude are numbers, they may be replaced with any other quantity (year as the longitude and imported and exported data as the latitude). Using this logic, he was able to create the first amazing visualization.

Also known as *The Lady With the Lamp*, Florence Nightingale (1820 to 1910) was a British nurse, social reformer, and statistician. She created the incredible *Diagram of the Causes of Mortality in the East Army*. This diagram illustrated the epidemic sickness that claimed more British lives during the Crimean War than battlefield wounded men. *Figure 7.3* illustrates the wonderful graphic created by the founder of nursing.

A Contribution to the Sanitary History of the British Army During the Late War with Russia was formally published by her. This book also included a beautiful and easy-to-read Rose diagram, as shown in *Figure 7.3*:

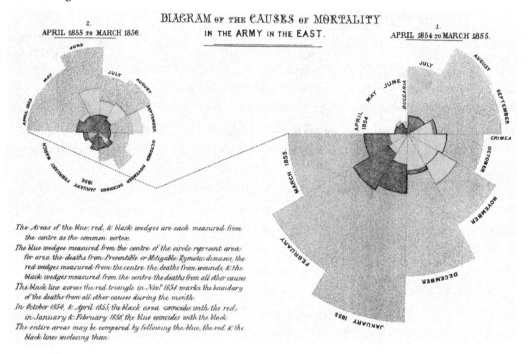

Figure 7.3 – Nightingale's Rose Diagram

> **Note**
>
> The source of the image can be found at `https://www.historyofinformation.com/image.php?id=851`.

She honestly informed the leaders that the losses from epidemic diseases could be better controlled by a variety of factors, such as improved ventilation, housing, and nutrition.

Before we go more into detail on how to design the various charts that we can use, we do not claim to be visualization experts. We simply enjoy telling you tales on how to represent and read insights correctly. This allows you to learn how to create visuals that your viewers will comprehend and read. We wish to do so because we have been misled many times by various people. In the next section, we will discuss some examples that we've encountered in our daily work lives.

Deceiving with bad visualizations

Why is it important to know how to read a visualization? Why is it essential to create accurate graphs? The objective and primary goal of data visualization is to facilitate the recognition and identification of trends, outliers, and patterns in small and big datasets. In this situation, we use the term data visualization to refer to the process of converting collected data into a visual representation such as a graph, table, or even a map.

According to Alberto Cairo, the following frequent fallacies surround visualizations:

- A picture is worth a thousand words
- A visualization is intuitive
- The data should speak for itself
- Show don't tell

And his statement is correct, if people don't know how to read, understand and interpret visualizations.

Unfortunately, we get misled and misinformed in a variety of ways; we will look at several examples to learn how to identify misleading graphs.

Figure 7.4 shows two different data forms. The figure on the left is from *FOX TV* and is several years old. Can you see the flaw in this figure? If you look attentively, you will notice that the "axis" is not displayed correctly. On the right-hand side, we constructed a graph with the values from the first figure. This is a correct depiction of the values, and the difference is not that large! However, when you look at the graph what was shown on TV, you will notice a more dramatic change, which is not the case!

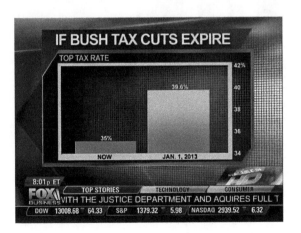
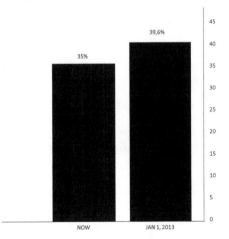

Figure 7.4 – A representation of a bad graph and the correct version

It is quite easy to be misled and misinformed by incorrect, badly constructed graphs. So, let us take a step back and demonstrate how to spot a badly drawn graph using some easy techniques. We will assist you with a simple basic rule for identifying charts that may mislead you. You will make a giant step forward in your data literacy learning journey when you understand the basic guidelines for recognizing difficulties with graphs.

Let us assume that a sales team meets to discuss the previous year's sales. The entire team is pleased when a graph similar to the one shown in *Figure 7.5* is displayed with the results of the previous year. We are all pleased with the upward trend of the growth curve. However, is this the case?

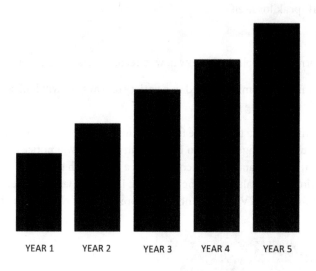

Figure 7.5 – Bad sales graph – 1

When we look at this graph more closely, we can see that some critical components are not designed or built correctly. To begin with, the Y-axis is completely absent!

In this instance, we should contact our graph developers and request that they add a Y-axis to the graph as shown in *Figure 7.6*.

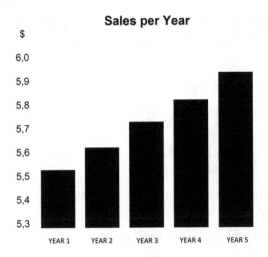

Figure 7.6 – Bad sales graph – 2

The Y-axis was added to the graph by our Data & Analytics team's designer (or developer). Even if we carefully examine the graph in *Figure 7.6*, it is still somewhat incorrect! Our lesson in building a bar chart is that the Y-axis of a bar chart should always start at "0" to provide an accurate picture of our sales (or other) performance. In this instance, we should contact the graph designers again and request that the axis be set to 0.

When we set the Y-axis to 0, the picture completely changed; our sales rose slightly but there was no steep growth, as was shown in the first two figures. *Figure 7.7*, where we changed the Y-axis from 5,3 to 0 demonstrates this! The context for our graphs is critical; we want to leave as little opportunity for interpretation as possible:

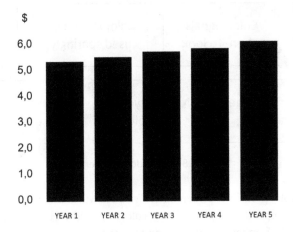

Figure 7.7 – Sales graph – final

To finish, there are certain basic guidelines to follow while visualizing data. We must always pay special attention to the graphs that we observe. The following are some common concerns that can arise (remember them):

- When a bar chart is used, the Y-axis needs to start at 0.

- When a pie chart is used, please do not use more than 4 to 5 slices (otherwise it won't be readable anymore).

- Don't turn your graphs upside down! Believe us when we say we've seen some during our work in the data and analytics world.

- Avoid using unusual items to look for correlations (pirates versus rock music, sold ice creams versus jellyfish stings, and so on).

- Poorly designed graphs can mislead you easily.

- Do not use dubious, incomplete, or insufficient data.

Many bad visualization examples can be found at `https://viz.wtf/`. We provide instances of strange and poor visualizations to our students and other trainees in our line of work, and to be honest, you will learn a lot from them! We must exercise caution and examine intently, ask questions, and be skeptical of what we see! The next section will go through how we look at graphs, how to interpret what we see, and how to utilize colors.

Using our eyes and the usage of colors

How do we pick a color for a data visualization? Color is used for more than merely enhancing an image or adding aesthetics to graphs. Color has emotional and cultural aspects that might enhance or hinder your visualization. *Figure 7.8* depicts a couple of features that will help you choose colors for your visualizations:

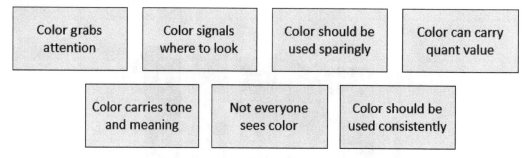

Figure 7.8 – Color does matter

Using the fundamental color guidelines presented in *Figure 7.8* will allow you to create fantastic graphs that enable you to create impactful graphs utilizing colors correctly. However, there is still much to learn about reading visuals. Stephen Few (our second top example) wrote multiple books and papers on displaying data insights. His books and website (`https://www.perceptualedge.com/`) are a great place to learn about how our brains operate, how our minds work, and how easily our eyes can deceive us. Do you know that we don't look with our eyes? We use our intellect to recognize patterns quickly. *Figure 7.9* depicts our eye-brain connection:

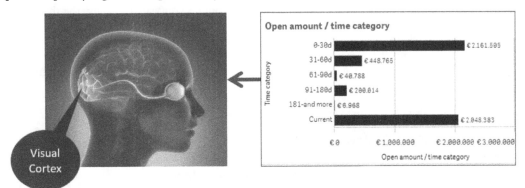

Figure 7.9 – Eye-brain connection

We accomplish this through the use of our iconic memory (our picture memory), which is very short-term memory. This explains why we recognize images so quickly. *Figure 7.10* shows how our brain is dedicated to processing information that our eyes collect to take you through some easy principles.

Many aspects of visual perception are not intuitive. When we look at these two sets of objects, we can immediately see that those on the left are convex (which means outward) and that those on the right are concave (which means hollow):

Figure 7.10 – Convex versus concave

But what do you see in the representation displayed in *Figure 7.11*?

Figure 7.11 – Concave versus convex

The effect has now been reversed, with the things on the left appearing concave and the objects on the right appearing convex. However, all we did was flip each group of objects. We did not change them. Because our visual perception learned to presume that light was shining from above, we now regard those on the left as concave. Because the shadows are on the top, we see the items on the left as concave (hollow), and the ones on the right as convex (rounded outward), because the shadows are on the bottom.

Stephen Few inspired this visual perception example in one of his presentations on his website, Perceptual Edge: `http://www.perceptualedge.com/files/VisualAnalysisCourse.pdf`.

While reading this chapter, you've discovered that color does matter and that our brain helps us notice patterns faster. It is also critical that we understand what will work, what will not, and why.

Stephen Few also explores visual perception characteristics that are directly applicable to our world of data visualizations. These are known as the pre-attentive qualities of visual perception. Understanding those factors allows us to understand what will work, what will not, and why understanding the pre-attentive qualities is crucial.

Figure 7.12 depicts a small list of pre-attentive features in the areas of form, color, position, and motion. There are many more to discuss, but those are the fundamental factors that will assist you and be the most useful:

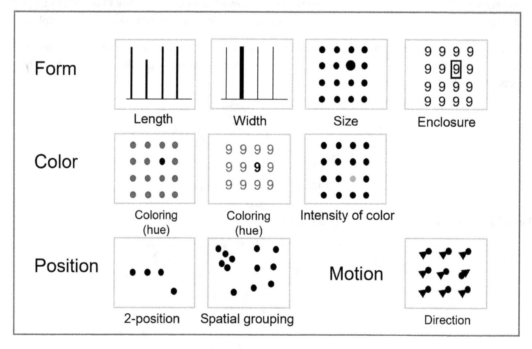

Figure 7.12 – Pre-attentive processing

When visualizing data, we must always keep colorblindness in mind. In reality, we must begin by asking several questions to our readers. If we understand our businesses and their aims better, we will be more equipped to picture what and how to visualize.

If you do not have a good eye for color, there are various tools available on the internet that we will introduce here to help you. If you go to the websites present after *Figure 7.13*, you may see all of the common color combinations, as well as take care of the corporate brand that you'll need to maintain.

When developing a dashboard, contrast should be considered. Colors opposite of one another on a color wheel have high contrast. You can also generate contrast by darkening one color and lightening the other. Because different screens display colors differently, contrast is equally crucial when designing digitally on a screen. As a result, make sure you use adequate contrast where it matters. *Figure 7.13* shows an example of a color wheel (in black and white) from one of the websites present after *Figure 7.13*. It will undoubtedly assist you in selecting the appropriate colors:

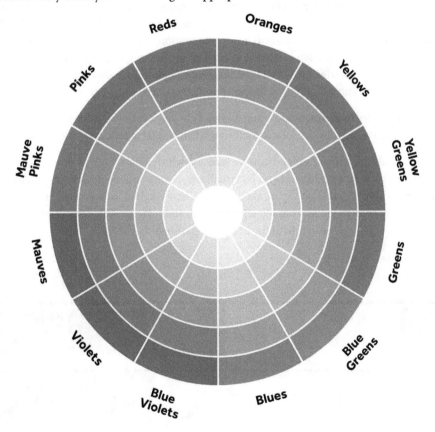

Figure 7.13 – Color wheel

You can find this color wheel at `www.colormatters.com`. The following are some other fantastic websites to visit:

- `https://color.adobe.com`
- `https://coolors.co/`
- `https://palettegenerator.com/`

You can utilize them to plan out the color schemes you want to use.

You're probably wondering, "How do I choose the right color?" So, how do you pick a color for a data visualization? Color is about more than merely enhancing an image or aesthetic. Color has emotional and cultural aspects that might help or hinder your visualization. When it comes to color, there are a few factors to consider. Many of our associations are debatable, and people's perspectives may differ. Symbolic meaning is frequently founded on cultural consensuses, such as connecting black with death. In Asia, red is associated with marriage and prosperity, but in the Ivory Coast, it is associated with death. Green is a wonderful color; we identify it with vegetation, mother nature, and money. On the other hand green in also associated in a negative sense with greed, envy, nausea, and poison. The color blue is commonly connected with the sea and the sky. From a cultural standpoint, it is associated with sadness in Iran. Did you know that blue is the most preferred corporate color worldwide?

So, using different colors in a presentation may have a huge impact on the appearance and feel of a visualization, and you should consider color associations when designing for a culturally varied audience.

Another fundamental idea is to understand how we read and which tools we use to view our dashboards and reports. When viewing a dashboard and its visualizations on a mobile device, keep in mind that all visualizations will be stacked on top of each other. When you look at a screen, you most likely (though not in every country) read from top left to bottom right. *Figure 7.14* depicts how we read by using an image from a *Google* search with the keyword "dashboards:"

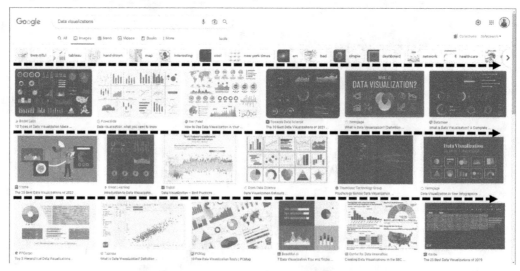

Figure 7.14 – When we read, we read from top left to right bottom

Of course, the existing data and analytics tools will allow you to adjust the reading methods for countries that do this differently. However, we utilize the reading view from the top left to bottom right in Europe and the United States.

This method of seeing information is something you'll need to consider as you design your dashboards and reports. Because of the way we read, the most important visuals must be positioned at the top of the line that we consume. The major KPI elements should not be placed on the bottom right; instead, they should be placed on the top left-hand side!

In this section, we addressed how faulty visualizations can mislead you and provided you with the first basic tips for recognizing bad graphs. We talked about the importance of colors and how we gaze and read, and demonstrated some of the pre-attentive attributes. In the next section, we will introduce the DAR(s) principle, as well as provide definitions of dashboards and reports.

Introducing the DAR(S) principle

We have standard reports, such as those that meet periodic information needs; these are reports that do not change greatly over time. Examples include financial status, inventory, employee availability, the number of products sold, and so on. These reports frequently feature a fixed layout with the option of drilling (more comprehensive material), being more aggregated (drilling up), and even slicing and dicing (selecting a different angle)

Dashboards for management (score carding) are displayed differently. Dashboards or scorecards are often one-page documents that provide an overview of several graphs, meters, and tables. This overview provides a quick snapshot of the present state of things in a specific region of an organization. They also show how a company performs from a strategic standpoint, as shown in *Chapter 6*, *Aligning with Organizational Goals*.

The key takeaways are that there are three angles to display information, like **dashboarding, analysis, and reporting**. This is known as the DAR principle. We've even added an S to allow you to choose dimensions (angles) and facts (measurements) to generate tables or other visualizations on your own. This is known as the self-service area. We offer some example questions in *Figure 7.14* to help you understand the DAR(S) principle:

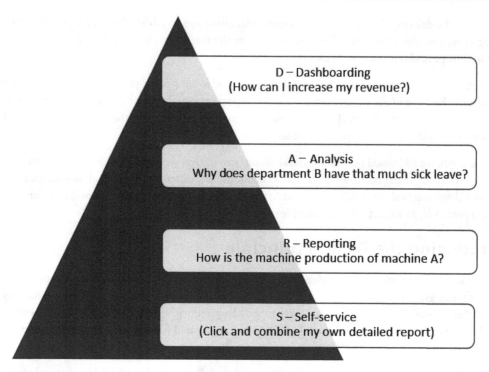

Figure 7.15 – DAR(S) principle

When we look at this informational pyramid, which we also addressed in *Chapter 6, Aligning with Organizational Goals*, we can see how it is related to the DAR(S) principle in a straightforward way.

From a **strategic perspective**, it is about assisting managers in making data-informed decisions by providing high-level knowledge about their specific firm. A dashboard's data is largely limited to the past and the future.

We would like to study complicated data and its connections from an **analytical perspective**. We'd love to discover new angles (dimensions) and facts (measures). The analytical portion is primarily historical, with plenty of data interaction.

From an **operational perspective**, we require straightforward and accessible data analysis with a high degree of detail. The operational section is largely historical and contains a wealth of comprehensive information. Self-service analytics can also be made available in this part; analysts like to dig deeper into data with a high level of detail, but they also want to develop tables and visualizations.

We normally ask a lot of questions to be able to understand what our readers and business want, but we also try to explain to them what type of users they are. By identifying the users, we may also debate the depth of analysis and so on. We use the *Bill Imnon user groups*. Bill Imnon, considered the father of the data warehouse, identified four types of user groups: Farmers, Tourists, Explorers, and Miners. Using this method helps us investigate what type of granularity is needed and what type of interactivity is necessary for our viewers. *Figure 7.16* depicts a table with many jobs that can exist in an organization; each function has its own set of requirements and preferences for how they want to use the insights for data-informed decision-making:

Who is my public	Farmers	Tourists	Explorers	Miners
Managing board	X			
Middle management	X			
Team manager		X		
Team lead				
Controler			X	
Process advisor			X	
Business Analysts			X	
Analists			X	
Data Analysts			X	
Data Scientists				X

Figure 7.16 – Inmon groups to identify the level of interactivity and detail

Farmers have defined, predictable requirements. Tourists are practically equivalent to farmers, but they must utilize filters to look at the data differently and understand the findings. Explorers seek to examine existing indicators from several perspectives (dimensions) and interact thoroughly with dashboards and reports for data-informed decision-making. Miners are from more of a scientific field; they are our data scientists, and they want a lot of freedom to investigate anomalies in the data (looking for the golden egg).

Using this strategy not only helps us design and develop our frontend but also helps us establish what detailed level is required from a data warehouse standpoint.

Defining your dashboard

The following is Stephen Few's definition of a dashboard (which we utilize in our daily lives):

"A single-screen visual presentation that presents the most important information required to fulfill one or more goals."

When we divide the definition into numerous parts, we find the following elements:

- *Presentation of visuals*: How should the data be presented to the eye and brain? It must have a well-organized interface and must summarize divergent and attention-demanding material.

- Is it *data used to achieve one or more goals*: KPIs are typically used. It is tailored to a certain user group (or audience) and requires a certain level of detail; it is for a specific user group (or audience) and we must be clear about what should be displayed on the dashboard.

- *It must fit on a single screen*: There should be no scroll bars or toggling between screens; it should provide a clear overview.

- *We need to see the results in the blink of an eye*: This necessitates a high level of detail! The dashboard should do nothing more than what it is supposed to accomplish and should not raise any concerns. The message must be clear and concise.

- *Putting all of those factors together, we can probably conclude that a dashboard is always custom-made*: It is designed for a certain audience and requires a certain amount of information. By addressing all of these points, you'll see that you'll need to take specific actions to acquire the ideal results while creating or developing a wonderful, amazing, and clear dashboard. The crucial factors will be discussed in the next section.

Inquiring with your customers or the general public is a vital step. Involve your business users from the beginning; this will provide you with the best support and assistance. As a result, you will have a product that meets all of the standards. You must also immerse yourself in the business users. Ask your audience's age, and remember, your audience may be from different age groups. Those from older generations may be less tech-savvy so it's best to then keep the visualization as simple as possible as they consume information in a different manner. Find out if there are any colorblind people! When creating the initial drafts, consider numerous concepts, such as A/B testing, what appears better, and what the user can read and understand! All of the consequences of the requirements package must be evident to the client, as well as the level of detail. Agree (provisionally) on the drawing or proof of concepts with your client. We like to use sketches in our first designs to better understand our clients; we call this approach sketching and chatting or chatting and sketching.

Figure 7.17 illustrates a visualization or a requirements session to help illustrate the sketching and chatting process. This chat session was focused on **Software Asset Management** because it is critical to managing your assets as you can save a lot of money here (such as by simply removing the not used licenses, cloud subscriptions that are not used, and so on). The initial stage in this process was to gather suggestions for the requirements that needed to be displayed and the filters that were most likely to appear in our dashboard:

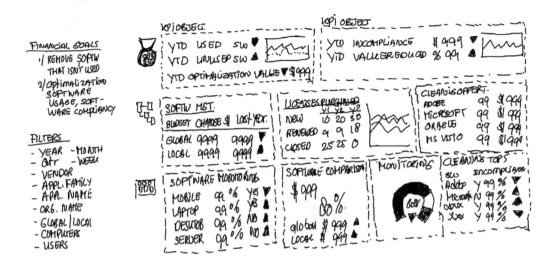

Figure 7.17 – Chatting and sketching

The next stage is to create a more detailed design for the new dashboard (while keeping the corporate identity colors and styling in mind). We like to do so in Photoshop or similar design software. *Figure 7.18* illustrates the outcome of some chatting and sketching sessions:

Figure 7.18 – Final result after a few chatting and sketching sessions

This is a true tale of how we devised this solution; however, we cannot show you the outcome because it is confidential. But what we'd like to state is that as soon as this image was presented in its original coloration, someone leaped up, got behind the laptop, and began clicking on it. Those are incredible moments that we will never forget because we knew we did the correct thing at the time!

We are frequently asked how we design a dashboard as per the DAR(S) principle. As one of our friends once stated (thank you Rob van Vliet), it is like *eating an elephant piece by piece or chunk by chunk*. When we look at those portions, we can discern some steps. We must identify the business questions, understand our target audience, locate the data, learn and define the measures, identify the analytical angles and filters, and then create the visualizations and necessary interaction.

Figure 7.19 shows the steps in the phases that we have discussed so far:

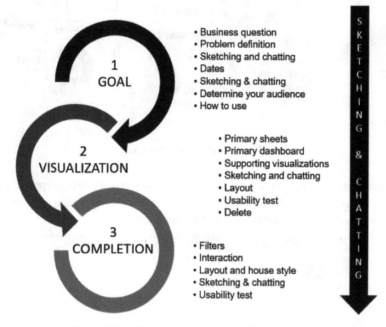

Figure 7.19 – The three phases of dashboard design

Figure 7.19 helps identify the steps of the sketching and chatting process. To conclude this section, here are some tips that we would like to share with you:

- Keep the screen quiet and readable.
- Preferably, the background should be off-white.
- No color gradients and no 3D effects.
- Use as few lines and borders as possible.
- No plot area background color.
- No frame around the object.
- No borders around the bars of a bar chart.
- Keep the lines on a line chart as thin as possible.

- Think of color blindness and how red and green are close to each other. For example, you could use a green up arrow instead of a green circle to indicate a positive metric (blue and green could also be an issue).

- Pay attention to signal colors: red is wrong, green is right, and yellow is in-between.

- Don't use bright colors, but work with hues and saturation.

- The font should be readable (we know it's a subjective thing, but don't use a small size or unclear font).

- Consider your audience. What is their age?

As we mentioned regarding the common fundamental guidelines for building dashboards and reports, it should be evident that color matters and that design is governed by basic laws. However, we see the situation visualized in *Figure 7.20* almost every day:

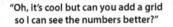

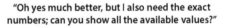

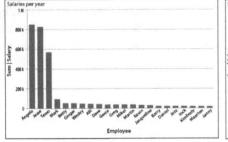

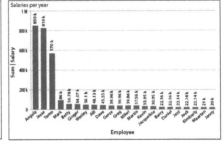

Figure 7.20 – This is how it usually goes

It is not strange to want to see the details. However, they should be displayed as a report (table or pivot table) or as a self-service component in your dashboard. In this manner, we protect and maintain the single point of truth. Exporting data from a dashboard to Excel does not work (several versions of detailed information, cleaned-up information, and so on) since it was saved in multiple spots by different people.

In this section, we spoke about the DAR(S) principle, the definition of a dashboard, and how to identify and find your dashboard readers. We also demonstrated the chatting and sketching technique.

In the next section, we will assist you with some of the most commonly used visualizations in our opinion (and the ones that we just love to use). We will go over the visualizations that you may use in your dashboard design as well as the underlying use cases in some detail. Of course, in between, we'll tell you some incredible stories about data journeys we've worked on.

Choosing the right visualization

The incredible world of data visualizations is booming, and we've seen some great, amusing, and tough graphs in recent years. In addition, there are more types of visualizations than ever before; to be honest, we adore all of these visualizations, but you must be able to understand them. So, in our opinion, keep things simple! *"Simplicity is the highest sophistication,"* Leonardo da Vinci famously observed. This is extremely true; make things basic, comprehensible, and readable. When we do this, we can embark on our data journey, which we depicted in *Figure 1.13 – The data-informed decision-making journey*.

We should strive to keep things as basic as possible. Alternatively, we could apply artificial intelligence to see what we could learn from our dataset (which is mostly available in the tools nowadays). From there, we can create fantastic, legible dashboards that will result in wiser decisions and more value for our organization, owing to better outcomes.

Nine types of functions can be visualized, as shown in *Figure 7.21*:

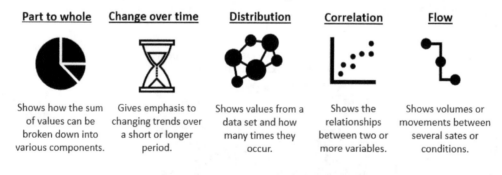

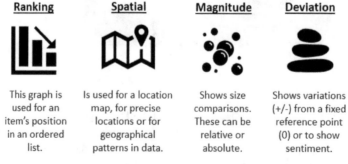

Figure 7.21 – The data visualization functional groups

The *Financial Times* has built an amazing **visual vocabulary**, which can be found at `https://ft-interactive.github.io/visual-vocabulary/`. *Figure 7.21* is a reference to the great visual vocabulary. When designing a data story, consider one of these nine functional groupings and select a form of visualization that will properly accompany your data story. In the following section, we will look at some of the most commonly used visualizations when a person or organization is just getting started with data.

Understanding some basic visualizations

Visualizations help demonstrate and visualize the data for descriptive analytics. There are numerous graphs you may use. This book will walk you through some of the fundamental visualizations found in the majority (if not all) tools. We will begin by providing a graphical representation of the visualization and explain when and why you should utilize it.

Bar chart (or column chart or bar graph)

The bar chart belongs to the *Ranking* functional visualization group. *Figure 7.22* shows two types of bar chart:

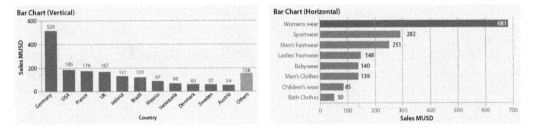

Figure 7.22 – Two types of bar chart

The most important aspect here is that the Y-axis of a bar chart should begin at 0 (if it does not, please contact the developers). A bar chart is used when an item in an ordered list can be positioned. It is utilized when the absolute or relative value is more essential. A helpful approach here is to emphasize the main topics of interest. When sorted into order, normal bar charts present the ranks of data considerably more readily.

When to apply

You should use this chart when specifying the number of incidents, items, and purchases made on a website by various sorts of users, wealth, deprivation, league tables, constituency election results, and so on.

`https://infogram.com/examples/charts/bar-chart` provides some fascinating examples of when to utilize a bar chart.

Line chart

The line chart is part of the *Change over time* functional visualization group. *Figure 7.23* shows two different types of line charts that you can utilize:

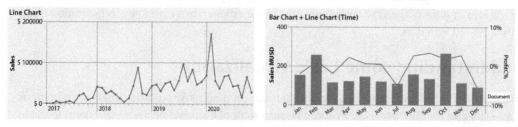

Figure 7.23 – Two types of line chart

A line chart allows you to display changing trends throughout time. This can be done on a daily, weekly, monthly, yearly, or other time scale. However, we've also seen some very complex time data displayed as a line chart. It is critical to select the appropriate period for your data story's viewers. The most common approach is to display a moving time series, such as a 90-day moving average. Consider using markers to denote data points if the data is irregular. *Figure 7.23 (the image on the right)* depicts a useful method for displaying the relationship over time between an amount (columns) and a rate (line).

Look for trends in the dataset that have been displayed for you or by you. A trend is typically defined as an overall movement in one direction. It may rise or fall, but there is usually a consistent flow. Steps (rapid and sustained changes) or spikes (short-term changes) can occur as a result of a sales promotion or an enhancement (step) to a certain procedure.

Figure 7.24 shows a combination chart, where we can modify the colors for each expression (measure) to give the viewers of our chart additional analytical ability:

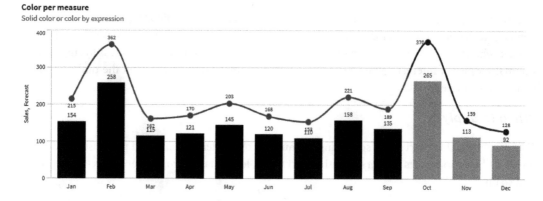

Figure 7.24 – Combination chart – colors per expression

Slope diagrams, area charts, fan charts with future projections, and connected scatterplots that show the movement of specific values are part of the other visualizations you may utilize in the *Change over time* group. An excellent illustration would be the numerous types of software vendor scores that are reviewed for the annual *Gartner Magic Quadrant* report. When you visualize multiple points across time, you can use a connected scatterplot. A great example can be found at `https://qap.bitmetric.nl/extensions/magicquadrant/index.html`.

When to apply

You should use a line chart to share information on price movements, economic time series, emerging market valuations, days on market averages by month, market sectoral changes, the average amount of payments over time, the number of sales categories (one line per category), and so on.

Pie chart

The pie/donut chart belongs to the *Part to whole* functional visualization group. In *Figure 7.25*, we have created two types of pie charts that you can use:

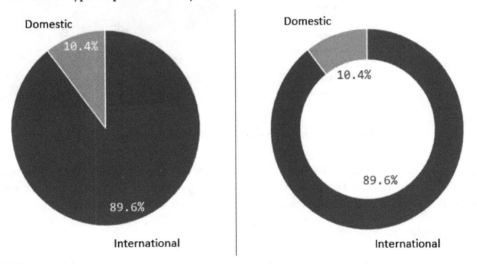

Figure 7.25 – Two examples of pie charts

William Playfair created one of the earliest documented pie charts in 1801. He authored a book called *The Statistical Breviary*, where he introduced both the pie chart and circle graph. His pie chart shows the proportions of the Turkish Empire located in Asia, Europe, and Africa before 1789. It is amazing to see how William Playfair used circle graphs to represent the data. You can find the complete story at `https://infowetrust.com/project/breviary`.

Let us discuss *Figure 7.25*, you can see that the total is 100% and that the slices are separated into values (the smaller slice is 10.4% and the larger slice is 89.6%). Pie charts function best with values of 25%, 50%, or 75%. In this approach, readers can more easily identify percentages in a pie chart than they would in other charts.

A pie chart is not a good choice when comparing slices or shares, or when there are many small slices. The general rule of thumb is 4 to 5 slices. Another rule of thumb is to avoid using distorted 3D visuals. Another typical error is that the data for a pie chart is not total, as it does not reflect 100%. The final issue is that pie charts are incorrectly used for groupings that are totaled up.

The second chart shown in *Figure 7.25* is a donut chart, which is similar to a pie chart but has a blank middle where you can add additional (contextual) information. Tree maps, grid plots, and other charts can also be utilized within the *Part to whole* functional visualization group. *Figure 7.26* depicts two examples – one of a grid plot (left) and one of a tree map (right):

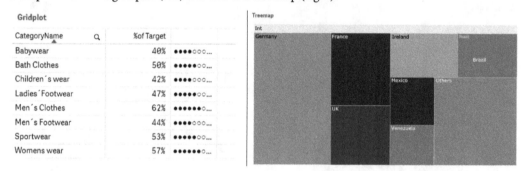

Figure 7.26 – An example of a grid plot and a tree map

Tree maps give a quick overview of the hierarchical structure. Tree maps are also good to compare the parts via their area size. These *Part to whole* diagrams are a great way for the viewers to make sense of a problem and see the relationship between the whole number and the components.

When to apply

To utilize a pie chart, you must have a complete quantity that is divided into numbers or discrete sections. When using a pie chart, your primary purpose should be to compare each slice's contribution to the overall. When this is not achievable, a pie chart is not the best option. Some examples are the number of sales by user type, the number of different types of responses in a survey or questionnaire, and the number of votes cast in an election.

Heatmap

The heatmap is one of our favorite and most powerful graphs; it belongs to the *Change over time* functional visualization group:

	Day						
	Sun	Mon	Tue	Wed	Thu	Fri	Sat
Q1	74	117	107	58	55	67	58
Q2	54	63	56	37	33	55	70
Q3	64	66	42	43	53	95	47
Q4	53	39	116	50	74	80	59

Figure 7.27 – A calendar heatmap

These types of graphs show the density of your data – for example, patterns per hour, per day, per week, and so on. When utilizing a calendar heatmap, you can detect flaws in planning versus requests or staffing versus requests, and even find the busiest times for a call center, and so on.

The bed cleaning story

Let us look at a real-life example of a hospital that was struggling with staffing, the number of requests, and delivering "clean beds" on time to demonstrate the effectiveness of a calendar heatmap. They agreed to provide clean bedding within 75 minutes. The cleaning department began by collecting Excel data, and we sought to discover a more convenient approach to do so. So, we began with some simple data to prepare (as we know it will be a journey) and a visualization solution. First, we provided some metrics to demonstrate the SLA data (did we meet the 75% mark?) and the number of requests, as well as a line chart displaying the number of requests over time. *Figure 7.27* depicts the first visualizations that were developed:

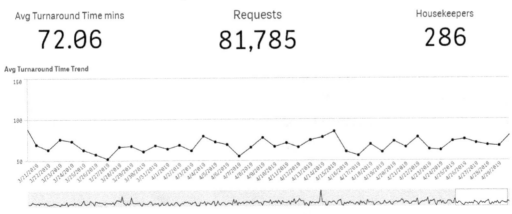

Figure 7.28 – The first bed cleaning visualization

This is interesting information, but it doesn't reveal much while providing a decent summary. The customer required more precise details. We knew that the agreed-upon SLA time was 75 minutes (a target), so we could add a target line. *Figure 7.29* shows the line chart with the newly added target line. Furthermore, we were able to detect requests that did not meet the SLA time frame. We did this by emphasizing the ones that did not reach the 75-minute mark but were above it. Being able to detect queries that took more than 75 minutes provided us with the opportunity to improve even more:

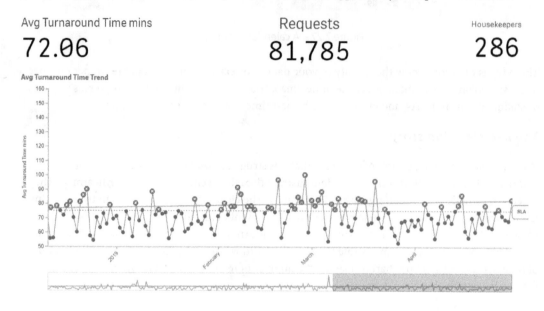

Figure 7.29 – Improving and adding a target line

From here, we identified more potential to expand the visualizations to a more detailed level and assisted the hospital's management in identifying planning difficulties. We used these incredible heatmaps to visualize personnel, requests, and response time.

Figure 7.30 shows the wonderful calendar heatmaps that helped us understand the issues that happened during the day and prevented us from meeting the SLA time:

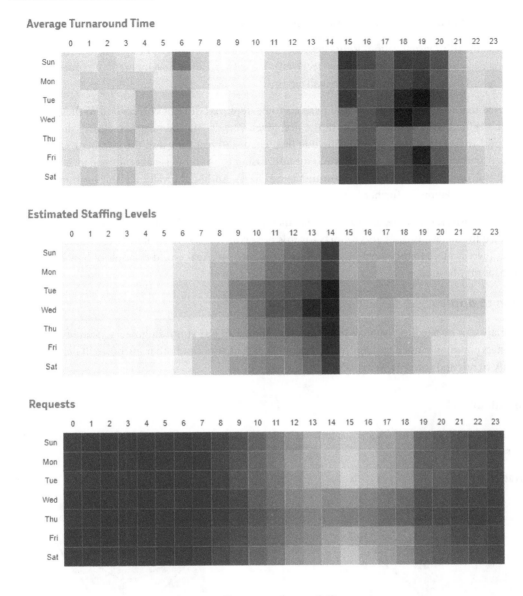

Figure 7.30 – The usage of powerful heatmaps

We discovered some significant findings when we utilized these calendar heatmaps to depict **Average Turnaround Time** and compared them to **Estimated Staffing Levels** and the number of **Requests**.

First and foremost, we can tell from the **Average Turnaround Time** chart that the time of delivery increases (the darker it is, the longer it takes) – that is, after 15:00 (3 P.M.). Second, from the **Estimated Staffing Levels** chart, we can observe that we have a high staffing level between 11:00 (11 A.M.) and 14:00 (2 P.M.).

After that, the number of employees drastically decreases.

However, the third visualization, **Requests**, also shows the total number of requests (the lighter the coloring becomes, the more requests are received). We witnessed the development of requests from 12:00 (noon) to 18:00 (6 P.M.) in this visualization.

We noted that the intended number of persons to be deployed did not correspond to the number of requests filed. We couldn't see this in the first given visuals, but the heatmap clearly shows this pain spot. Therefore, it is natural to conclude that when staff planning and the number of requests received are out of sync, the average time for addressing those requests exceeds the SLA timings (which is shown in the **Average Turnaround Time** chart). Adding the values to this heatmap could be a recommendation for further improvement.

Using these visuals, they were able to better plan their personnel, as well as with the other visualizations we added to the dashboards and reports for this hospital, and improvements were made fast. Of course, there is more to this story, but we wanted to show you a real-world example of how calendar heatmaps may be used.

When to apply

Heatmaps can be used to visualize time series, as shown in our story. Engineers, academics, and marketers commonly use heatmaps for comparative data analysis and other purposes. It helps them identify trends and patterns, as explained in this section.

Radar chart

The radar chart is part of the *Magnitude* functional visualization group. *Figure 7.31* shows two instances of a radar chart:

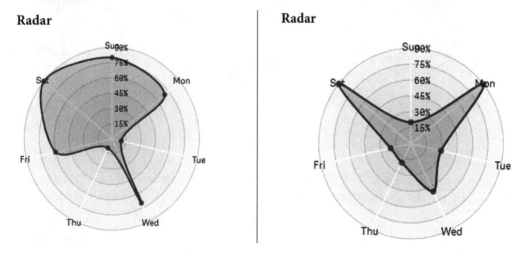

Figure 7.31 – Examples of radar charts

A radar chart is a chart that uses a small area to display several variables. When comparing two or more values, items, attributes, or features, you can utilize a radar chart. When using these types of charts, be sure you structure the chart in a way that makes sense to your readers. Radar charts are commonly used for illustrating commonality, exhibiting outliers, and ordinal data.

We once utilized a radar chart to depict differing responses from two different groups based on questionnaire responses. When we positioned the groups atop each other, it was amazing to see the distinctions between them.

To avoid a cluttered radar chart, plot no more than three sets of a group. When we employ too many, the chart becomes crowded and thus unreadable.

When to apply

You can use a radar chart to compare two types of pharmaceuticals from the same class along numerous dimensions, such as the most prevalent adverse effects, alcohol use, addiction, client expenses, and so on. You can also use this type of chart to show weekly sales figures/revenue by product category and the competitive analysis of your services in comparison to others. Last but not least, you might utilize a radar chart for human resources and to present, for example, the results of a soft or technical skill evaluation.

Geospatial charts

A geospatial or spatial chart is part of the *Spatial* functional visualization group. Some examples of geospatial charts are shown in *Figure 7.32*:

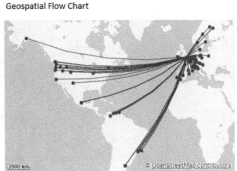

Figure 7.32 – Examples of geospatial charts

We've seen a lot of excellent geospatial charts over the years. We've seen plain basic charts, heatmaps on charts, flow charts, and contour charts (showing a city, a part of a city, and so on). The dots or bubbles of a chart depict the cities and their population, for example. When you use geographic data, it is commonly referred to as geospatial data, and it can contain various kinds of data. Geometric data and geographic data are two types of spatial data that are more widely employed.

Spatial data can help you understand a variety of topics, and there are numerous resources available on the internet. The main advantage of using spatial data is that the visualization may effectively illustrate the geographic distribution of key variables connected to location or region. The disadvantage here is that it can be tough to gain a decent overview when there are many values. By zooming in on specifics, the values can be visualized. Geospatial data can be presented in a variety of ways. As an example, imagine adding numerous layers to a geographical map and visualizing diverse types of information on the same map. Alternatively, you can establish a hierarchy of areas by using drill-down measurements to zoom in to a detailed level.

The story of Dr. Snow – death in the Pit

Outliers are individual values that differ significantly from the majority of other values in a set, and they can be identified using tools such as maps. Identifying outliers is always one of the first things you should look for when trying to get a sense of the data. The definition of an outlier is fairly subjective. Many people define an outlier as any data point that is three standard deviations or more out from the dataset's mean. Early identification allows you to understand what they are, analyze why they are outliers, and then decide whether or not to eliminate them from the analysis.

Dr. John Snow is a well-known example of how an anomaly might help you identify practical ideas. Dr. Snow was researching a cholera outbreak in London in the nineteenth century. While the most widely held belief was that the cholera outbreak was caused by airborne bacteria, Dr. Snow hypothesized that it was spreading through the water supply via microscopic bacteria. On a map of London, he depicted the cholera deaths, as shown in the following figure:

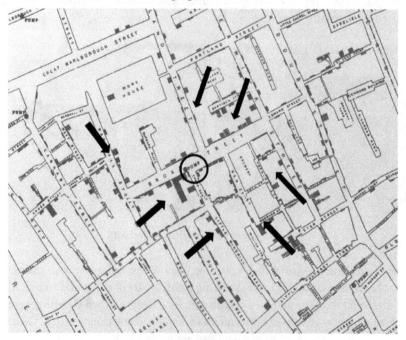

Figure 7.33 – The story of Dr. Snow

At first, no patterns surfaced and everything appeared to be random. What eventually contributed to the hypothesis's validation? Only one outlier! The map indicated that someone had died who lived outside the city, far from the other deaths. He started to look into the anomaly and discovered that the individual used to live in the heart of the city, where there had been several deaths, and she used to enjoy the taste of the water there. She was so concerned that she would have the water transported to her new home. With this new information, there was enough proof to halt the water pumping from that water station, eventually putting an end to the epidemic.

Who knows how long the pandemic would have lasted and how many more people would have perished if Dr. Snow had dismissed the anomaly instead of using it as an opportunity to learn why it was an outlier? While not every business decision is as critical as this one, it emphasizes the significance of looking for outliers to understand more about why they exist rather than simply ignoring or filtering them out of your dataset.

When to apply

Some examples of when to use geospatial charts include visualizing population density in certain areas, localities, or countries, visualizing election results, identifying walking routes (on floor maps), detecting crime in cities (based on various criteria), and so on. It is also feasible to utilize a geospatial chart to indicate the distribution of offices, shops, and other important areas. They are not limited to places; sales values and other types of measures (bubbles and color) can also be added and shown.

KPIs in various ways

Key performance indicator (KPI) items are not mentioned in a single functional group but are usually closely linked to a company's strategic objectives. *Figure 7.24* depicts two forms of KPIs:

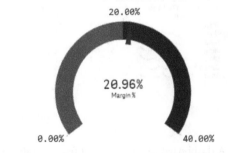

Figure 7.34 – Two types of KPIs

On the left-hand side, a KPI for summarized measures is displayed, while on the right-hand side, a more often-used KPI (gauge meter style) is displayed.

KPIs can be displayed in a variety of ways, with two of the most frequent types of visualizations shown in *Figure 7.33*. But there's a catch! There are several methods for visualizing measures against a target. Summarized metrics are shown simply as a textual graph, as shown in *Figure 7.33*. In this example, we compared the sales amount of 2020 to the sales amount of 2019 at that time. This is known as "Year-to-Date." In *Figure 7.33*, we even colored the amount of 16,28M slightly and added a small triangle pointing upwards in green, indicating that we had converted more sales than the previous year.

When displaying a KPI more traditionally, several KPI items can be used (a gauge, a horizontal gauge, and more). Typically, we do so by using the standard gauge chart, as shown on the right-hand side of *Figure 7.33*. In this example, we used three colors to show the good, neutral (you must act), and bad options (you have to take action as it's wrong, bad, and so on).

Nowadays, we can configure triggers to send automated messages to our cell phones, send emails to get people's responses, and so on. However, the human side must also lead to action; action to analyze, see what's wrong, and enhance your operations (in the broadest way).

When to apply

You should apply KPIs to all metrics with a goal. We explored many types of examples in *Chapter 6, Aligning with Organizational Goals*.

Tables

Tables are not included in a single functional area, but they are commonly used to display detailed information, and mini-charts are occasionally added to such tables to indicate trends or patterns. We don't think detailed tables belong in a dashboard, but when combined with mini-charts, we can present patterns and trends more simply, and they could end up in a dashboard as well.

Figure 7.34 depicts an example of a table that employs mini-charts:

Year to Date Division Scorecard (thousands)								
Region	YTD Sales Trend	YTD Sales 2015	YTD Sales 2014	%	YTD Fresh Food Sales 2015	YTD Fresh Food Sales 2014	%	YTD Customer Satis 2015
Total		$99,171	$105,812	-6.3% ▼	$83,991	$80,947	3.8%	89.40%
USA		$22,156	$21,785	1.7%	$18,937	$18,103	4.6%	89.86%
Nordic		$21,299	$23,885	-10.8% ▼	$17,922	$17,119	4.7%	89.16%
Japan		$17,490	$20,512	-14.7% ▼	$18,124	$17,619	2.9%	88.82%
UK		$17,217	$18,154	-5.2% ▼	$13,326	$12,730	4.7%	89.52%
Germany		$10,712	$10,721	-0.1% ▼	$7,786	$7,705	1.0%	90.08%
Spain		$10,297	$10,756	-4.3% ▼	$7,897	$7,671	2.9%	89.13%

Figure 7.35 – Table with mini-charts

A dashboard can also benefit from highly aggregated data and the use of mini-charts. A table, on the other hand, is used to present more precise information. Tables are often used to lay out and organize detailed or complex data. However, by utilizing our DAR(S) defined format when generating dashboards and reports, we can provide our readers with a specific level of detail.

When you use tables, you should consider the following basic rules:

- Tables can show raw values or aggregated values (like in a pivot table).

- Use a table when you want to give your dashboard's readers more detailed and specialized information.

- It is recommended to use a table when comparing data in many directions.

- Avoid using too many columns when building a table. This allows you to make the table more readable for your readers.

- Shorten the number format or round your figures (for example, 2.7M rather than 2,700,000).

- Even though we read from left to right, most individuals look at tables from top to bottom (vertically). This occurs more frequently when the data is ordered from A to Z or from 1 to 100.

- For slightly longer tables, please use a light gray color for every second row. This will help readers avoid jumping between rows while trying to read the values. Zebra shading is another name for this phenomenon.

- When designing a table, consider the height and width of the rows. When a table contains a lot of rows, a more compact layout may be preferable, while when it's a smaller table, a wider layout may be preferable.

- Highlight important information by coloring the background or numerals. But don't overdo it; it won't help you make the message obvious. Coloring is typically used for parts that require more attention, such as a value that is almost on target or crossing a target. This is referred to as "management by exception." Use subtle tones rather than bright hues.

- Nowadays, most tools will automatically sort your tables. It is a good idea to make your tables sortable and searchable so that your readers can discover the information they need more easily.

- We've already talked about heatmaps (*Figure 7.27*). Tables are a useful way to efficiently visualize your data. You could employ colors, as shown in our examples.

- The final piece of advice is to consider how you want to arrange your table. When you create a lengthier table, the vital values may get concealed and inaccessible to your readers. In this scenario, you may employ a form of custom sorting.

In this section, we discussed the most used types of visualizations and helped you understand when and how to utilize them. In the following section, we will go over some of the more sophisticated visualizations.

Presenting some advanced visualizations

As mentioned previously, when you learn to read visuals, your curiosity will grow and you'll want to learn more about visualizations. From that curiosity, you can progress and learn to use more advanced visualizations. This section will cover some sophisticated types of visualizations that have been chosen from a huge list.

Bullet charts

Bullet charts are part of the *Magnitude* functional visualization group and represent progress toward a specific value (goal). One of the benefits of a bullet chart is that it displays the actual and desired values together. Another benefit is that if you align multiple bullet charts on top of each other, using the same range, you can also compare them (which you cannot do easily with multiple gauge charts). You can also add ranges for good, bad, and average values; these are represented by colored bands. *Figure 7.36* depicts an example of a bullet chart:

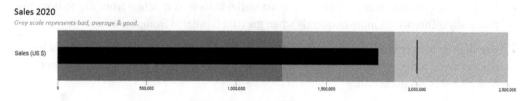

Figure 7.36 – An example of a bullet chart

The following are the benefits of using a bullet chart:

- Presenting the results in the shape of a bar makes it simpler to compare the different values with one another

- When comparing performance against an objective and a simple performance evaluation, you may provide the appropriate context (scaling and target)

- Using a bullet chart saves space on your dashboard

Scatter and bubble charts

Scatter and bubble charts are part of the *Correlation* functional visualization group. A scatter chart depicts the association of two or more "quantitative" values. We can size the bubbles with a third value when utilizing a bubble chart.

Figure 7.37 shows an example of a scatter chart (left) and a bubble chart (right):

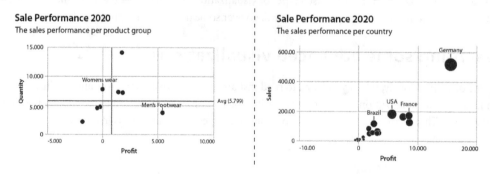

Figure 7.37 – Example of a scatter chart (left) and a bubble chart (right)

In the first example (*Figure 7.37 – the left-hand side of the chart*), we have visualized sales success by plotting quantity on the Y-axis and profit on the X-axis. The bubbles on the graph inform us that four of our articles had a negative profit, but that items in the Men's Footwear category did not sell as well, even though we made a bigger profit. The remaining four goods, which are practically on the zero line, have a higher sold quantity but a smaller profit. In this scenario, we should delve further and examine what is going on with the negative profit cases.

The second example (*Figure 7.37 – the right-hand side of the chart*) shows our sales revenue on the Y-axis) and profit on the X-axis. But, in addition, when we look at the bubble sizes, we've included a measure in our bubble to see the total quantity sold. In the end, we can see a negative or poor profit and decreased sales quantities. It is also worthwhile to evaluate and go further into our dashboard charts to see how we can improve them.

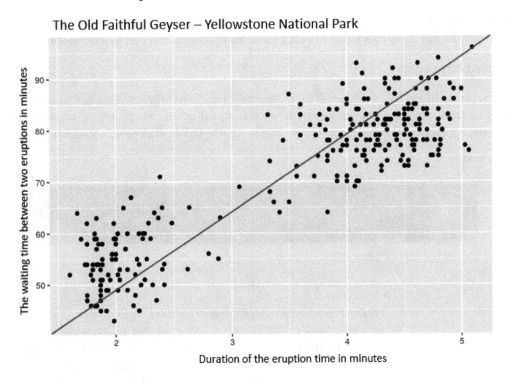

Figure 7.38 – A scatter plot of the Old Faithful geyser

The scatterplot of the American Geyser *Old Faithful* is another real-world example we can look at. The eruption of Old Faithful occurs every 50 to 80 minutes. When this occurs, the geyser emits hot water for several minutes:

- When we view all of the collected data points, we can see some intriguing things – for example, there is a link between the waiting period and the length of the eruption. The more you wait for an eruption, the longer the eruption lasts.

- *Figure 7.38* depicts two distinct data point clouds, the first of which is a 2-minute eruption followed by a 50-minute pause. After an 80-minute wait, the second cloud erupts for 4.5 minutes.

- We find a correlation between the waiting duration and the eruption length in this situation since we've learned that the longer the waiting period, the longer the eruption.

Finally, please ensure that you are displaying the correct comparison or correlation. We've seen several awful graphics that relate rock music to eating ice cream or pie consumption to jellyfish stings.

Stacked bar charts

Stacked bar charts are part of the *Part to whole* functional visualization group. A stacked bar chart is a straightforward approach to depicting a part-to-whole relationship, but it can be difficult to understand when there are too many components (parts). *Figure 7.39* depicts an example of a stacked bar chart:

Figure 7.39 – An example of a stacked bar chart

A stacked bar chart can be used to display information such as market shares, fiscal budgets, organizational available funds, and process phases. We've visualized the steps of the "Call to Balloon" process in the following example, which is represented in *Figure 7.40*. We told this narrative in *Chapter 2, Unfolding Your Data Journey*. We were able to assess the process steps with the help of the developed visualizations, which included a stacked bar chart, so that we could improve our results. We refer to this technique as the flipping technique, as it's good to show the top performing items but when we turn it around (flip it) we can draw attention to the items that need to improve! *Figure 7.40* depicts an example of using a stacked bar chart to visualize the process steps:

Analysis of Extreme Times in period 201308 t/m 201706

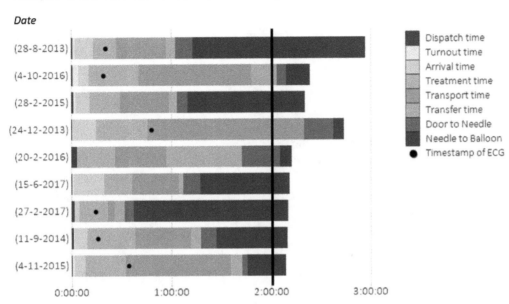

Figure 7.40 – Call to Balloon process breakdown with a stacked bar chart

We were able to discuss what happened and what caused the delay by simply looking at the different parts of the stacked bar chart and identifying the step that took too long. We were able to click on that specific bar so that a detailed report could unfold; by doing so, we could discuss what happened and what caused the delay. Following that, all the required steps can be made to improve the process. And, as shown in *Chapter 2, Unfolding Your Data Journey*, the Safety Region was able to improve our time by 20 minutes!

Sankey charts

The Sankey chart is a member of the *Flow* functional visualization group. A Sankey chart allows you to construct and display the flow and divides in your data. It also shows how changes progress from one to the next stage or category and so on. You can predict the possible outcomes of processes. *Figure 7.41* depicts the flow of consumer products and market share (domestic versus international):

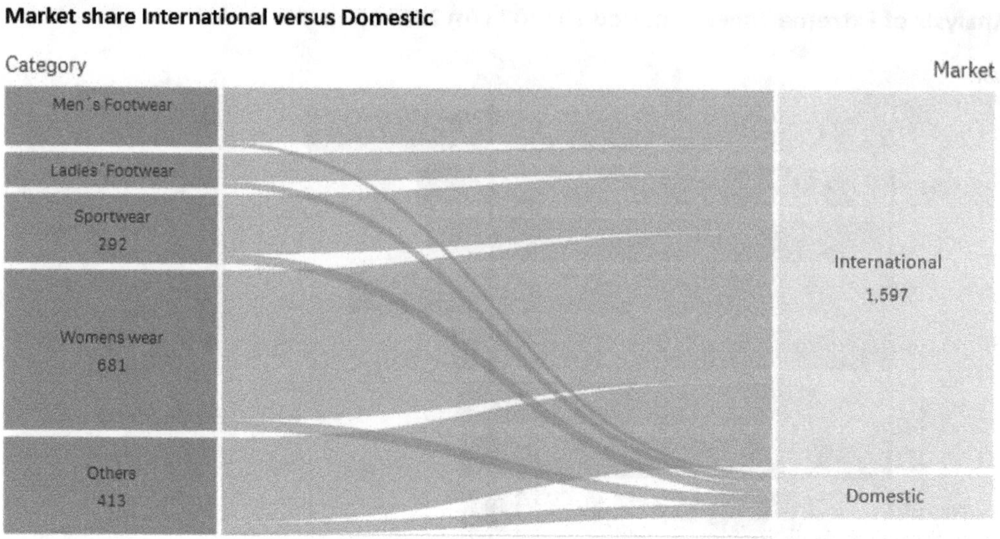

Market share International versus Domestic

Figure 7.41 – The flow of consumer goods and the market share (domestic versus international)

Sankey charts can be applied to a variety of processes, including consumer goods, money flows, prescription flows, call center flows, and energy flows, among others. The width of the arrow, which represents the flow of energy or material, is proportionate to the magnitude of the flow in a Sankey chart. Common blunders to avoid include the position of the flows, which is critical, and aiming to reduce the number of crossings (which makes the chart very unclear).

When your visualization is cluttered and unreadable due to too many flows, attempt to avoid weak connections.

There are many process flow charts on the market, and we've seen some incredible ones. It is critical to consider what to envision and whether your readers will understand what you are attempting to demonstrate.

Waterfall charts

A waterfall chart is a financial tool that belongs to the *Part to whole* functional visualization group. For example, if you want to compare forecasts to actuals, a waterfall chart can display the running totals and allows you to subtract or add data. *Figure 7.42* depicts an example of a waterfall chart:

Financial result 2021

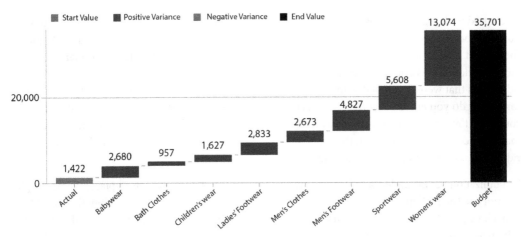

Figure 7.42 – An example of a waterfall chart

It is particularly important, for example, to see how a value at the beginning of the year is changed by monthly positive and negative values. You can display negative or positive values by coding the floating sections. When used correctly, waterfall charts are incredibly useful for displaying changes in financial or other data.

Here are some examples of when to use waterfall charts:

- A waterfall chart can be used to display an organization's net income, as well as rises, declines, revenue, and expenses over a quarterly or yearly timeframe
- A waterfall chart can also be used to represent cumulative product sales over a year as well as an annual total

With this chart, we bring this section on more advanced sorts of visualizations to a close. We are certain that there are more visualizations than those discussed in this chapter. As previously said, there are numerous other sorts of charts that may be created using various methodologies or computer languages. From our perspective, the sorts of visualizations that we have shown you are the most commonly used in our professional lives.

In the final section, we have an intermezzo from a global corporation called AmbaFlex. AmbaFlex has created an incredible spiral conveying technique for material handling systems. These systems are utilized in logistics, packaging, bottling, and printing. This one-of-a-kind approach is employed in a variety of businesses and is particularly well known for the vertical transportation of goods and other packaged products.

Intermezzo – AmbaFlex and its data and analytics journey

We chatted with AmbaFlex's Business Intelligence Solutions Manager, Bart Koning. We've talked about data before, including how to work with visualizations and data literacy. Bart was unambiguous when asked how he assisted his business users to grow and function using the dashboard that his team provided. It was critical to teach the staff how to deal with data and how to use the dashboards and reports that were developed. Simply throwing them over a wall and wishing them luck does not work! How do you ensure that the tool is set up so that people can work with it and find their way around it? It must be done in such a way that the user is proud of what they do, what they do with it, what they see, and how they form their activities. And now, the team is using this dashboard in talks and presentations, which is a fantastic advancement.

Data utilization has expanded, and insights must be available at all times and in all places. Some people may not use the insights daily, but they do use the environmental data weekly. Nonetheless, it has been a long path to this point, and it has not always been simple. Growth has arrived, and users have an increasing number of questions, and they truly expect this solution to address all of them. When the moment arrives and users understand how to find the information, we have the buzz. The "Aha, oh wow!" moments are similar to the opening of a flower. That is incredible and the time to excel in a professional manner of working!

Bart organized numerous training courses, such as a data visualization workshop for the entire data and analytics team, to teach them the fundamentals of data visualization. There is also an "AmbaAcademy," where users can access online tutorials and physical workshops on how to use the dashboards and reports regularly. In addition, Bart organizes inspiration sessions to answer the topic of how you may use this instrument most effectively. The nice thing here is that dashboard viewers may also provide input on dashboards and reports. According to Bart, there is a significant difference in dealing with data and analytics between various professions (user groups) such as HRM, ERP, and CRM. Most supporting departments are increasingly process-focused, and data and analytics is the shell that holds everything together.

In response to this topic, what are your favorite kinds of visualizations?

Bart made it quite clear that he has a favorite: the bullet chart. A bullet chart provides a wealth of information about the current situation in comparison to the previous state. It also specifies the objective or bandwidth you wish to attain with your team or organization. A bullet chart can provide insights on the spot and takes up less space than a gauge meter. As Bart points out, while driving your car, you will have all of the relevant information in front of you. It's not much, but it gets you from point A to point B. A bullet chart provides a lot of useful information in a single glance and saves space on your dashboards. Bart suggests altering the use of the bullet chart between current and expected situations, so long as it is extremely apparent to the user what they are looking for. As a result, the bullet chart is the most commonly used.

To conclude this section, we've discussed several types of visualizations and how to use them. A beautiful story has been told by AmbaFlex's Business Intelligence Solutions Manager Bart Koning, and why he loves to use bullet charts. But when we want to fuel our visualizations even more, we can use a technique called contextual analytics. In the next section, we will look at this in a bit more detail.

Addressing contextual analysis

When it comes to data visualization, we've dealt with a lot of fundamentals. We've learned that context is essential for understanding what your image is about. Context is sometimes overlooked or not included in visualizations, leaving us to assume what the visualization is about. Context can take many forms, and this section will discuss how to provide context to your visualizations to help your readers grasp the information you want to convey for their data-informed decision-making.

There are various ways to provide context to your reports or dashboards, including employing text components (that is the simplest way). However, including more contextual information in your visualizations is also an option. *Figure 7.43* shows an example of adding context to a graph so that elementary time intervals, or timestamps, contain contextual information. In this particular visualization, we have the clinical trials data that we collected from `https://www.clinicaltrials.gov/` and we've added some interesting time stamps to give our readers more information:

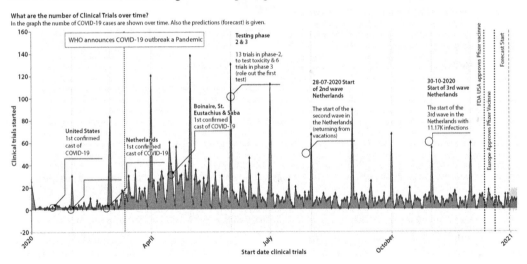

Figure 7.43 – Adding context to your charts

By using contextual elements, it helps our readers understand when peaks occur, or when important occurrences took place. We have added the important start of the COVID-19 pandemic and the moment the **Food and Drug Administration (FDA)** and **European Medicines Agency (EMA)** approved the various vaccines that were developed.

Another way to add extra contextual information is to use titles, subtitles, and footers. *Figure 7.44* shows an example of this:

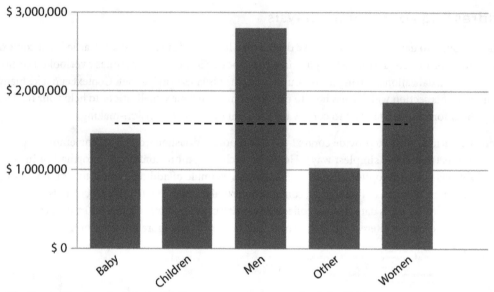

What is the Revenue per Main Category for the year 2020?
This graph shows the sales over the year 2020 for our productgroups in the USA market

The linear line is calculated with the average amount of sale in 2020

Figure 7.44 – An example of using a title, subtitle, and footer to give context

Here, we utilize the title for the business question we want to answer and then put that extra information in the subtitle. Alternatively, we can explain the goal colors, empty fields, and so on here. Then, by including extra information in the footer, the viewer of your visualization will have a better understanding of the visualization. And, with today's tools, we can even add calculations as necessary.

To summarize this section, every reader must understand how to read a visualization and the message that we wish to convey for their data-informed decision-making. You can comprehend what they are looking at and how to interpret the dashboards and reports by including context. You can do so in a simple and meaningful way.

Summary

After reading this chapter, you should have a better grasp of data visualization and the basic rules to follow when developing dashboards and reports. This skill set allows you to develop better visualizations and read charts. We've learned that charts may readily be used to tell lies and that we should always consider the context of a representation. In this way, we can identify and question the good, terrible, and inaccurate visualizations.

Then, we discussed the most commonly used data visualizations and provided some examples of how to apply them. We've included some noteworthy success stories in this chapter and finished with some of our favorite advanced visualizations.

We concluded with a fantastic tale of one of our clients who went on that path a long time ago and learned to work with data insights. In addition, we discovered how they were able to be successful in their data and analytics journey.

In the next chapter, we'll discuss questioning and its relationship to data literacy and data-informed decision-making. The next chapter will guide you through the many stages of questioning, as well as cover some best practices that you could use.

Summary

8
Questioning the Data

There is an old saying: *Curiosity killed the cat*. This is often mentioned as a way to highlight to individuals who ask too many questions that they may not like the answers they get. People tend to hear this quote and think that curiosity is seen as a bad thing, because it may have unintended consequences. However, did you know this is not the full saying? The saying goes on: *but satisfaction brought it back*. This highlights that people should embrace curiosity, even if it does have some unintended consequences.

This saying highlights the critical data literacy skill of questioning. The most important part of the process of working with data is ensuring you understand what is being asked. There's no such thing as asking too many questions when making decisions using data.

In this chapter, we're going to cover the following main topics:

- Being curious and critical by asking questions
- Questioning based on the decision-making stage

Being curious and critical by asking questions

Data is not black and white; there is so much you can do with it. Accordingly, two people with the same data can come up with very different insights. This is because so much depends on the specific problem to be solved and the approach you take to solve it.

Perhaps, counter-intuitively, this process starts with questions, not answers. We don't actually learn anything unless we truly question it. Most schools use a paradigm where they teach kids to answer questions asked by their teachers, but they don't teach them how to question. The outcome of this is it forces kids to learn only facts.

Two things are wrong with that approach. First, we live in a world today where facts and other information are in abundance and are immediately accessible. We no longer have to find the nearest encyclopedia to look something up. We have this at our fingertips. In fact, we have much more information available at our fingertips, from many more sources, and some of those sources are either missing critical context or are not accurate. If we do not have the skills to question the information, we end up believing the information and insights are true when they are not.

When we take the COVID-19 pandemic as an example, most of us never anticipated that the pandemic would shine a spotlight on the need for data literacy. As stated earlier, we often start with questioning and seeking the answers that we need. During the pandemic it was no different—we all needed to make sense of it and what all the data meant. In this way, we were able to make better data-informed decisions from all kinds of levels. Let's have a look at *Figure 8.1*, which shows types of questions from different perspectives through the COVID-19 pandemic:

Personal questions:	Work-related questions:	Government/municipality questions:
• Can I visit my elderly parents?	• How can I keep my employees safe?	• How do we prevent people to get infected
• How can I protect myself and my loved-ones	• How can I arrange a safe working environment for my staff?	• How do we arrange the wellbeing of our inhabitants?
• Is it save to travel by public transport?	• Is it save for my staff to travel by public transport?	• Who are our vulnerable elderlies and how can we protect them?
• Should I go to the office or do my shopping at the mall?	• Can we safely have clients at our office (or in our shops)?	• What do we need to have testing facilities?
• When will I be able to travel again abroad	• Will my business survive when we must close?	• Should we close shops, schools and other facilities?
• Will I lose my job when my office must close?	• How can we ask for support to our government?	• What should we arrange to be able to vaccine our community?

Figure 8.1 – COVID-19-related questions

Insights from data can be useful in making sense of the COVID-19 information and answers that we need when we take the time and read the questions, search for the right data, and try to make sense of it all. Likely, we are then able to make an informed decision instead deciding from our gut feel or impulsivity.

We have to start at the base of it all, so let's go back to our personal questions listed in *Figure 8.1*. In order to answer any of these personal questions, we actually have to start with more questions specific to COVID-19:

- What is being positive, or what is a positive case?

- What is a PCR test or an antigen test?

- Where can I find information about the number of active cases in my region or town?

- I have read in the newspaper that elderly people need to be protected. Does this mean the older you are, you are most likely to get very sick with this virus, or worse?

When we look at the trends of confirmed (positive) cases, it gives us a good sense of what is happening in our neighborhood, region, town, or country. It gives us a good idea of where to go and where not to go. Finding that data should be found on the official channels.

From a business perspective, there are most likely some other questions besides the personal ones:

- What if my government or municipality gives the order to close our businesses? How will I get my income?

- If we remain open or open back up, which regulations do we need to take care of (disinfecting materials, coronavirus tests, contact tracing, fewer tables in our restaurant, and so on)?

- The news states that the number of positive cases is rising. What should we do, which advice should we follow, and what regulations will we face?

- What about my financial status—what is coming in and what is going out? Where can I get support for my financial matters?

For those questions, the owners of organizations might be interested in trends and hotspots for positive or confirmed cases. But then, organizations will need to know what to do when an outbreak occurs and what they can do to reopen or get the needed funding to survive. Having that information and those insights available will give them a broader understanding of what is happening with the COVID-19 pandemic in local areas or towns where those businesses are situated. It will help them to get a better sense of trends and effects from it and make better-informed decisions about what to do.

From a governmental, municipal, or safety region perspective, there are other kinds of questions that needs to be answered:

- What kind of measures do we have to take to protect our people?

- How many people can we test in our local test location?

- Do we have enough beds in our local hospital?

- Do we have enough ICU beds available, or are we able to transport people by air to other hospitals?

- How will we inform and convince the public to be vaccinated in order to protect themselves and others?

The people from those types of organizations should be watching the trends in their areas, the parts of towns where clusters of infections could occur, and so on. They should investigate the testing capacity and the development of the virus and see if there is enough capacity to administer people to hospital, have medication available, and so on.

When this information is available to them, people can make better data-informed decisions, but there is a danger of getting too much information from too many sources, which may show different answers. To avoid information overload and drawing incorrect conclusions, we need to question all the data and information we see. We need to question the source, the relevance, and the context, among other things, before we use it to make decisions.

And this is exactly what we are seeing out in the world today with massive amounts of misinformation being treated as truth. Many people are not questioning it. Second, the world is continuing to evolve and change at a rapid rate. The half-life of facts and information is shorter than it's ever been. We don't really know what information we need in the future. A better skill to teach kids is the ability to find their own insights when they need them, by asking the right questions. This is not just a problem related to teaching kids. As we grow up and join the workforce, it sometimes is even harder to teach and apply questioning as there are many cultural reasons why this is perceived as a negative.

What, then, are some key things we can do to help people ask the right questions when they are looking to gain insights from data?

Starting with the problem – not the data

Most people work backward when it comes to data. They begin with the data they have available, then leverage a set of tools and analytic techniques, and come out with some insights. The problem with this is they end up using very simple, closed, and leading questions, which then leads to uninteresting insights at best, and in the worst case what is called a type 3 error, where you are working on a solution to the wrong question. When you build a house, you don't start building before you think about the requirements for the house, and then build a blueprint. Starting with the data, without doing much preliminary questioning and thinking, will give you the same results as building a house without any requirements. This is one reason why people who are good at questioning use systems thinking. The starting point has to be the full problem from a systems perspective—not the tools or which transformations to apply to the data.

It is not only critically important that you define the problem properly, but if you are a leader, it is also critically important you frame the problem appropriately as well. Thomas Wedell-Wedellsborg (a globally recognized innovation and problem-solving guru) gives an example of a problem where the organization needs to increase innovation. Wedell-Wedellsborg highlights that if the "*problem is defined and communicated as a lack of motivation or an incomplete understanding of the company's strategic imperatives, as examples, that can drastically change how the organization tries to find a solution.*"

Intermezzo – systems thinking

Systems thinking within organizations helps to oversee and address the whole. The basis of systems thinking is that we consider an organization as a set of complex processes and opinions that adapt to each other, react to each other, and influence each other. The belief behind systems thinking is that the whole is greater than the sum of all of the parts. In the context of an organization, this means an organization is more than just all the various parts within it. It has to include the actions and relationships between the parts. To think systemically is to understand these actions and relationships and how decisions will impact all of them. The opposite of thinking systemically is to make a decision based on one part of the organization and not consider how that will impact other parts of the organization.

Identifying the right key performance indicators (KPIs) ahead of time

Ideally, organizations have already established a measurement framework with the proper objectives and KPIs before they even look at the data. If they haven't, they won't be able to ask the right questions, as they will be too focused on metrics, which may be irrelevant or not important to the situation or the organization.

Questioning not just the data, but also assumptions

Proper questioning to achieve the best insights requires the ability to not just question the data, but also assumptions and other information (that is, context) related to it. Data can provide us with different insights when we have different assumptions. Asking open-ended questions is a great way to make hidden assumptions visible. This is akin to how kids are asked to write out their work when solving math problems, as it provides an opportunity to understand the thought process and see where there may be assumptions that will impact the insights.

Using a questioning framework

There are multiple questioning frameworks available on the internet that help with asking the right questions. One, in particular, is introduced by Max Shron in his book *Thinking with Data*, and is outlined here:

1. **Context**: Start by asking questions related to the context, such as: *What is the problem or situation? Who are the stakeholders? Are there any related projects or dependencies?*

2. **Need**: Then, ask questions related to the need, such as: *What will this give us that we did not have before, and why is this important to the organization?*

3. **Vision**: Then, ask questions related to the vision, such as: *What will the results look like? How is the logic related to the insight?*

4. **Outcome**: Finally, ask questions related to the outcome, such as: *What does success look like? Who will use these insights, and what will they do with them?*

The diagram in *Figure 8.2* helps us to see how we can address questions to a particular set of data. In this example, the data is around sales from a retail organization:

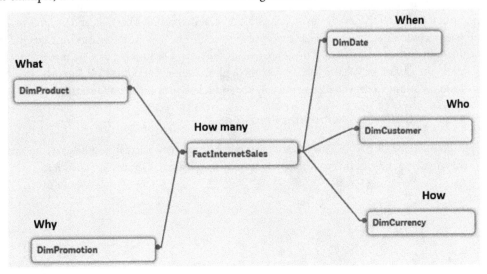

Figure 8.2 – Typical questions

Specific questions include the following:

- What kinds of products did we sell?

- When did we sell this particular product?

- How many products, or how many of those products did we sell?

- Who has bought our products and when did they buy them?

- Why did they buy this product? Did we have a promotion?

Although there are certainly plenty of wrong answers, there are not nearly as many wrong questions. Be inquisitive; approach problems with a 360-view in mind; continually ask why, what, who, and how—simply producing something by rote or a formulaic command won't get you to the insight you need. Embrace the art of questioning.

Questioning based on the decision-making stage

Questioning is important throughout the entire journey from data to insights to decisions, no matter which role you play. If you are responsible for preparing data, you need to question things such as the validity and relevance of the data and aggregated information. If you are responsible for making decisions based on insights gleaned from the data and analytics, you need to question the insights provided to you and not just take them at face value. The questions are not meant to just help you understand when the insights may not be correct, but they will also help you identify why they may not be correct for the specific situation. For example, they were missing relevant data that would have materially changed the insight, or maybe the insight is accurate, but it answers a different question than what you need answering.

It is important to apply healthy skepticism and critical thinking here. What makes questioning even more important is the fact that everyone is susceptible to misinterpreting what data and insights really mean to your decision because we all are susceptible to cognitive bias. These biases make us think we have the right answer when, in fact, there are usually other data or insights that are more relevant or accurate to the situation. What we will cover through the remainder of this section are specific strategies and questions to help challenge the validity and relevance of data and insights.

Intermezzo – COVID-19 – removing emotions

In *Chapter 1, The Beginning – the Flow of Data*, we showed you a news article and discussed a small part of removing emotions. In this way, the picture becomes clearer, as shown in *Figure 8.3*:

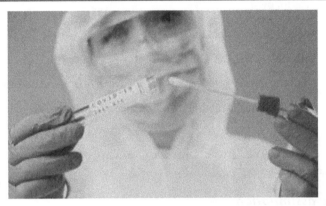

Figure 8.3 – News article and removing emotion

What is the news article trying to tell us? We truly have to dig deeper and try to answer some more questions. What does the rise of confirmed cases actually mean? If we look at 45%, where does it come from? What is the region where the increase was calculated? How was it calculated? How many positive cases were represented there? We need to question the things that we read, see, and consume a bit further than just reading the words in the article.

To understand the need to question things, let's understand the process of questioning data and information.

Questioning data and information

When you are presented with data and information, before undertaking any analysis on it, you should follow a process to question it, to ensure it is OK in its current form to work with. This includes validating whether the data is trustworthy, orientating yourself to the data to understand it, identifying the lineage of the data and which transformations have been applied to it, and then validating the relevance of the data to the question or problem at hand.

Let's understand all the aspects of data before diving deep into understanding and believing the data that is in front of us.

Data trustworthiness

When you are presented with data and information, you should assess whether you find the data to be credible and trustworthy. This means you should consider the source and examine the quality of the data, as follows:

- What is the source of the data?

- Is the data accurate? Can we trust it?

- Does the data or information align with facts from related sources?

- What is the quality of the data? Data quality can be measured in terms of accuracy, completeness, consistency, and whether it is up to date.

Related to the COVID article from *Figure 8.3*, can we trust the data? Is *Amsterdam News* a trustworthy news agency?

Data assimilation

After you have deemed the data trustworthy, you should orientate yourself to the data to ensure you fully understand it and consider the following:

- Do you and your colleagues have a collective agreement on what the definitions and words mean that are used?

- Do you understand the units of measurement being used?

- Do you understand the descriptive statistics for the data, including central tendency, measures of spread, and frequencies?

Related to the COVID article from *Figure 8.3*, many words were not given a definition, and many of them can be misleading. For example, even the word "case" as it relates to COVID-19 cases can be a bit misleading. How does someone become a positive case? Is it only when they test positive? Does it include patients who are assumed to be positive cases, but did not test? Are they only looking at current cases? Does it include people who had COVID-19 but have since recovered, or died?

It also includes emotional words such as: "*staggering, dramatic, dramatically, most likely, this much,* the *highest level ever, dramatic rise*". Is that accurate? How do you quantify those?

Data lineage

The data provided to individuals to perform an analysis is commonly transformed and manipulated from its raw state to something else by the time it reaches the analyst. Data can be filtered out and excluded, whether it be specific points in time only or various categories being excluded, or maybe it's a sampling from a larger dataset. Understanding data lineage, including which data was modified, how it was modified, who modified it, and why it was modified is critical. Consider the following points:

- Which transformations were applied to the data? If so, do you understand how the transformations were applied or calculated?

- Was any data filtered out (outliers, time-based, other selections)?

- How large is the data (sample size) compared to the population?

- If the data was collected via a survey, how was this data selected (random sampling, and so on)?

The COVID article from *Figure 8.3* states that in some areas there was "*a dramatic rise of 45%*". What were the sizes of the populations in those areas? If there were—say—50 people, then a rise of 45% means something different than a similar rise in a population of a couple of million citizens. The article also states the coronavirus has been diagnosed 209,073 times in the past 7 days. Does this include just positive test results, or also diagnoses from a doctor as presumed positive cases? If so, it is important to understand the lineage to ensure that the data is not double-counted for patients who have been diagnosed by a doctor without a test but then, later on, took a positive test as well.

Other examples related to COVID-19 deal with how some authorities handled data related to patients who died while they were infected with COVID-19. If a person died from a heart attack, it could have been a result of being infected with COVID-19, or it could have been completely unrelated. If an authority chooses to filter out all deaths that cannot be directly attributed to COVID-19 in their data, that context is extremely useful to share with the consumers reading this information.

You heard earlier in the book about a famous example of outliers with Dr. John Snow and the insights about a cholera outbreak in London back in the 19th century. Had Dr. Snow ignored the outlier, rather than using it as an opportunity to understand why it was an outlier, who knows how much longer the epidemic would have continued and how many more people would have died. While not every business decision is life or death like this one, this clearly highlights the importance of searching for outliers to learn more about why as opposed to just ignoring them or filtering them out of your dataset.

Outliers are individual values that differ greatly from most other values in a set. Identifying outliers is always one of the first things an individual should look for when trying to orientate themselves to the data. What defines an outlier is somewhat subjective. Many people treat an outlier as any data point that is three or more standard deviations away from the mean of the dataset.

Identifying outliers early on in the process allows you to understand what they are, investigate why they are outliers, and then decide whether to exclude them from the analysis or not.

Data relevance

Finally, the data may be trusted and understood clearly, but before you proceed, you should ensure the data is relevant to the question or problem at hand by addressing the following points:

- Is this data meaningful to help answer the problem/question?
- What other data and information is relevant that is missing (think systemically)?

The COVID article from *Figure 8.3* states 32,149 positive tests were the highest number reported for a Wednesday. Is that relevant? It may be in some situations, but in general, COVID does not have favorite days of the week to infect patients.

Removing noise

When referring to analytics and statistics, noisy data is data that is meaningless to the problem or question at hand. It could be accurate data, but just irrelevant to the problem at hand, or it could be data that has quality issues. Noisy data complicates your ability to identify trends and patterns that will impact your question or problem. The goal is to pick the signal in the noise. The signal represents meaningful data. Whether it is at the raw data level or the insight level, it is important to remove any noise so that it does not distract you from interpreting the real insights.

Now that we have identified how to question the data and information, we will turn our focus to techniques to help us interpret results from any analysis or statistical experiments and the insights obtained from them.

Questioning analytic interpretations and insights

As a reminder, **insights** are derived from data and information, usually through analytics. Insights should consider the context of the problem/question at hand, and then draw conclusions that will lead to decisions and actions. Insights are typically shared just as words in written form, or along with data visualizations. This process is especially important to everyone working toward data-informed decisions. You may not be the person responsible for performing the analysis or coming up with the insight, but if you plan to use the insight and make a decision from it, you need to be sure you can critically review and evaluate it.

The process of questioning insights includes three steps:

1. Questioning the relevance of the insight
2. Questioning the words and visuals used in insights
3. Applying healthy skepticism to insights and balancing with the human element

The next few sections will dive deeper into these three steps, starting with questioning the relevance of insights.

Questioning the relevance of insights

As with data relevance, you should review insights to ensure that they are relevant to the problem or question at hand. Even if you have already done this step when reviewing the data for relevance, it is important to also review insights for relevance. There are many situations where relevant data may be used, but insights that were obtained end up being irrelevant or not actionable. In other situations, the opposite is true, meaning there was other relevant data related to the situation that was not included in the analysis. Consider the following:

- Is this insight meaningful to help answer the problem/question?

- Does this insight align with your goals and objectives?

Questioning words and visuals

Once you question the analysis, you should then move on to questioning how insights are being shared and communicated. This includes checking the visual properties of any data visualizations and ensuring you understand the words used in insights.

Checking the visual properties (checking the time and scale)

Are the scales used in any of the visualizations confusing or misleading? Is the time frame specified long enough? Data visualizations are supposed to give us a clear and visual description to communicate insights. Visualizations are powerful in that they make insights more consumable than just via text, making it easier to see things such as patterns, trends, and outliers. This allows us to not only understand and interpret the information but also reflect and infer new information and insights to help us understand the situation and make a decision. However, all visualizations should be carefully reviewed to ensure they are not misrepresenting the situation. The last chapter focused on how people who create data visualizations should design them, and the scope of this section is for people who are trying to consume the visualization and draw conclusions from them.

Follow these three best practices for critically reviewing the configuration of data visualizations that have been shared with you:

1. **Identify the information contained on each axis**: It is important to understand what data or information is used on each of the visualization's axes. Pay special attention to any calculations used—for example, if a pie chart adds up to over 100%, or if a visualization is using a cumulative calculation.

2. **Identify the ranges and scales used (Is the time frame specific enough? Is the range altered?)**: Interpretations can be skewed simply by changing the ranges and scales used in visualizations. Suppose a visualization is set up to change the y axis to not show the entire range—for example, starting at the low end at some point in the middle of a range. This can be used to highlight differences but can make the differences seem bigger than they really are.

Potentially the visualization is trying to highlight a change, but the range shown in the visualization is for a condensed period of time. Is it possible to infer that our sales revenue has materially changed when we are only looking at 1 day's or 1 week's worth of data?

3. **Watch for misleading constructs (for example, does a pie chart add up to over 100%?); dates go from right to left**: Visualizations are supposed to lower our cognitive load. Cognitive load is the amount of effort required by our brains when thinking, such as when trying to interpret a visualization. When the cognitive load is high, it can interfere and make us miss important information. The reason we want visualizations with low cognitive load is so that we can focus on only what is important and relevant in the visualization to be able to interpret it. In doing this, there are certain constructs that the human brain uses to subconsciously aid us in our interpretation. For example, a pie chart should add up to 100%. A line chart with time-series data should be read from left to right. A line chart should not be used with discrete data. We do not typically consciously think about these points, but when visualizations are set up that violate these constructs, they can be very misleading.

In the three visualizations shown in *Figure 8.4*, *Figure 8.5*, and *Figure 8.6*, we are all showing the same data insights. However, there are critical flaws in the first two that lead people consuming this visualization to draw incorrect conclusions. *Figure 8.4* is not showing the *y* axis, so we cannot tell what it is showing or what the scale is that is used. We would draw a conclusion from this that the sales per year are rising, but how much and to what extent?

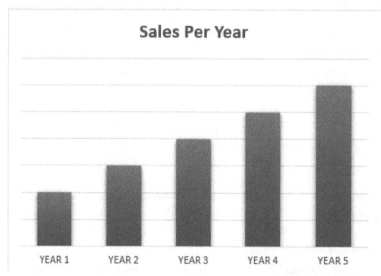

Figure 8.4 – Visualization without a y-axis scale

In *Figure 8.5*, we added *y*-axis labels and the range. However, we can see that the *y* axis here does not start at 0, so it artificially makes the increase bigger than it really is:

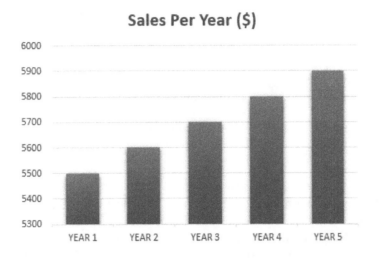

Figure 8.5 – Visualization with a scale not starting at 0

This is resolved in *Figure 8.6*, and you can see the true insights are less distorted than in the previous visualizations:

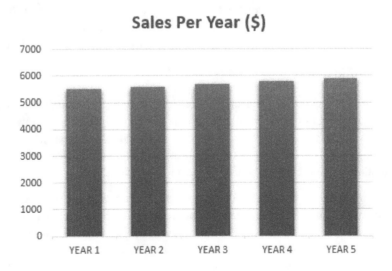

Figure 8.6 – Visualization with proper scaling

Now that we have discussed strategies for how to question visualizations to avoid misinterpreting them, let's move on to the next step, which is to question the words that are used.

Words matter

There are two questions that we should be asking ourselves about the words that are used in insights:

- Do you understand the words that are used in insights?
- Are the words used leading you to a misleading conclusion?

As you continue to orientate yourself to insights, you should pay special attention to the words that are used in any of the verbal or visual descriptions. Interpretation of insights can be swayed easily based on the words that are used around them.

COVID-19 has given us tons of examples where this comes into play—for example, seeing visualizations and reports with the title *The percentage of positive tests*. What does this really tell us? Can we use this information to identify patterns or how prevalent the virus is? Not really, as it is not a random sample. In fact, most testing at the beginning of the pandemic was provided to those who had the worst symptoms or those who were at risk due to their job, medical conditions, or age.

In another example, a visualization shows *"The total number of cases"*, but that is not really accurate. It is the total number of confirmed cases, but there are many cases where people had COVID-19 but did not test for various reasons. If you're using this visualization and insight to help make decisions on safety protocols to limit the spread of the disease, this can be misleading. Suppose there is a testing shortage, which was something that happened; then, the total number of cases will show a drop. However, it is not a real drop—it is an artificial drop since the reason for this was due to a shortage of tests. In both of these situations, the words used matter and can lead you to a less-than-ideal decision.

Being skeptical of insights

How many times have you made a decision and later realized that you either misunderstood the data or the insights or that you did not fully think through the impact of the decision? How many times did you realize after you made a decision that you were missing important context? In these situations, the data is not wrong. The data is correct, but it is your interpretation of the data and what it means related to the question at hand that leads to a less-than-ideal decision.

What is the solution? After you interpret the results of any analytics and statistics executed on the data, you will have an insight that you are ready to act on. But before you can act on it, you need to still be skeptical of the insight and apply the human element to it. It could very well be that the analysis performed is accurate but becomes skewed due to a bias, an incorrect assumption, or an outdated mental model. It could also very well be due to the fact the analysis did not include all the data that was truly relevant to the situation. This critical step is all about applying the human element to insights. Consider the following:

- Have you got multiple perspectives?

- Did you consider possible alternatives?

- Have you considered situations when the insight may not actually be true?

We make a lot of decisions and are bombarded with millions of pieces of information every day. Our brains are limited when processing information from the environment. We can hold only a small portion of those millions of pieces, and the information we manage to retain is done so on our own terms or based on our own subjective experiences and knowledge. The good news is that our brains are relatively efficient at making decisions due to heuristics. Heuristics are rules of thumb and mental shortcuts that the brain applies to guide decision-making based on a limited subset of the available information. These modes of thinking demonstrate how our brains classify objects, assess probabilities, and predict values based on automatic judgments that can be skewed. The bad news is that heuristics can lead to poor decisions.

While heuristics enable us to make snap decisions without constantly stopping to think about them, when it fails to produce a correct outcome, the result is known as a bias or, more specifically, an unconscious bias. An unconscious bias is a tendency to draw incorrect conclusions due to cognitive factors embedded in our brain and according to our culture, interests, knowledge, experiences, and even our feelings.

While there are hundreds of biases, we wanted to introduce three of the most common ones that impact decision-making: confirmation bias, survivor bias, and first-conclusion bias:

- **Confirmation bias** describes the tendency of the human brain to seek out data and information that validates our existing beliefs and hypotheses about a situation. At the same time, the human brain tends to ignore or skip over information that contradicts our beliefs. This is one reason why we say data literacy and data-informed decision-making is a team sport, as getting different perspectives from others who may not have the same initial belief or hypothesis as you can help challenge your thoughts.

- **Survivor bias** describes the tendency for the human brain to remember only part of the relevant data to make a decision. Those parts that are remembered tend to be ones that are still active— for example, using data from projects that succeeded as opposed to including those projects that failed too. A famous example of survivor bias is when a military in World War II wanted to minimize aircraft losses to enemy fire. The intent was to examine aircraft to see where they had the most damage and then fortify those areas. Survivor bias would cause the investigators to focus only on the planes that had not been shot down. However, looking at planes that were shot down would be the most useful data, as the planes that had damage but returned safely at least returned safely. Since the investigators did not have access to planes that had been shot down, they examined areas on returning planes where there was no damage, inferring that any plane that was hit in those areas resulted in a crash.

- **First-conclusion bias** describes the tendency of the human brain to give more emphasis to the first solution that comes to mind. Even if new data and information are presented later on that contradict the first decision, the brain will still be more inclined to go with the first solution. This is where the term "*to a man with a hammer, everything looks like a nail*" comes from, as carpenters' first thoughts about problems tend to be within the lens of what they do, which is to use a hammer to hammer nails.

For more detailed information on these heuristics and biases, read *Turning Data into Wisdom* by Kevin Hanegan.

Tapping into our unconscious thoughts and improving our decision-making ability starts by recognizing that we are all biased. To ensure we are not making decisions based on bias, it is important to identify bias in our thinking and then work toward mitigating it as best as possible. Next are four strategies that can be applied to help mitigate bias.

PAUSE

A popular approach that can help us slow down our thinking is the **PAUSE** model, created by consulting firm Cook Ross. The PAUSE model is a five-step process, with each step named after one of the letters of the word PAUSE:

1. "**P**" stands for **pay attention**. We must consider what's happening beneath our judgments and assessments.

2. "**A**" stands for **acknowledge**. Accept that our reactions and interpretations may not be proper.

3. "**U**" stands for **understand**. We should try to learn more about alternative reactions, interpretations, and judgments that may be possible.

4. "**S**" stands for search. Explore the most empowering, productive ways to deal with a situation.

5. Finally, "**E**" stands for **execute**. We can now implement our action plan.

Let's move on to the next strategy, the Ladder of Inference.

Ladder of Inference

One tool that can be used to try to identify and mitigate bias is the **Ladder of Inference**. The tool, created by organizational psychologist Chris Argyris, helps you avoid incorrect inferences in your decision-making process by using a step-by-step reasoning process.

The *Ladder of Inference*, as shown in *Figure 8.7*, describes the thinking process that we go through, typically without even realizing it, to go from data or information to a decision or an action:

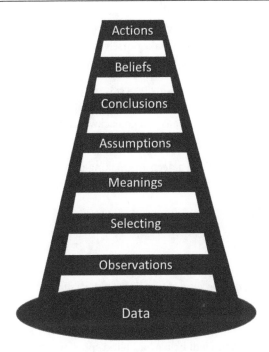

Figure 8.7 – Ladder of Inference

Let's go through each step of the ladder from the previous diagram and identify what is included in each step:

1. At the base of the ladder is all the possible data for a given situation.

2. Individuals then see a subset of the data based on their observation of the situation.

3. From there, individuals select a subset of the data that they feel is relevant, and they discard any data that they feel is irrelevant.

4. Individuals then interpret the remaining data to add meaning to it.

5. Individuals then make assumptions about the remaining data.

6. Individuals then draw conclusions based on their assumptions and on what is good for them and their friends and family.

7. Individuals then adopt beliefs based on their conclusions.

8. Finally, individuals act on their beliefs as if they are proven facts.

The human brain typically takes less than a second to go through the steps just listed, and it often happens subconsciously for the individual. The actions from this process and the results are then all stored back in the brain's long-term memory and will influence future situations when something similar arises. This can have a kind of tunnel-vision effect that leads us to ignore certain facts when we are presented with them and to potentially jump to conclusions. Using the Ladder of Inference as a tool can help us slow down this process and make ourselves aware we are going through each step. It also allows us to work backward down the ladder to see where we may have drawn a wrong conclusion.

This is tremendously helpful for decision-making processes as you can leverage it to help look at data without any preconceived thoughts or judgments. If you want to learn more about the Ladder of Inference and what questions to ask yourself as you go backward, you will find them in the book *The Fifth Discipline Fieldbook: Strategies and Tools for Building a Learning Organization* by Peter Senge.

You can also use this tool in the middle of a decision-making process before you draw a conclusion. It can be used to identify which level of the ladder you are currently on.

Getting diverse perspectives

Author Maya Angelou once said,

"You are the sum of everything you've ever seen, heard, eaten, smelled, been told, forgot — it's all there. Everything influences each of us, and because of that, I try to make sure that my experiences are positive."

This same concept relates to decision-making as well. If individuals are the sum of everything they have seen, heard, and so on, then getting input from other individuals who have seen and heard different things related to the decision at hand will help avoid blind spots, will give a clearer picture, and will ultimately allow you to make better-informed decisions.

However, it is not natural in the business world to reach out to others to get their perspectives. Sometimes, this is due to a hierarchical organizational culture that does not foster getting multiple perspectives. In other cases, individuals do not understand that other perspectives are relevant to their decision. When organizations support getting perspectives from others, and when individuals believe in the value of this, collective genius occurs, which results in a better decision.

Scott E. Page, the author of *The Difference*, highlights:

"When looking at diverse perspectives within decision-making, it is important to look at cognitive diversity."

According to Page, cognitive diversity is as follows:

"the inclusion of people who have different styles of problem-solving and can offer unique perspectives because they think differently."

Page goes on to identify four dimensions of cognitive diversity:

- **Diverse perspectives**: Individuals look at problems in different ways and have different perspectives. As a result, individuals also have different solutions to improve those situations or problems.

- **Diverse interpretations**: Individuals interpret the world differently by putting things into different classifications. For example, some people may think of me, the author of this book, as a teacher. Others may think of me as a parent, a coach, a data-literacy expert, or something else. They are all different interpretations of who I am.

- **Diverse heuristics**: Heuristics are rules of thumb or mental shortcuts that the brain uses to quickly assess a situation and make a decision. Individuals have their own heuristics unique to them, so that means that they also have unique and different ways to solve a problem.

- **Diverse predictive models**: Individuals have different ways of assessing a situation or problem. Some people may analyze the situation, while others may listen to a story to understand how to act.

Let's move on to the next strategy.

Leveraging systems thinking and lateral thinking

We introduced the concept of systems thinking earlier in this chapter. This way of thinking can be incredibly useful with decision-making, as it helps you recognize unintended consequences. It does this by looking at the system as an entire component, rather than breaking it down into components to analyze separately.

In addition to systems thinking, individuals and organizations can also leverage lateral thinking to help question data and insights. Lateral thinking is the ability to think about solutions to problems in a new and indirect way. This is where the phrase *"think outside of the box"* comes from.

This approach is especially useful when trying to challenge an insight to see if there is any situation where the insight is not true. Next is a summary of an example from Paul Sloane's book *Lateral Thinking Puzzles* of where lateral thinking can be useful.

In the example, when the military was analyzing data on head injuries during a war. The uniform at the time used a cloth helmet. In an attempt to minimize the number of head injuries, they decided to replace the cloth helmet with a metal helmet. To their surprise, the data showed that the number of head injuries increased after the change to metal helmets. The number of soldiers in battle and the intensity of the battle were the same as before.

It would be hard to challenge the insights that the metal helmets were not working. However, thinking laterally and thinking about situations in which the insight would not be true, the military's reached another conclusion. In reality, the number of recorded head injuries increased, but there was another relevant data field that should have been included: the number of deaths. When looking at the data, we can see that the number of deaths decreased over that same time span. This is because if a soldier was hit on the head during battle, it would have most likely killed them. This was recorded by the military's as a death, not a head injury. After helmets were updated to metal, fewer hits on the head would cause death. In those situations, they could very easily still create head injuries such as concussions or lacerations. When lateral thinkers ensure that the data for deaths is included in the analysis, the conclusion drawn is that metal helmets are working to minimize deaths.

Challenging your assumptions

It is not uncommon for an individual or an organization to follow a proper decision-making process, to use the right data, and yet still come up with a less-than-ideal decision. In those situations, usually what happens is the individual or the team making the decision makes an incorrect assumption about something related to the decision. It is critical that all aspects of a decision are questioned, including any assumptions. The following list of questions will help you challenge your assumptions:

- Have you written down all assumptions or things you think are true about your business and related to the question at hand, no matter how "obvious" you think they may be? And then, have you challenged the assumptions and asked when they could not be true?

- What would be required to happen for the insight to not be true?

- Has anything changed related to the environment or similar that could make your mental model not accurate?

As with our tendency to make biased decisions, we also easily make the wrong assumptions. Assumptions are inferences we assign to observed facts without proof. There are explicit assumptions, which are stated out loud, and implicit assumptions, which are hidden and not spoken about. We naturally make implicit assumptions as we reason about the world around us. Implicit assumptions include what we may infer about people's motives and abilities. For example, a common assumption in business would be that people will pay for your new product. While that may be true, without any evidence to support that opinion, it can easily be overstated and become a false assumption.

Rather than overstating, some famous examples of incorrect assumptions understated the impacts of technological innovation. Back in the late 1800s, Western Union, the leader in telegraphs, declined an offer from Alexander Graham Bell for his patent for the telephone. Western Union leaders stated that the telephone would not be seriously considered as a means of communication and so the device was of no value to them. While this was incorrect, at least Western Union articulated its assumption so that people could potentially challenge it. Implicit assumptions are even harder to challenge as they are ones that are never stated out loud. This is why it is important to list out all assumptions that are made as part of the situation and problem at hand.

Summary

In this chapter, you have learned why it is important, as a data-literate individual, to critically evaluate everything, ranging from the data all the way to the insight and the decision. You can accomplish this by asking questions. Better questions will lead you to better insights and, ultimately, better decisions.

This process requires you to think critically and not accept any of the information at face value. This is important so that you can develop skills to properly examine and inspect data critically to benefit your organization. You learned how to question various components of the data, such as its trustworthiness, its lineage, and its relevance. You also learned how to question and critically evaluate both the words and visualizations shared with you.

Now that you have done this, you can now move on to the next step in the process, which is to choose the right visualizations for your data. This is discussed in the next chapter.

References

Please go through the following references for more information:

- *Wahl, D. (2016). Designing Regenerative Cultures. Triarchy Press.*

- *What's Your Problem?: To Solve Your Toughest Problems, Change the Problems You Solve. Thomas Wedell-Wedellsborg, Harvard Business Review Press, 2020.*

- *Shron, M. (2014). Thinking with Data. O'Reilly Media.*

- *Wald, Abraham (1943). A Method of Estimating Plane Vulnerability Based on Damage of Survivors. Statistical Research Group.*

- *Hanegan, K. (2020). Turning Data into Wisdom: How We Can Collaborate with Data to Change Ourselves, Our Organizations, and Even the World. Kevin Hanegan.*

- *Ross, Howard J. Everyday Bias: Identifying and Navigating Unconscious Judgments in Our Daily Lives. 2014.*

- *Senge, Peter M. The Fifth Discipline Fieldbook: Strategies and Tools for Building a Learning Organization. Crown Publishing, 1994.*

- Maya Angelou interview. *O, the Oprah Magazine.* April 2011.

- *Scott, E. P. The Difference: How the Power of Diversity Creates Better Groups, Firms, Schools, and Societies. Princeton, NJ: Princeton University Press, 2008.*

- *Sloane, Paul. Lateral Thinking Puzzles, 1991.*

9
Handling Data Responsibly

Today, data and analytics are present in every aspect. As a result, data and analytics play a huge part in our daily lives. As stated in *Chapter 1, The Beginning – The Flow of Data*, we constantly generate and collect data. It has been estimated that we generate more than 2.5 quintillion bytes of data every day (`https://www.vpnmentor.com/blog/data-privacy-security-stats/`), sometimes in ways that we cannot control or see.

Companies use our data on the internet, on websites, on our watches and phones, and even on our smart devices at home for a variety of purposes. Our information is used to improve customer service, provide a better customer experience, send us personalized advertisements, and more. However, we are not even aware of the potential risks that may arise. What should we think about our privacy? Or do you not wonder what others might do with your data, and whether it is used safely and ethically when, for example, algorithms and/or business rules are used? Do you know whether your data is safe? Do you know what others do with your data?

There are some obstacles that we must overcome and identify. This chapter will cover a variety of topics, with the goal of providing you with food for thought about how to handle data in a correct and ethical manner, as well as how to care for personal data, identify personal data at the start of a project, and more. We do not claim to be ethics, privacy, or security experts, but we have witnessed how our data world has evolved over the last few decades. In addition, we have seen an increase in the number of potential risks that we must address at the start of our projects.

In this chapter, we will cover the following topics:

- Introducing the potential risks of data and analytics
- Identifying data security concerns
- Identifying data privacy concerns
- Identifying data ethics concerns

Introducing the potential risks of data and analytics

Over the years, we've seen a lot of movies with artificial intelligence elements. We've seen *Mr. Arnold Schwarzenegger* in the movie *Terminator*, where computers took over the world and the movie ended with things returning to how they were. What do you think of the *Matrix* movies starring *Keanu Reeves*? The *Matrix* is a computer simulation of the world in 1999, designed specifically to control people on the planet. Or what about the *Sandra Bullock* film *The Net*? Angela Bennet (Bullock) used to be a systems analyst. When a coworker sends her a floppy disk with a game on it, she looks at it on her system and the trouble begins, and her entire identity is erased. There are many more movies such as this, with programs, computers, and more describing the world and telling humanity what to do, or, in the best-case scenario, saving the world. Sometimes, the movies and series that were made depicted rather dark and bad scenarios. Some are even worse than others when it comes to using data in a bad way, using virtual worlds, and more.

Looking back in time, what should we think about East Germany? For four decades, until the Berlin Wall fell (November 9, 1989), the *Stasi* spied on millions of people. They even forced loved ones to spy on their own families and friends. They amassed an incredible amount of information about their inhabitants. They are said to have collected and stored 111 kilometers of documents in their previous archives (`https://www.pieterjanssen.eu/2020/06/15/transitieproces-van-de-stasi-documenten-in-volle-gang/`). We do know that people are working on restoring and digitizing those documents. In this way, history is saved and preserved for future generations. Can you imagine what kind of analysis can be done when documents, films, and other media are digitized? When this project is completed, it is possible that amazing, interesting, or harmful things will be discovered.

It's all here: data, analytics, big data, artificial intelligence, machine learning, deep learning, natural language processing, neural networks, and more. It is used in many ways; we even described some solutions in *Chapter 2, Unfolding Your Data Journey*. But what will happen when we use that data to classify people? For example, consider that a university only wants students with grades higher than 8 out of 10 to enter that particular university. As they say, to influence the level of entrants at that university to have better-qualified students (that is, a better success rate).

Think about sorting resumes based on algorithms, where women above 40 will be dismissed for a job at a certain company. Or that your data is stolen and your credit card is used to purchase expensive goods.

Nonetheless, as a result of various ethical, security breaches, or privacy issues, people have been robbed, injured, banned, or labeled as fraudulent. The question here is whether we need to protect data and protect people from unethical use of our data. The answer is yes! During our discussions, it occurred to us that we needed to consider data privacy, data security, and data handling in an ethical manner before beginning our data and analytics projects. This is why we felt it was important to address how to handle your data responsibly, and we chose to write a chapter about it. *Figure 9.1* depicts three specific data concerns when it comes to handling data responsibly:

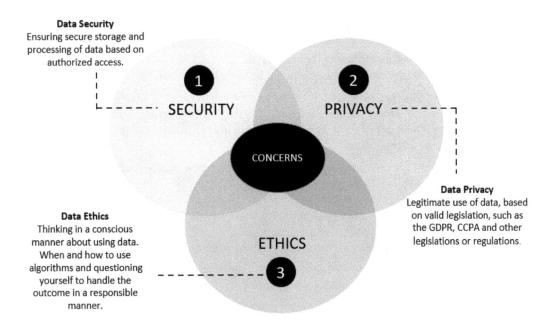

Data Security
Ensuring secure storage and processing of data based on authorized access.

Data Ethics
Thinking in a conscious manner about using data. When and how to use algorithms and questioning yourself to handle the outcome in a responsible manner.

Data Privacy
Legitimate use of data, based on valid legislation, such as the GDPR, CCPA and other legislations or regulations.

Figure 9.1 – Three important data concerns

When we look at those three concerns, we are able to define them a bit further in more detail:

- **Data security**: Data security is the process of protecting data and ensuring that the data in your organization is secure. It is concerned with the security of infrastructure, software, and procedures. It also handles data access with the necessary permissions that you are authorized to look at specific data.

- **Data privacy**: Data privacy, also known as privacy management, is concerned with the protection of data through legislation and regulations. With the assistance of these laws and regulations, everyone can take privacy regulations into consideration so that personal and confidential data is properly collected, shared, and used.

- **Data ethics**: Data ethics is about managing information in a transparent, fair, and respectful manner, which is required for responsible data handling.

According to the *Internet Society* (`https://www.internetsociety.org/policybriefs/responsible-data-handling/`), when we want to handle data responsibly, we should not ask ourselves, *can we do this?* The question that needs to be answered here is *should we do this?*

The concerns of data security, data privacy, and data ethics will be discussed in the following sections. We address those concerns from a more pragmatic standpoint, and we are well aware that those are not the only concerns that could exist. They simply mean that you will be able to address questions about security, privacy, and ethical data handling earlier in your project initiatives (such as an intake).

> **Intermezzo – a retailer uses buying history and artificial intelligence to personalize coupons**
>
> A United States retailer was interested in doing more personalized marketing for its customers. It had previously sent out monthly coupon books in the mail but had an idea to try and send out personalized coupons that each shopper might be more likely to use.
>
> To start the project, the retailer looked at all the historical purchases to analyze what items are commonly purchased together. Once it figured this out, it then planned to find customers who may have purchased one of those items recently, but not the others, and then send them coupons for those other products.
>
> It was able to accomplish this and launch the project. A few months later, the organization received a complaint from a father saying that his 16-year-old daughter was being sent coupons for items that relate to pregnancy. While the father was upset that his daughter was being sent coupons for pregnancy, what he did not know at the time was that his daughter was, in fact, pregnant and in the first trimester. The organization's personalized marketing project had correctly identified the daughter was pregnant, even before her father was aware.
>
> Did the organization violate the privacy of the girl? Had the organization done its due diligence to ensure these ethical dilemmas would not happen?

Identifying data security concerns

When a security breach occurs, sensitive, private, personal, or confidential information is exposed to untrustworthy or unsecured parties. This is exactly why we are of the opinion that data security (just like privacy and ethics) should be at the forefront of our minds and that we need to pinpoint it.

> **Intermezzo – data security facts**
>
> In the United States, 1,767 data breaches were reported in the first 6 months of 2021, with over 1,000 data leaks exposing more than 155.8 million records containing sensitive data (`https://www.vpnmentor.com/blog/data-privacy-security-stats/`).
>
> *The Dutch Data Protection Authority (AP)* published the Data Breach report for 2021 on May 24, 2022. The number of Data Breach notifications was 24,866, a 4% increase from the previous year. Malware, phishing, or hacking were the sources of those breaches.

Data breaches can occur unintentionally or intentionally. When this occurs and there is no control over the use of that data, that data can be used to cause harm to persons in question, such as spending on their credit, identity theft, and selling personal data on the dark web for other bad guys. When a security breach occurs, it can be extremely painful and cause significant harm.

We should always consider data security elements, especially when we work with data and share insights. Therefore, we should identify them upfront, for example, during the initial data and analytics project initiatives. We can do this by using checklists in our project intake forms or adding a checklist to a project plan.

An example of such an intake form with included checklists is available in *Appendix A*:

Data security check

A data security incident is a serious security breach. When protected, sensitive, or confidential data is stolen, used, viewed, stored, or transmitted by someone who is not authorized, a breach occurs. Other security concerns include data leaks, information leaks (who can see what), sensitive information leaks, and data spillage. As a result, when it comes to data and information usage, we must identify some specific elements.

Application/model/app Dashboards and reports are critical for any organization, team, or department. The work cannot be completed without this information.	Essential | Important | Desirable | Unclassified
Confidentiality The dashboards and reports are private and only available to a select group of managers and employees.	Essential | Important | Desirable | Unclassified
Access control What type of access control is required when confidentiality is required? What are the rules that we must follow? (For example, the manager of team A can see information about team A and so on.)	Add information:
Integrity Incorrect information will not be tolerated (accountable environment). The organization suffers significant damage if the information is incorrect, incomplete, or late. Inaccurate data, such as financial transactions, undermines trust in the organization.	Essential | Important | Desirable | Unclassified
Availability Dashboards and reports are essential. The organization will suffer severe consequences if the information is not available.	Essential | Important | Desirable | Unclassified
Additional information and/or explanation	

Intermezzo – a data leak at an airplane carrier

The **Dutch Data Protection Authority** *(AP)* fined an airline carrier 400.000 Euro for failing to secure personal data. In 2019, a hacker was able to penetrate the systems of this airplane carrier due to a poor security process. The hacker gained access to systems and was able to view the personal information of over 25 million people. It has been determined that the hacker downloaded the personal information of approximately 83,000 people.

According to the AP, when you book a flight and enter personal information, the airliner must use that information correctly. Because you cannot book a flight without providing your personal information, you must be able to trust that an organization will handle your data with care and protect it thoroughly. In this case, it was discovered that the airliner did not adequately protect the data.

In 2019, the hacker gained access to systems by using two IT department accounts. That proved to be far too simple.

The airline failed to address the following three data security issues:

1. The password was simple to figure out. Only one easy-to-guess password was sufficient to gain access to the airline's systems.

2. There was no use of multi-factor authentication (for example, using a password and a code received via text message).

3. Once the hacker gained control of the two accounts, they were able to access a large number of the airline's systems.

The hacker gained access to the systems in September 2019 and retained access until the airliner closed the leak at the end of November 2019. They promptly reported the breach to the authorities (AP) and informed those who were involved. The airliner took immediate action and measures to better protect passengers. The press release is available at `https://autoriteitpersoonsgegevens.nl/nl/nieuws/ap-beboet-transavia-om-slechte-beveiliging-persoonsgegevens`.

This previous section described the elements of data security and how important it is to address them at the start of data and analytics projects. We've provided an overview of a checklist and added stories from real life to support the importance of data security. In the next section, we will discuss the concerns of data privacy.

Identifying data privacy concerns

When it comes to data usage and data privacy, some countries have special legislation and regulations in place. For example, in European Union countries, there is a law known as the **General Data Protection Regulations** (GDPR). Regulations in the United States are a patchwork of rules. Except in the case of children, there is no specific privacy law; but the state of California has implemented the **California Consumer Privacy Act (CCPA)**.

Data privacy is the process of handling personal data in accordance with data protection regulations, laws, and common data privacy best practices. We can define who has unrestricted access to what data or information with the help of data privacy, and who has restricted access to data (see also *Identifying data security concerns*). One example of sharing data (as we described in *Chapter 2, Unfolding Your Data Journey*) is the usage of smart devices such as a smartwatch for monitoring sports activities. What if the home address of a military member could be found by sharing data from their smartwatch, which poses a potential threat to the personnel and their family? This is exactly why we should take care of privacy concerns at the start of our data and analytics initiatives.

We will address some concerns that we should take care of when we work with data for our data-informed decision-making processes:

- Designed-in privacy (using a clear framework, a written and internal data protection policy, and described organizational and technical measures). Privacy needs to be at the forefront of our minds!

- Processing registers (describe the processes, type, purpose, data security, users, and retention period).

- Is it necessary to do a privacy impact assessment with our Privacy Officer or responsible privacy staff member?

- Take care of procedures and processes in place for the *right of access*, *right to transfer data*, and *right to be forgotten* for data (typically done by the Privacy Office or other departments responsible for data privacy).

- Have a register to report data leaks. When an authority is in place, we should report the data leak within the given regulations.

- Larger organizations, such as healthcare organizations, banks, and governments, should have a Privacy Officer and data privacy processes in place.

To be able to identify data privacy elements, the preceding concerns/elements must be verified and checked during the initial project initiatives (for example, via an intake form). A checklist example can be found in the data privacy check table (the complete intake form and checklist are available in *Appendix A*):

Data privacy check

When it comes to using personal data, we should take precautions or be aware from the start of our project that we must adhere to privacy regulations. We need to identify and categorize several categories.

For example, in the Netherlands, we handle the following criteria:

- You may not just process personal data unless you have a legal basis.
- You will need the consent of the person in question.
- The processing serves a general, legitimate interest.

Note here that simply moving, copying, or linking data is already a process of digesting or assimilating data.

Name, Address, and City data

(Name, Address, Postal Code, and City of Residence)

Yes

No

Identification data	Yes
(Passport, Driver's license, or Social Security number)	No
Application details	Yes
(Application letters, Resume)	No
Contact details	Yes
(E-mail address, Phone or Fax number)	No
Salary details	Yes
(Salary details, Social Payments, Income Taxes, Expense reimbursement)	No
Social Media accounts	Yes
(LinkedIn, Twitter, WhatsApp, Facebook)	No
Image and sound recordings	Yes
(Video, Photos, Passport photographs)	No
Payment details	Yes
(Bank name, Account Number, Name of Account holder)	No

Addition and or explanation	
When a checkbox is answered with "yes," it is advised that you arrange a legislation and regulations check with your Privacy Officer.	

Legislation – Regulations check	
Privacy Impact Analysis (PIA) needed?	Essential | Important | Desirable | Unclassified
Register of Data needed?	Essential | Important | Desirable | Unclassified
Addition and/or explanation	

Data privacy regulations are governed by national or state regulations or laws. To ensure that we work in a correct, legal, and ethical manner it is necessary to address privacy concerns like we described in this section. This especially is important when it comes to processing personal data. It is a fact that some (the bigger ones) European organizations face a significant administrative burden to do so, they have to set up their Data Registers, perform Privacy Assessments and act responsibly based on the regulations that are set. If they don't they could face significant problems and fines from the controlling authorities.

> **Intermezzo – it is unavoidable; companies are using our private data**
>
> There are over 100 data and security statistics displayed on the *vpnMentor* website (`https://www.vpnmentor.com/blog/data-privacy-security-stats/`). One of the issues here is determining what the percentage of data collection is for some large companies. These are companies that we most likely use every day. For example, did you know that Facebook collects 79.49%, Instagram collects 69.23%, Tinder collects 61.54%, and Airbnb collects 33.33%?
>
> It's impossible to hide from this phenomenon. If you don't want your data to be collected through your interest behavior, you should not go on the net! As Edward Snowden once said, the NSA knows it all – you are not aware of it, but you are being monitored! To be honest, it's hard to control our data. Do we really read all the information of an agreement when using an app or using a website for purchases and more? No, we don't think so, and once companies have our data, they are able to sell it to other companies. Those companies can use your data to sell more products or services. But what happens when our data falls into the hands of someone who doesn't have the right intentions?

This previous section described the concerns of data privacy and how important it is to address them at the start of data and analytics projects. We've provided an overview of a checklist and added stories from real life to support the importance of data privacy. In the next section, we will discuss data ethical concerns.

Identifying data ethical concerns

When it comes to ethical concerns about data, we see that this topic has grown in prominence in recent years. This is because, in our digital big data era, we create masses more data every day, as discussed in previous chapters. But this data, whether pertaining to an individual or a business, can often be personal or sensitive, and open to exploitation by cybercriminals or others looking to exploit or use this information for negative gain.

Initially, this was a kind of gray area as there were no particular rules defined. People just did amazing things, such as predicting when a website visitor booked an airplane ticket online that they also would buy insurance (a sort of classification was used here). Wherever we could lay our hands on data from an internal and external perspective, we could do amazing things without even worrying about rules or ethical concerns.

But today, the data ethics landscape is different. Issues such as the ownership, privacy, and transparency of data now come into play. In this chapter, we'll discuss a few examples. We'll begin by exploring how ethics pertains to algorithms and business rules.

Algorithms and business rules are a set of instructions that can be used to solve specific problems, connect data, and connect logic. While they are commonly used interchangeably, for the purposes of this book, we will define business rules as any logic that you might use to run your business processes, whether those processes are automated or not. For example, a store's return policy can be an example of a business rule.

An algorithm is a rule or procedure that can be used for solving problems, or when a computation is needed. When we think of algorithms, we think of them as coded formulas. Once the rule and process are automated, it is typically a set of instructions that can run automatically. Like using an algorithm to recognize the faces of people, or identify outliers in data sets and correct them, and so on. With both algorithms and business rules, they take in data and information, apply some logic or math to it, and provide data or information as an output. The output of the business rule or algorithm is the knowledge that aids in the formulation of a solution to a problem.

When viewed in this way, business rules and algorithms are nothing more than a recipe or a detailed set of instructions. Because of technological advancements, particularly in our data field, business rules and algorithms are increasingly capable of learning based on the knowledge they generate.

With the help of *Figure 9.2*, we give you a definition of ethics and the essence of behaving ethically:

Ethics is one of the basic subjects of philosophy. From the Greek ἦθος (èthos - norm or custom), ethics refers to norms, values, customs, or habits. Ethics, then, is the doctrine of what is ethical or moral.

Figure 9.2 – What is ethics?

To be able to identify data ethical elements, they must be verified and checked during the initial project initiatives (for example, via an intake form). We have an example of a checklist in the data ethics check table (the complete intake form and checklist are available in *Appendix A*), which you could use when performing an intake for your data and analytics projects.

When it comes to data ethics, we simply mean that you should think about what you create from data and how you handle data. Following a number of incidents involving data, algorithms, and business rules, an algorithm supervisor has been established to monitor transparency in the use of algorithms as well as the implementation of effective European regulations. Some industries are developing frameworks and standards for ethical data handling, such as *The Council on the Responsible Use of AI* by *Harvard Kennedy School's Belfer Center for Science and International Affairs* and the *Bank of America Corporation*. Singapore is also working on ethical data use in the financial sector. Last but not least, *Meta*, *Microsoft*, *Apple*, *Amazon*, *IBM*, and *Google* are all working on the ethical side of data usage. Europe is also working on new legislation and regulations when it comes to handling data in an ethical manner.

When it comes to handling data ethically, businesses must have a transparent, structured data strategy that includes the data ethics strategy. When we use algorithms or business rules that affect decisions that then affect people, organizations, and more, the following three elements must be present:

- **Trust**: Organizations must apply key data ethics principles to their models, such as transparency, fairness of use, accountability, and privacy. For example, creating risk models in which people are classified as risky based on data from others while they themselves have not done anything to get that label.

- **Fairness**: Bias, most likely unintended and unknown, can have a negative impact on data-informed decisions. Organizations can provide documentation of fairness when the fairness of use is in place and ethical processes are followed. For example, Amazon was recommended to hire white male applicants based on data from the past, because the data showed that IT professionals had those characteristics (`https://amp.theguardian.com/technology/2018/oct/10/amazon-hiring-ai-gender-bias-recruiting-engine`).

- **Compliance**: When it comes to data, we must adhere to privacy legislation and regulations such as the *GDPR* in Europe and the *CCPA* in California, USA. Beyond legislation and regulations, organizations have a moral obligation to implement ethical rules. When organizations (or countries) do not have specific ethical rules, it could be a rather scary world. For example, in China, a massive amount of data is collected. Some people call it Big Brother 2.0. Your *social score* determines your life. When your social score is low, it will affect your complete life. And when this is the case, it could be that people have to face inequality, discrimination, and get hurt.

As mentioned earlier, addressing data ethical concerns, especially when we work with data and share insights, is important. We should do so upfront, for example, during the initial data and analytics project initiatives. We can do so by using checklists in our project intake forms or adding a checklist to a project plan. An example of a checklist is in the following table which is also available in, *Appendix A- Templates*:

Data ethics checklist		
Data generation, use, collection, analysis, and dissemination are all aspects of working with data. We can do this with both unstructured and structured data. When we do so, there is a chance that the decisions we make will have an impact on individuals and the world. As a result, we must be open about how we use data in our projects.		
1	**Do we have to take care of laws and regulations in this data and analytics project?** The first critical step is to determine whether any legalizations or regulations are applicable to the project.	Yes No **Write extra/additional information here:**
2	**Is the data that we want to use available in an ethical manner and is that data suitable for usage?** We must be mindful of who owns the data and ensure that it is used in the manner intended by the owner!	Yes No **Write extra/additional information here:**
3	**Is it possible to identify and check bias in the data that we have collected or used for our models?** People can be biased by their origin, and the same is true for data and the application of algorithms and business rules. The data we collect and store is not as objective as we believe! When using algorithms and business rules, we should be aware that the data we use to train the models can have an impact on people and possible human bias magnifies, which results in undesirable outcomes. To conclude, we must be able to identify, test, verify, and discuss the results.	Yes No **Write extra/additional information here:**

4	**Can we identify and demonstrate bias in our created model or in the used data?**	Yes
		No
	When we use data and apply various models, we may have used data that is biased. When we use that specific dataset and apply the learning models, the model produces biased results; for example, a bias based on gender, age, equality, or racial elements.	**Write extra/additional information here:**
	We must be aware that we must consider documenting, discussing, and evaluating our data usage choices. The message here is to avoid doing things simply because you can!	
5	**Can the legal rights of individuals be impinged by the use of data?**	Yes
		No
	When individuals' legal rights are at stake, the organization must have permission and the right to use data for specific purposes. For example, suppose an organization provides data to its direct partners, but privacy conditions other than the internal data usage may be addressed here. In the event of an incident, for example, they know address details and more detailed information about people, but certain data is not shared to protect those people's privacy (such as names, address details, and other things by which someone can be individually identified).	**Write extra/additional information here:**
	It could also happen internally, for example, through logging information that is known at the employee level but is shared with users at the department or concern level. We should be aware of this in order to protect the privacy of each individual employee.	
6	**Are we able to understand that the data that we want to use is suitable for the purposes of our project?**	Yes
		No
	When we begin an analytics or data science project, we must understand and ensure that the data we intend to use is appropriate for the purpose of our projects. Following that, we should be able to verify and validate the data for our project.	**Write extra/additional information here:**
	For example, when records or values are missing, the outcome or our algorithms and business rules can have a significant impact on the results, potentially producing a biased result.	

7	**Do we have a multi-disciplinary team present to discuss the apparent dilemmas regarding the possible usage of algorithms and the possible outcomes?**	Yes
		No
	When it comes to assessing and discussing our own work, we need to discuss the dilemmas and outcomes that can occur with a multi-disciplinary team.	**Write extra/additional information here:**
8	**Explainable AI by Design. Are we able to define the role of the algorithm used and what processes are being followed (procedural transparency)?**	Yes
		No
	It is critical for data engineers and data scientists who train models to understand the model's behavior in order to detect errors or weaknesses. This is why we must correctly describe the used algorithms or business rules.	**Write extra/additional information here:**
	When data scientists and data engineers train a model, it is critical to understand the model's behavior. They must identify any flaws or errors.	
9	**Explainable AI. Are we able to explain the algorithm or business rules to the guardians, stakeholders, and others with whom they are concerned?**	Yes
		No
	Explainable AI is defined as the ability of a person to comprehend the reason for a decision. The decision is influenced by algorithms and business rules. To be able to understand the model's decision, we must be able to explain the decision. We can do so by design, but we can also do it post hoc by using an algorithm to understand the black-box model.	**Write extra/additional information here:**
	Addition and/or explanation	

Intermezzo – tax office profiles ethnically

This is a translation of news articles and reports published in the Netherlands and beyond. We've cut those articles and news flashes down to the essentials of the story.

The *Tax and Customs Administration* was already aware, at the start of 2019, that a selection was made based on non-Dutch ancestry in fraud investigations involving childcare allowance. Despite repeated questions from the House of Representatives and the media about possible ethnic profiling by the service, the tax authorities continued to deny this for more than a year.

Several organizations performed an investigation into how this situation could occur. Amnesty International concluded (just like the other investigators) that a majority of things went wrong in this particular case. Therefore, thousands of people were affected wrongly. Above 30,000 people were accused of fraud and they had to repay the received allowances back to that tax office. As a result of this situation, people lost their homes as they could not pay their mortgages or rent anymore and their jobs. The children's protection organization got also involved and due to the earlier-mentioned issues, children were displaced from their parents and homes..

The risk model was used to estimate the risks of fraud or improper benefit utilization. For example, in the algorithms, *Dutch citizenship* was used to identify and estimate the possible risk. However, having Dutch nationality is not a condition (or business rule) for receiving a childcare allowance. The model was also used by a special team within the allowances department. This team assessed signs of abuse and then determined whether additional investigations by special fraud teams were required. The *Tax and Customs Administration* determined which applications for rent or childcare allowance had to be processed manually using the contentious risk model. Employees of the *Tax and Customs Administration* examined nationality, family composition, and income level, among other things. But using a nationality (or a second nationality) is discrimination and, therefore, prohibited. The *Authority* previously found the *Tax and Customs Administration* to be discriminatory. The good action here is that the model has not been used since July 2020.

The key message here is that using algorithms for classifying people is an ethical concern. When those initiatives are planned or discussed, we should take the mentioned concerns and potential risks into account. Determining the danger of risks when using personal data, outdated data and lack of control are key elements to consider, and by all means, be vigilant.

Here is a list of the websites we've used for this intermezzo:

- `https://www.amnesty.nl/actueel/toeslagenaffaire-is-mensenrechtenschending-zegt-amnesty-international`

- `https://autoriteitpersoonsgegevens.nl/nl/nieuws/werkwijze-belastingdienst-strijd-met-de-wet-en-discriminerend`

- `https://nos.nl/artikel/2364658-nooit-meer-een-toeslagenaffaire-wat-moet-er-nu-gebeuren`

Let's move on and summarize the chapter next.

Summary

After reading this chapter, you should have a better understanding of data security, data privacy, and data ethics. We've discussed the various topics from a more pragmatic standpoint.

We took the three topics and created tables with questions that you can use when you are about to begin a data and analytics project. It is prudent to address and answer these types of questions because incorrectly applied outcomes can cause harm to individuals.

Additionally, we included some real-life stories that were published online by newspapers or other news sites to help you understand what can go wrong when you use data incorrectly.

As we need to act on the created insights (see *Chapter 7, Designing Dashboards and Reports*), we will help you understand how to turn insights into decisions. We will do so in the following chapter. We will cover a seven-step framework to help you to turn insights into decisions.

Part 3: Understanding the Change and How to Assess Activities

In this section, we will focus on the action part of the journey to dive deeper into the process of change for individuals and organizations to increase their data literacy. We will discuss how to scope out typical BI projects, how to put decision-making with a data process and framework into action, and how you can increase your individual data literacy competency level.

This section comprises the following chapters:

- *Chapter 10, Turning Insights into Decisions*
- *Chapter 11, Defining a Data Literacy Competency Framework*
- *Chapter 12, Assessing Your Data Literacy Maturity*
- *Chapter 13, Managing Data and Analytics Projects*
- *Chapter 14, Appendix A – Templates*
- *Chapter 15, Appendix B – References*

10
Turning Insights into Decisions

Now that we have introduced data literacy and talked about how to tie it to organizational goals, we can move forward to discuss how to put it into action. Insights are great, but they need to be acted on. This chapter focuses on phases and steps to action your insights. You first need to turn those insights into decisions. You will be introduced to a seven-phase, data-informed decision-making model you can use. Then, you need to rally support and action for the decision by managing the change. You will be provided with best practices for managing change as a result of data-informed decisions. A big part of proactively dealing with change is by being resilient, so you will learn how to develop your resiliency skills. Another critical part of the change is how you communicate the insights and decisions via storytelling, so an entire section of this chapter is focused on this topic.

We will cover the following topics in the chapter:

- Data-informed decision-making process
- Storytelling

Data-informed decision-making process

What does being data literate enable you to do? What is the outcome? The outcome is gaining insights from your data so that you can make decisions and take action. This is what a data-informed organization does. It is able to obtain insights and knowledge from its data to enable effective data-informed decisions.

As defined in Kevin Hanegan's book *Turning Data into Wisdom*, data-informed decision-making is "*the ability to transform information into actionable and verified knowledge to ultimately make business decisions.*"

A data-informed organization is an organization that systemically and systematically utilizes data and analytics to make the best possible decisions across all levels within the organization.

There are various processes and models out there that can be followed for data-informed decision-making. The one covered in this book is an evolution from the seven-phase process introduced in the book *Turning Data into Wisdom*.

This seven-phase process, shown in *Figure 10.1*, focuses on ensuring you are asking the right questions of your data, you understand the data that is being used, you analyze the data using the appropriate analytic techniques, you critically appraise the data and insights, you effectively communicate the insights and decisions to be made, and you evaluate the decision after it has been made.

Figure 10.1 – Data-informed decision-making process

The seven phases in the process are the following:

1. **Ask** – Identifying decisions to be made and interpreting requirements. Formulating and asking focused analytical questions.

2. **Acquire** – Understanding, acquiring, observing, and preparing relevant data.

3. **Analyze** – Analyzing and interpreting data so that you can transform it into insights.

4. **Apply** – Validating the insights. Apply the experiences and beliefs of yourself and others to the data, including being aware of any bias you or others may hold.

5. **Act** – Transforming insights into decisions. Evaluate the information and insights provided, understand whether there is risk or uncertainty, and choose the decisions that are most likely to achieve the desired outcome.

6. **Announce** – Communicating decisions with data to all relevant stakeholders in a way that they can understand.

7. **Assess** – Evaluating and assessing both the outcome of the decision and the process used to come up with the decision. Leveraging this systematic and systemic process will reduce impacts from bias, foster diversity and inclusion, minimize unintended consequences, and allow you to improve on your decisions by failing fast, fixing fast, and learning fast, including improvements to your data and measurement frameworks, increased accountability, and better data-informed decisions.

We will now go into more detail about each phase to help explain it.

Ask – Identifying problems and interpreting requirements

The first phase of the decision-making process is to define the problem or decision that needs to be made. This includes not just highlighting what the problem is, but also understanding the context as well as all the requirements and constraints. Albert Einstein once said that, *if he had an hour to save the world, he'd spend 55 minutes defining the problem and 5 minutes solving it*. This highlights how critical this phase is. Failure to properly define the problem can result in what is called a type 3 error. A type 3 error occurs when you make a decision but the decision is based on the wrong question or problem that needs to be solved. It is critical, before we proceed, that we are in fact trying to solve the right problem. Let's take a look at a non-business example of type 3 errors. Suppose your partner is mad at you, and you infer that it is because you have not done anything special for them in a while, so you go out and buy an expensive item for them. However, in reality, the issue is they are mad at you because you seem to always be spending money and not saving it. In this case, you answered the wrong question. In fact, buying an expensive item had the opposite impact. It made the situation even worse because you failed to understand the context of the problem.

Let's now look at a business example of type 3 errors. Suppose a company needs to make a decision on how to increase its lead generation, as it believes the reason they are not selling as much is due to not having enough leads. In reality, the reason they are not selling as much has nothing to do with not having enough leads, it has to do with executing on the leads they do have and not converting enough of them into a sale.

These types of errors are the costliest in business, as you have invested tons of time in the process without actually spending any time on the actual problem. These errors typically occur when the organization does not work well across teams. It could be that the decision was designed just by upper management without any discussions below them, or it could be that the decision was made by the team focusing on the data model and analytics, without much collaboration from the business team.

Defining the decision includes not only identifying the decision itself but also identifying what brought you to this point where a decision needs to be made, as well as what your motive is for the decision. You should also define how you will measure the success of the decision.

Once the problem is defined, it then needs to be classified. Not every decision is the same, and as such, the effort and approach should match the need.

One classification system that can be used is the *Cynefin framework*, created by Dave Snowden. This framework can be used to assess the situation in which the decision needs to be made. The framework classifies the decision into one of five domains:

- **Clear** situations are stable and predictable, and cause-and-effect relationships are known to be involved. A simple example of a clear situation is when you decide to make dinner following a recipe. You have the ingredients, you have the equipment, you have the knowledge, and you have the process (the recipe).

- **Complicated** situations are much harder for us to determine the true root cause, so the cause-and-effect relationships are not clear to everyone. Rather, they require experts to solve. A good example of this would be the decisions a coach makes when coaching a sports team. The coach has all the skills, but those skills need to be applied to the players on the team. A decision with one set of players may not work for another set of players. This goes for managing employees at an organization as well. A common error in decision-making is when a manager tries to apply what they did at a previous organization to the current situation. Many things will be similar, but the employees themselves and the organizational culture are different, and the decisions need to factor that in.

- **Complex** situations involve multiple relationships and interdependencies, with multiple unknown factors. It may be impossible to identify one correct solution. Examples of this situation include making investments in the stock market and playing poker. Both of those situations require skills and strategies, but luck also plays a big part, which cannot be predicted.

- **Chaotic** situations occur when there is no way to truly understand the root cause and what may be happening with the relationships. What is clear is there are relationships that appear to be dynamic and changing. As a result, decision-making in chaotic situations is very difficult and requires a trial-and-error approach. A good example of this relates to decisions that were made at the start of the COVID-19 pandemic. Another example is the decisions that were made when the first iPhone launched. There is no historical data for a new innovative product like the first iPhone.

- **Confusing** situations are when you have no clarity about which of the other four domains apply.

A component of the classification is to understand the time required for the decision. Time is an important criterion for classification. Approaches for decisions that are required in terms of seconds or minutes, compared to decisions that need to be made in hours, to those that need to be made in days, weeks, or months are different.

Finally, you must define the importance of the decision. Importance is typically classified in terms of the importance of the outcome and is based on whether the decision is strategic, tactical, or operational. Strategic decisions typically have a long-term or material impact on the entire organization. Tactical decisions typically support a strategic decision and are usually for outcomes that are expected within the year. Operational decisions tend to be day-to-day decisions that typically have only a short-term impact on the organization.

Another way to look at the decision's importance is based on the questions they answer, as shown in *Figure 10.2*. For example, if a company is looking to change its business model, or grow its revenue by 15%, those decisions would be strategic and would impact the entire organization. The company would then need to make a series of decisions to establish initiatives to achieve the new strategic goals. These include decisions about the supply chain vendors to use and how much of the goods to keep in inventory. Those are examples of tactical decisions. Then there are many day-to-day decisions the company would need to make that need to align with the strategic and tactical decisions. These include things like defining the return policy and other logistical decisions, such as the work schedule for the employees in the manufacturing plant. These are examples of operational decisions.

Strategic	Tactical	Operational
Increase organization's revenue by 15%	Selecting vendors as part of the organization's supply chain	Employee's schedule
Change organization's business model	Number of goods stored in inventory	Return policy

Figure 10.2 – Decision importance levels

Another framework to use to classify decisions is one created by *McKinsey & Company*. They classify decisions into four categories, based on two dimensions: the frequency, and the scope or impact, as shown in *Figure 10.3*:

The ABCDs of categorizing decisions.

Figure 10.3 – McKinsey & Company's decision categories

Let's move on to the next phase.

Acquire – Understanding, acquiring, and preparing relevant data

After the decision to be made is defined and classified, the next phase is to identify and acquire the right data and get it in the right format. When gathering the right data, ensure you are looking systemically at anything that is relevant. This includes data that is not only internal but also external to the organization, as well as structured and unstructured data. The data will most likely not be in the right format for analysis, which is the next phase. Therefore, you, or someone within the organization with the right skill set, must clean and prepare the data, using techniques to clean the data and transform it.

This phase typically has two different approaches, depending on whether the decision to be made is brand new or whether a data model and measurement framework already exists. If those already exist, then the existing data is typically visualized, and this part of the phase has you reviewing those visualizations to think about what additional data may be relevant or needed to help. If this is a brand-new request with no existing data model or visualizations, then the process starts by documenting all the data that you believe is required to make the decision.

Analyze – Transforming data into insights

The Analyze phase is where you leverage the data from the Acquire phase as input and perform some analysis on the data. The goal of the Analyze phase is to find insights. There is a large toolbox of analytic techniques that can be applied, depending on the need. These range from various analytic techniques, such as descriptive and diagnostics, to inferential statistics, to more advanced analytic techniques such as machine learning and optimization techniques. More details about analytic techniques were covered in detail in *Chapter 7, Designing Dashboards and Reports*.

Apply – Validating the insights

After the data is analyzed and insights are obtained, the insights need to be validated with the human element of decision-making. You should apply reflective thinking at this stage and ask a number of questions about the insights to ensure that you challenge any assumptions, validate your mental model, and work to mitigate any cognitive bias that may have entered the decision-making process.

In Sydney Finkelstein's book, *Why Smart Executives Fail*, he studied 51 corporate failures and identified 4 patterns of destructive behavior that affect executives and led to the collapse of their organizations. Three of the four patterns relate to the human element, which is covered during the Apply phase: flawed mindsets, incorrect assumptions, and cognitive bias:

- **Flawed mindsets** – Leveraging data and insights to make decisions requires a data-informed mindset. Individuals and leaders alike need to think critically about data and information, to understand what data is relevant and what is not, and how to interpret what it really means. This requires everyone to question the data and information we receive. In the next chapter, *Chapter 11*, we will discuss in greater detail what a data-informed mindset is.

- **Incorrect assumptions** – Like our tendency to make biased decisions, we also easily make the wrong assumptions. Assumptions are inferences we assign to observed facts without proof. There are explicit assumptions, which are stated out loud, and implicit assumptions, which are hidden and not spoken about. We naturally make implicit assumptions as we reason about the world around us. Implicit assumptions include what we may infer about people's motives and abilities. For example, a common assumption in business would be that people will pay for your new product. While that may be true, without any evidence to support that opinion, it can easily be overstated and become a false assumption. More details on incorrect assumptions were covered back in *Chapter 8, Questioning the Data,* in the Be skeptical of the insights section.

- **Cognitive bias** – We make a lot of decisions and are bombarded with millions of pieces of information every day. Our brains are limited when processing information from the environment. We can hold only a small portion of the millions of pieces, and the information we manage to retain is done so on our own terms or based on our own subjective experiences and knowledge. The good news is that our brains are relatively efficient at making decisions due to heuristics. Heuristics are rules of thumb and mental shortcuts that the brain applies to guide decision-making based on a limited subset of the available information. These modes of thinking demonstrate how our brains classify objects, assess probabilities, and predict values based on automatic judgments that can be skewed. The bad news is that heuristics can lead to poor decisions.

  While heuristics enable us to make snap decisions without constantly stopping to think about them, when it fails to produce a correct outcome, the result is known as a bias, or more specifically, a cognitive bias. A cognitive bias, also called unconscious bias, is the tendency to draw incorrect conclusions due to cognitive factors embedded in our brain and according to our culture, interests, knowledge, experiences, and even our feelings. More details on incorrect assumptions were covered back in *Chapter 7, Designing Dashboards and Reports.*

Act – Transforming insights into decisions

The process does not end in the previous stage, where you have validated your insights. Insights are useless if they cannot be acted on by making a decision. The goal of the Act phase is to make a decision. These decisions should not just be made solely from the provided insight, but they should include qualitative judgments as well.

During this phase, the decision-maker needs to be able to do the following:

- **Interpret probabilities** – Making decisions based on the data and insights you have received typically involves making a prediction about whether something will happen. These predictions are many times based on probabilities. Understanding the basics of probabilities is an essential data literacy skill for individuals trying to make decisions from their insights. Probabilities are typically calculated by looking at the frequency with which something has happened in the past.

For example, imagine the weather forecast says there is a 7% chance of rain today. This does not mean that if it ends up raining today, the weather forecasters were wrong. It means that, based on the previous days with similar weather patterns and events, it ended up raining on 7% of the days. The other 93% of the days had no rain.

- **Discern between uncertainty and risk** – In the previous example, if you decided to leave the house without an umbrella given there is only a 7% chance of rain, that is a risk. It is a risk because, on 7% of the days historically similar to this day, it did end up raining. With these decisions, you do not know the outcome (whether it will rain or not) but you do know the possible outcomes (either it will rain or it won't) and the probability of each outcome. With uncertainty, unlike risk, you either do not know all the possible outcomes or you do not know the probabilities of the outcomes. Let's look at a different example of this. Let's assume you work for a restaurant and have to make decisions on what perishable food items to purchase. Similar to the example with the weather, you can look at historical data to understand the consumption patterns of those items, and then make a decision based on that. However, decisions are hardly ever that simple and one-dimensional. There is always some level of uncertainty as we are trying to make decisions about the future. Suppose the next week there is the start of another pandemic, and a majority of would-be customers stay home. Suppose there is an announcement about a change in the economy that causes would-be customers to rethink whether they want to eat out or not. The point is, very few decisions are ever made without some level of uncertainty. We are always tasked with making decisions without all the information, and we often do not properly take into account how uncertain the world is today. This often leads to less-than-ideal decisions, especially when the decisions are strategic decisions, as they are harder to course correct. It is important to be aware that there is uncertainty, and factor that into your decision.

A famous example of this is from the 2016 United States presidential election. Most polls had a probability of between 71-95% that Hilary Clinton would defeat Donald Trump. This does mean that those same polls said Donald Trump had a 5-29% chance of winning. On the surface, this looks purely like risk. However, there was a lot of uncertainty with the polls and sampling that was used. Time has changed and many locations in the country have had lots of changes in their preferences for a political party. Remember, uncertainty occurs when things happen in the future that could not be assigned a probability. Another key change, which had not happened before, was that some of the polling was off because people were reluctant to state which candidate they supported. These are examples of uncertainty, which lead to the probabilities being lower than what they should have been in reality.

- **Identify alternatives** – When faced with a decision, you always have options. It is important that, during the Act phase, you properly identify all alternatives. Many times, decisions will be decided upon as a yes or no answer. We need to go beyond that and look at the full spectrum of possible alternatives. This includes potentially doing things differently or in a new way that has not been done before. When Airbnb wanted to get into the lodging business but did not have the upfront capital to purchase facilities, the decision was not yes or no as to whether they take out a loan to purchase facilities, it was to do something that has not been done before.

They chose to make a strategic decision to leverage houses and other facilities from existing homeowners. This is an example of lateral thinking, which was introduced back in *Chapter 7*.

- **Weigh the insights based on outcomes** – Now that you have identified and understood the risks and levels of uncertainty, it is important you factor those into your decision and weigh them against the potential outcomes. This process does not just look at the outcomes when they are accurate, but also at the outcomes of making an incorrect decision. For example, going back to the weather analogy, if you decide to risk it and not take an umbrella, and it rains, your outcome will range from things like you and your clothing getting very wet to potentially leading you to get sick, or potentially, if you are carrying electronics, they can get destroyed. All of those potential outcomes and more need to be weighed based on each situation and context. My guess is if you are just going out for a walk in the park, you are more likely to not bring an umbrella if there is a 7% probability of rain than if you are going on an important job interview. This is where lateral thinking comes in, as we do not want to just focus on only answering the very specific question that is asked. In this case, should we bring an umbrella or not? Many times, the answers evolve into something in between. For example, a plausible decision could be to not bring an umbrella but take a taxi instead of walking to avoid getting wet.

Announce – Communicating decisions with data

Once the decision has been made, it needs to be communicated to all involved stakeholders. This process includes not only communication but identifying all stakeholder groups. Then, for each stakeholder group, crafting and delivering the communication, which includes the right data and insights, the right visualizations, and the right narrative.

This phase also includes the start of the change management process if the decision requires a deliberate change management approach. Details about how to communicate data and insights are covered in much greater detail later on in this chapter.

Assess – Evaluating outcomes of a decision

The process does not end with the Announce phase. After the decision is made and the action has kicked off, you must go back and evaluate the outcome of the decision. If the decision has not improved the problem or the identified need, you should take your lessons learned and go back to the beginning of the process and re-evaluate the decision and future actions to take.

While it is important to know whether the desired outcome of the decision was obtained, it is also important to not just focus on the outcome, but also focus on the process followed. Focusing on the impact alone and forgetting about the decision process is a common bias. The quality of the decision should not be measured just by the quality of the outcome and impact. The quality of a decision should be evaluated on the process, not the outcome. Just because a decision leads to a less-than-ideal outcome, it does not mean it was a bad decision. Conversely, even with a good outcome, the decision process may have been poorly designed. Take the feedback from what you learned during this evaluation and use it as a continuous improvement in the process and information at the start of the process.

Making a data-Informed decision in action

Now that we have identified the seven phases in the data-informed decision process, let's look at an example using this process in action. In this example, let's assume you were debating on whether you should go on a family vacation during the COVID pandemic. There is an abundance of data and information available on COVID, as shown in *Figure 10.4* with a listing of news headlines, but how can you turn that into something actionable that is specific to your needs and your desired outcomes? You can use the model we just discussed to understand the right questions you should be asking, find the right data to help answer them, and then use your skills to analyze, interpret, and understand the insights and ultimately make a decision.

Figure 10.4 – Identifying the right questions to ask

Phase 1 – Ask

There are tons of metrics out there specific to COVID, but as you learned earlier, metrics and indicators serve different purposes. The right metrics really depend on the questions and decision. As we discussed earlier, it all starts with the decision to be made. In this case, the decision would be whether the family should go on a family vacation to a specific resort during the COVID pandemic. The questions can be further expanded to be specific analytic questions about the risk involved:

- What is the risk of catching COVID for me or a family member?
- What is the risk of serious illness for myself or a family member?

To properly make a decision on whether to go away or not, you will need to also determine what is an acceptable risk. There will never be no risk, so the analysis you will do later in the process will help you determine whether the risk is acceptable enough to still go forward.

Phase 2 – Acquire

Before you can answer these analytic questions, you need to understand *how* you can answer them. What data and information is required? To do that, we need to know additional data points:

- What are my personal risks and those of my family members?
- How is the disease spreading specific to the location in which we are planning the vacation?
- What is the transmission related to the specific activities planned (hotel, beach, concert, amusement park, and so on)?
- How well is the healthcare system able to provide care?

You should ensure you find credible places to gather this data. For example, in the USA, we have the Center for Disease Control, and in the Netherlands, we have the Centre for Infectious Disease Control. Both of these capture a lot of useful COVID data.

You will next need to build out a set of indicators into a measurement framework, as we discussed back in *Chapter 6, Aligning with Organizational Goals,* specific to your four questions.

Personal risk

Personal risk is an indicator that will place everyone in the family who plans to go on vacation into a risk category. For these purposes, it could just be low, medium, or high. The indicator uses other data, such as age, gender, and the number of co-morbidity conditions. You can create the indicator just based on this and use some logic, such as any co-morbidity conditions automatically puts you at high risk, anyone over 60 puts you at high risk, 40-59 puts you at medium risk, and so on. An alternative approach could be to find data from similar profiles and understand what percentage of them got infected and experienced serious illness.

Prevalence

There are tons of metrics that highlight prevalence. One of the most common ones that were used at the start of the pandemic is the total number of confirmed cases, as shown in *Figure 10.5*. This metric can be deceiving as it shows cumulative cases:

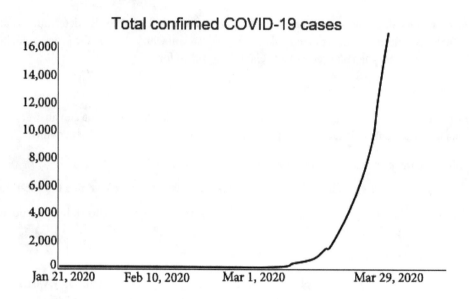

Figure 10.5 – Confirmed COVID-19 cases

To best answer our questions and make a decision, it is more relevant and important to know specifically about the current trends. *Figure 10.6* shows a representation of daily new cases in a graph:

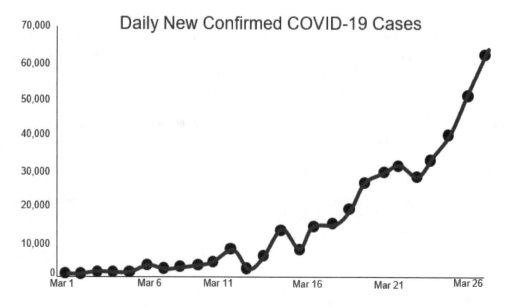

Figure 10.6 – Daily new confirmed cases

Questions you should ask include the following:

- What does the increase represent and what does that mean?
- Does that help you answer your question?
- How was the information calculated?
- What is the population used for the visualization?
- What was the period of time used for each calculation in the visualization?

Rate of transmission for specific activities

Another variable that needs to be measured to answer your question is specific to the location(s) you will be traveling in. We are not talking about the region where you will be traveling, but more specifically, the activities you will be doing and the risk of getting infected, as shown in *Figure 10.10*. Will you be traveling by airplane, will you be at an indoor concert with 20,000 other people, will you be at the beach, and so on?

Figure 10.10 – Questions about the rate of transmission

Certain locations and activities have higher rates of transmission due to a combination of environmental conditions such as being indoors next to a lot of people, and preventative measures put in place, such as masking mandates, social distancing, and onsite required testing. In these cases, it may be hard to get quantitative data for your decision. It may come down to qualitative data and information. For example, you may not be able to find anything that says there is a 25% risk of getting COVID if you are attending an indoor concert with 15,000 other people, but you will most likely be able to find insights that tell you it is a higher risk. So, this variable may not be best served with a set of visualizations, but rather with verbal insights. For example, there is a high risk of getting COVID based on the fact that this is an indoor concert with 15,000 other people and the concert venue does not require social distancing or mandate masks.

Health systems support

In order to properly assess the risk, it is not just sufficient to assess whether someone will get sick. It is also important to assess the scale and scope and quality of the healthcare system in the area you are visiting. How many beds do they have that are available, what type of equipment and medicine is available, what is the quality of the healthcare team, and so on?

Phase 3 – Analyze

Your measurement framework may end up looking similar to *Figure 10.11*:

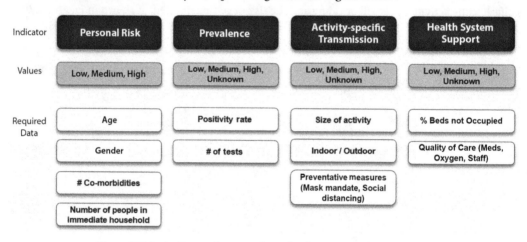

Figure 10.11 – Indicators for assessing a family vacation during COVID

You may perform various analytic techniques to obtain your insights. Those insights will be the values for each indicator: low, medium, high, and potentially, unknown.

Phase 4 – Apply

At this point, you have your indicators and understand the values. Here is where you use the Apply stage and try to challenge the data to see whether there are any gaps or misunderstandings. You should also get different perspectives. Potentially, there are other sources of data or information that are relevant. Maybe a new variant has just emerged that makes the data less relevant and accurate, at least related to prevalence and activity-specific transmission.

Phase 5 – Act

During the Act phase, you need to apply the decision criteria and understand whether there is any uncertainty or risk. The decision criteria would generally involve some type of logic, such as the decision is yes if prevalence and health system support are low, and activity-specific transmission is low or medium. Anyone in the family who has a personal risk of *high* would not partake in the specific activities that are considered high risk.

All of the indicators except the personal risk one have a possible value for *unknown*. It could be that the data does not exist for a specific region, or it does not exist from a trusted source. In those cases, this is not a risk – it is an uncertainty. When you are making the decision, you need to know what the risks are, and what is uncertain.

Phase 6 – Announce

After the decision is made, you communicate it to all the involved stakeholders, which include the people going on the vacation, as well as other friends and family. For the stakeholders going on vacation, you can explain the criteria used, the decision made, any exceptions that are included (such as specific events that were planned that will not be attended), as well as any criteria or situations for when the plans will change during the vacation.

Phase 7 – Assess

This type of decision is more of a single-use decision, but you should still take everything you learned about the process and the outcomes after the vacation, and then ensure you apply them the next time you have to make a similar decision.

Using a data-informed decision checklist

When making a data-informed decision, you can leverage the following checklist to verify you have followed the steps just discussed.

Ask

1. Did you define the decision to be made or the problem that needs to be solved?
2. Did you convert the decision or problem to be solved into a specific set of analytic questions?
3. Did you identify what your motive is for the decision or what brought you to this point where a decision needs to be made and what problem it is trying to solve?
4. Did you ensure the decision fits into the strategic plan and align it with the organization's strategy?
5. Did you describe the potential outcomes?
6. Did you document any boundary conditions – for example, understanding what is the most you are willing to invest to obtain the desired outcome?

7. Did you define how you will measure the success of the decision?

8. Did you classify the decision using either the Cynefin framework, the McKinsey ABCD decision classification, or similar?

9. Did you determine the timeframe needed for the decision (seconds, minutes, hours, days, weeks, or months)?

Acquire

1. Did you interview relevant stakeholders about what data is relevant to the decision?

2. Did you search for relevant qualitative data as well as quantitative data?

3. Did you search for data both internally and externally?

4. Did you prepare the data by transforming it into the specific data needed to answer the questions and make the decision?

5. Did you document where there were any gaps in data that would have been helpful but were not available?

Analyze

Did you analyze the data using one of the various techniques to come up with insights (analytics, statistics, machine learning, or optimization)?

Apply

1. Did you question the insights and consider situations when the insights may either be misleading or not true?

2. Did you apply your perspectives and experience to the insights to apply meaning to them?

3. Did you list out every assumption that you have related to the decision and questions?

4. Did you get input and perspectives from diverse people?

5. Did you leverage any techniques to mitigate any cognitive bias that could have crept into the decision?

Act

1. Did you identify what portions of the decision are risks and what are uncertainties?

2. Did you weigh up at least one alternative for the decision?

3. Did you think about worst-case scenarios for the decision you chose?

4. Did you look out for unintended consequences both with your direct team as well as with other departments or individuals?

Announce

1. Did you identify all involved stakeholder groups?

2. Did you build communication with each stakeholder group that included data, visuals, and stories that were relevant to them based on their background with data and how they are impacted by the decision?

3. Did you consider whether the decision is consistent with other decisions made in the past? (If not, it will require more change management.)

4. Did you develop a change management plan if needed?

Assess

1. Did you assess the outcomes against the anticipated outcomes?

2. Did you update the decision-making process or insights based on any learnings related to both the outcome and the process to get to the outcome?

Now that we have introduced the seven phases and provided you with a checklist that you can use with any upcoming decisions you need to make, we will move on to learn about why we call this a data-informed process and not a data-driven process, and what the difference is.

Why data-informed over data-driven?

It is intentional and deliberate that we call this a data-informed organization and a data-informed decision, as opposed to data-driven. Data-informed is about combining the data elements with the human element. Data and machine learning and artificial intelligence are extremely powerful. However, they are only working on the dataset that is available to them. Human abilities are broader than this. We can anticipate, and we can judge when a situation is about to change, even if it has not done so before. We can imagine future possibilities that do not exist in the data yet. We can shift our focus between short-term and long-term. This is why humans and machine intelligence complement each other perfectly and is the essence of data-informed decision-making. Let machines do the crunching and analyzing, and then provide those insights to a human who knows the business and can apply the human side of decision making to ultimately make the decision.

Storytelling

As you just read in the previous sections of this chapter, communicating with data is absolutely essential and critical, as it relates to your change management process. This skill applies across multiple phases of the process. You may have just come up with a decision that will save your organization millions of dollars, save countless lives, or something else just as spectacular. However, if you cannot communicate the right information at the right time in the right way to the right people, your decision may be ignored or ostracized. Your ability to come up with key insights to help with your decision is one skill but communicating it is another completely. Good communication of your data-informed decision can help stakeholders understand, accept, and then act on the decision.

As shown in *Figure 10.12*, appropriate and skillful communication of data includes an approach called analytic storytelling. This approach includes contextual design to achieve proper communication, a well-constructed narrative to bring your story to life, the right level of data and insights, and the right visualizations to support the decision. You do not want to overwhelm or bore your audience. Most importantly, you should not only present the data but also add in the appropriate context. Give the audience the idea, the picture, and then the applicable details.

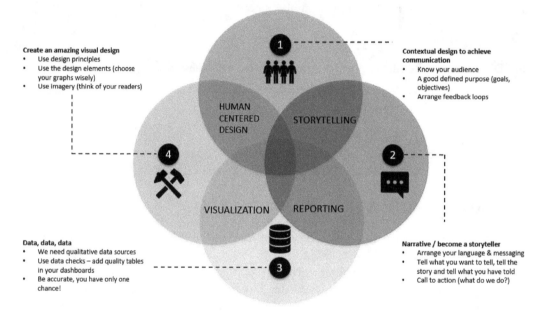

Figure 10.12 – Approach to analytic storytelling

We will learn about these various components in greater detail later on in this section. But before we go into those, it is important to understand why communicating with data is so hard.

Why is communicating with data so hard?

We have all been involved in some type of presentation where the theme and message just don't stick with the audience. There are many reasons why it may not stick with the audience. Maybe the data is not something they are familiar with. Maybe the visualizations used are too hard to understand. Maybe there is no context provided. Even if all those are present, it could be that the message is not memorable, persuasive, and engaging.

When we are younger, we learn in school how to speak, read, and write our native language. Independently, we learn how to use numbers in math class. However, we never learn how to connect the two. We do not learn how to tell stories with numbers. It is a different approach and a different skill.

Communicating with data is a method of delivering messages derived from data analysis in a way that allows the audience to quickly and easily assimilate the material. This will help the audience to avoid information overload. It should also allow the audience to easily identify what the communication is trying to tell them, without leaving any room open for misinterpretation.

Three key elements of communication

The goal of communicating with data is to get buy-in on a decision. Ultimately, the stakeholders will need to not only buy in but also act on the decision. The communication should resonate with the stakeholders and result in them taking action, usually in support of a change. There are three key elements involved in communicating with data: the data, the visuals, and the narrative. They all work together to aid in getting the message across, as well as helping with the change management process.

The data combined with the narrative will help explain to the stakeholders the context, including what the data or insight is, what the interpretation is, and why it is relevant to them. The data combined with the visual will help the stakeholder see the insights and interpretation clearer than just if you were showing the data in a tabular format. The narrative combined with the visuals will draw your stakeholders in and engage them.

Why include a narrative?

One reason why narrative and story are so important when communicating with data is that research has shown that stories make communication more memorable, more engaging, and more persuasive.

Memorable

Research highlights that stories are 22 times more memorable than when just data is used alone. Chip Heath, the author of *Made to Stick*, asked a classroom of 25 students to present a 1-minute persuasive pitch to their fellow classmates. Across all of those presentations, there was an average of 2.5 data points included. Only one of the presentations included a story. The teacher continued on with the class and intentionally moved to a completely unrelated topic. Ten minutes later, he then asked the entire class to pull out a sheet of paper for a pop quiz. The students were asked to write down every idea they remembered from the student presentations earlier in the class. Only 5% of the students remembered any of the 2.5 data points, but 63% of the students remembered the story.

You can make a story even more memorable by including emotions in it. Whenever there is a story that includes emotions, more of the message is embedded in the listener's memory, ultimately making it stick. Emotions make something more real. The stronger the emotion, the deeper the impact, to the point that it gets etched into the listener's long-term memory. The emotion does not have to be a negative emotion, such as fear; it could be a positive emotion as well.

Engaging

When you have an audience that is curious, their attention is focused on the speaker, and they are actively listening to you and the message. They are not disengaged, as they are putting their distractions aside to listen. Research has also concluded that when people are listening to engaging communication, they actually enter into a trance-like state where they drop their intellectual guard and want to see where the story leads them.

When following a proper arc of communication in a story, the brain gets activated much more than with data alone. Listeners' brains have their neurons fire in the same patterns as the storyteller's brain. This process, called mirroring, creates coherence and allows the listener to turn the story into their own ideas and experience. Listeners' brains also release dopamine when they experience an emotionally charged event, including a story. This makes it easier to remember with greater accuracy. When processing facts, typically, only two areas of the brain are activated. When listening to a well-told story, many additional areas of the brain are activated, including the motor cortex, sensory cortex, and frontal cortex.

Persuasive

It is important for the communication to be memorable and engaging, but it also must be persuasive if it is going to help as part of the change management. In another study, the *Save the Children* organization sent out two different types of requests for monetary donations. One of them was a brochure that just listed data and factual information about the plight of children in sub-Saharan Africa. The other request was a story about a 7-year-old girl named Rokia. The story talked about her plight and how she was at high risk of severe hunger and starvation. The results were that the communication that just listed the data and facts was far less persuasive than the communication that included the story. The average donation from the group that got the story of Rokia was double that of the average donation from the group that just got the data.

Stories are memorable when you provide just enough details, but not too many. Providing just enough details will allow the listeners to visualize the situation. In the example earlier in the chapter with the CEO of Intel, how many of you tried to visualize a car going half a million miles per hour on a highway?

To summarize, when communicating data and insights to stakeholders, if you focus only on the data, without a compelling story, it will typically deplete the attention of the audience. The audience will try to evaluate the data and think critically about it, and they will begin to ask questions about the data as they will be skeptical of it. However, if the communication includes a proper and engaging narrative, it will capture the attention and enchant the audience, causing them to be inspired and move to action.

The process

The process for communicating with data includes the following three parts:

1. **Defining the audience** – This part includes identifying all the stakeholder groups.

2. **Planning the story** – This part includes planning out the story and mapping it to the audience.

3. **Crafting the story** – This part includes identifying the right data, the right visualizations, and the right narrative.

Let's now go through each part in detail next.

Defining the audience

As you plan out your story, you need to take time to understand each unique stakeholder group. One of the most common issues that occur during this process is when you treat every one of the stakeholders the same, and provide them the same story, with the same data and visuals. Not only because each stakeholder group may have various levels of their own data literacy, but your story also needs to make an emotional connection with them too. In order to do that, you need to identify each unique stakeholder group. Consider stakeholders that are internal to the organization, such as your peers and your leaders, as well as stakeholders who are external to the organization, such as the consumers of your offerings. Also consider stakeholders who are upstream, including individuals who are involved in the implementation of whatever you're discussing or trying to change, as well as stakeholders who are downstream, including the individuals who are consuming what the upstream stakeholders are implementing.

Planning the story

To start, you should write down the goal of the communication, meaning what are you trying to get as an outcome. What are the key insights and decisions that you want to share with this stakeholder group?

Then, you should describe the role of the stakeholder group. Therefore, you need to tailor the communication to each unique stakeholder group. The consumers who are going to be impacted by the decisions are probably going to have different answers to, say, the developers who are implementing the actions driving the decision. It is important to put the communication in the perspective of the stakeholder. What is in it for them? What questions will they most likely ask? Why should they care and listen and act? What decisions do they need to make because of this communication? Structure the communication so that it easily and directly answers anything you believe will be a high-priority question from that stakeholder group.

As we mentioned earlier in the chapter, the story should include data and visualizations. Many times, the data will not just be KPIs, but they may be the results of some analytics or statistics that have been executed against data. You must understand how knowledgeable each stakeholder group is with interpreting these outputs and then match the right data, the right visuals, and the right words to the audience. For a group that happens to be data scientists, you could go deeper into the visualizations and the complexities of the algorithms used. If they are not comfortable with data, you should stick to giving high-level descriptive analytics such as KPIs. In addition, you need to understand the industry they work in to understand how familiar they may be with the terminology and other words used in your communication. If they are a business leader, they may not understand all the data, but they do know the business, and they should have a grasp on what the KPIs mean and how to interpret them.

One surefire way to lose an audience is to use business-level terminology and acronyms that they have no understanding of. If they are not likely familiar with the terminology, avoid acronyms and add clear and concise definitions.

Crafting the story

Now that you have planned the story, it is time to craft and create the story. This includes the three components we have discussed: the data, the visual, and the narrative. We already discussed a lot about visualizations in *Chapter 8, Questioning the Data,* so the focus of this section will be mostly on including the right data and creating the right narrative.

The right visualization

There are two reasons to use data visualizations. You use them to explore and gain insight and to describe and diagnose. You also use them to communicate those insights to your stakeholders. One of the most common mistakes that we see is that people will use the same visualization for both purposes. You may need to use a more advanced visualization to find your insights, but when you share them, you should prioritize what needs to be shown to the stakeholders and, ideally, use a simple visualization that just focuses on that. You will also want to design and configure the visualization that you are using to communicate to ensure the insights are easily understood.

The first step is understanding what the right visualization for your audience is. You want to ensure you are picking a visualization designed to visualize the data and answer the question you asked. This was discussed in the *Choosing the right visualization* section of *Chapter 7, Designing Dashboards and Reports.* You then want to ensure that the visualization prioritizes what is required to share with the audience. Anything that is not directly relevant to highlighting the insights into the questions asked should be removed. This will greatly lower the cognitive load of your audience, allowing them to interpret and comprehend the visualization more easily.

The right data and insight

Back in *Chapter 7*, we discussed the topics of thinking critically about the data and insights. When you are crafting your story, you will want to ensure you bring information obtained during that phase into your communication. If you do not show the details that are relevant for the audience to understand the insights, they will draw their own conclusions, which are not accurate.

Let's look at one famous example of this. This example comes from another book by Chip and Dan Heath, called *Switch.* In the book, they tell the story of a Cornell University study, where movie-goers were served stale popcorn. Half of the movie-goers were given a medium container of popcorn and the other half were given a large container. The study was trying to explore whether people with the larger bucket would eat more popcorn than the ones with the medium bucket. The results highlighted that the movie-goers with large buckets ate 53% more popcorn than those with medium buckets.

This research is fascinating yet has nothing to do with data literacy. However, the Heath brothers used this to highlight a key element of the story and communication with the stakeholders. They asked the readers to imagine that someone showed them the data from the research but failed to mention the different bucket sizes. The visual in the story would look something as shown in *Figure 10.13*:

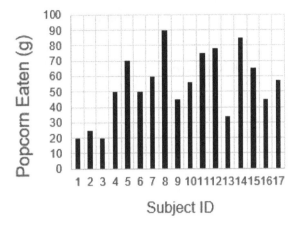

Figure 10.13 – Popcorn eaten by subject

Looking at this, most interpretations would highlight that there are some people who ate a bunch and some that did not each much. It would have been interpreted very differently if you had included the data that highlighted the various categories of the buckets, as shown in *Figure 10.14*:

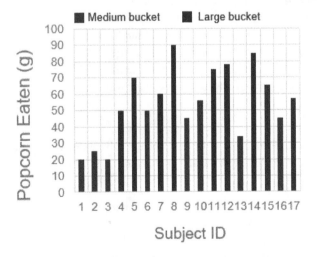

Figure 10.14 – Popcorn eaten by subject and by bucket size

Taking what we learned in this chapter into account, however, can the visual used be updated to make it even more clear to the stakeholders? Yes, in something like what is shown in *Figure 10.15*:

People with larger buckets ate 53 percent more popcorn than people with the medium size

Figure 10.15 – Does bucket size matter?

This is an oversimplified example, of course, but still serves a good point to remind everyone that it is important to not only pick the right visuals for communicating but also ensure you include the right data and insights to highlight.

The right narrative

The goal of the narrative is to provide context to the data and the visualizations. Context augments the audience's understanding, and it drives their ability to see the insights. Don't just show the insight but explain your interpretation of it and how it aided in the decision.

Another best practice is to ensure you use comparisons when needed, to avoid the audience thinking "*so what*?" The data and numbers you share in your narrative may not mean anything to the audience. You can make a comparison by using the same numbers but in a different context, a context that is understood by the stakeholder group. A perfect example of this approach was used by Intel's CEO, Paul Otellini, in a 2010 presentation. He was talking about his new company's new microprocessors and the speed of their innovation. He understood the audience and knew the stakeholders would not really understand the importance of the numbers he shared. He shared them, but then gave a comparison to the auto industry and how fast cars can go, which all the stakeholders could relate to.

Types of narratives

Proper narratives for communicating with data usually follow one of two flows. There is a flow when you are communicating an **explanatory** journey and one when you are communicating an **exploratory** journey.

In an explanatory journey, the speaker walks through the narrative in chronological order:

1. It starts with the context of what is happening and the current state.

2. Then, it lists out the challenges that were faced, followed by the conflict statement or business question that needs to be answered.

3. Finally, the narrative lists the resolution, which includes the insight found and possibly, the decision made as a result.

In an exploratory journey, the speaker walks through the narrative following the analytical and discovery process in order:

1. It starts with the expectations.

2. This is followed by the findings.

3. Then comes the conclusion.

4. And finally, the action.

The research firm Gartner recommends the exploratory journey, as shown in *Figure 10.16*:

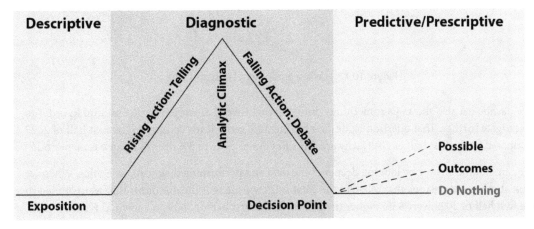

Figure 10.16 – Gartner's approach to storytelling

They take it one step further when they are talking about storytelling or communicating with data. They tie in the four levels of analytics that you learned about earlier in the book:

1. Start with the exposition where you are describing the situation.

2. Then you are trying to diagnose the problem so you perform diagnostic analytics to find the root cause.

3. Then, you are telling the story of the insights you obtained from the diagnostic analytics that becomes the climax of the story, and, at that point, the communication opens up for debate with the audience, including discussing what the audience thinks about the insight and why it happened.

4. That is followed by a decision point, where the communication potentially goes into predictive or prescriptive modeling to talk about possible outcomes.

Let's take a look at an example using this model. The example follows a company that sells commercial coffee-making equipment to restaurants and businesses. The company builds a dashboard to show that its sales appear to be dropping in the first half of 2022 compared to the first half of 2021, as shown in *Figure 10.17*:

Figure 10.17 – Coffee equipment leads and sales

The dashboard also shows us something confusing that we can create a question around in order to investigate further. That question is, despite having 38% more leads coming in the first half of 2022 compared to the first half of 2011, why are our sales down close to 3% over that same time period?

We can find the answer by looking deeper at the data and performing diagnostic analytics. When we look at other dimensions that relate to the total sales, we see that the discounts that were offered in the first half of 2022 were 93% higher than those in the first half of 2021, as shown in *Figure 10.18*:

Figure 10.18 – Coffee equipment sales discount

Now that we have identified the probable cause for the sales to drop, despite an increase in leads, we still want to understand whether the leads were useful. It is appropriate to communicate the insight about higher discounting to the stakeholders, but those stakeholders will most likely wonder what would have happened if the discount was the same as in the first half of 2021.

To answer that, we can use analytics to ask what if the average discount in the first half of 2022 was the same as the first half of 2011. You can see in *Figure 10.19* that the sales for the first half of 2022 would have been 4.2 million rather than 3.96 million; 4.2 million is also higher than the first half of 2021 sales of 3.96 million:

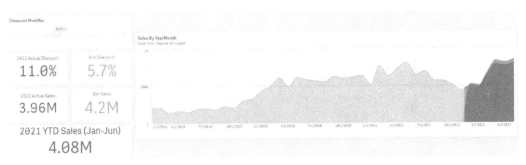

Figure 10.19 – Coffee equipment simulated sales

This provides a valuable story from the data that we could have easily missed if we did not use visual analytics. The story is that even though our leads were increasing year over year, our sales were not growing. In fact, they were down 2.93%. Only by investigating the data deeper and more systemically were we able to see that the organization was actually selling more units, it is just that their discounting had dramatically increased. This insight and communication allowed the organization to continue with its investment in leads but put tighter processes in place for discounts.

The SUCCESs model

We introduced Chip and Dan Heath earlier in the chapter. In their book, *Made To Stick*, they created a model called the SUCCESs model to help to get ideas to stick when communicating them.

The model has six principles that map to the acronym **SUCCESs**:

1. **Keep it Simple** – The brothers mention that simplicity isn't dumbing things down. It is all about prioritizing. This means if you have a ton of data and information, only show what is the most important and relevant to the question.

2. **Make it Unexpected** – Don't waste the time of the stakeholders by sharing information and insights with them that they already know. This will not be engaging for them and will cause them to zone out. Instead, get the audience's attention by ensuring the information and insights are not things that they are already aware of.

3. **Be very Concrete** – To help a message stick with the stakeholders, you cannot just cite theories and talk in very abstract terms. Ensure the message is very concrete and realistic. Concrete messages are less likely to be misunderstood.

4. **Show Credibility** – For the insights to stick, they need to be believable and also credible. If stakeholders do not either believe the insights or they do not find the speaker credible, they will zone out very quickly. Many times, it is hard to gain credibility, so if you are in a situation where you do not currently have it, you can gain credibility by using outside sources and best practices. This can include examples where the same insight and change have worked before, or it can be getting insights that come from leading innovators or analysts in your industry.

5. **Don't forget the Emotion** – Remember earlier in the chapter with the story of Rokia from Africa? People care about people, not numbers. Emotions will help the message stick with the stakeholders.

6. **Tell a Story** – As we have discussed throughout this chapter, stories will help you deliver your insights and decisions to your stakeholders, along with the right data and visualizations.

Summary

Insights are great, but they are useless unless they can be acted on in a way that helps drive you toward your goal. In this chapter, we learned about the importance of using a data-informed decision-making process to turn your insights into decisions. We also learned that the decision is not the endpoint. Typically, it is just the starting point of a change management initiative. Then, we learned about the importance of following a change management process and how to increase resilience in people to help the actions take place. A critical part of change management is effective communication and storytelling with data.

Now that we have learned various best practices for taking action on your insights, we will focus on what skills and competencies you will need to make this happen in the next chapter.

Further reading

- Snowden, D. and Boone, M., 2007. *A Leader's Framework for Decision Making.* [online] Harvard Business Review. Available at: `https://hbr.org/2007/11/a-leaders-framework-for-decision-making`

- Heath, C., & Heath, D. (2009). Made to stick: *Why some ideas take hold and others come unstuck. Random House Books*

11
Defining a Data Literacy Competency Framework

One of the most common questions we get asked is, what skills are required to be data literate? Everyone has heard about data literacy, but few are aware of the various skills and mindsets that make up data literacy. Data literacy is not a unique skill all by itself. It is an aggregation of specific technical skills and specific soft skills, along with a mindset to listen, be curious, and think critically. We have introduced a variety of topics related to data literacy already throughout this book, and this chapter intends to bring them all together into a cohesive framework. This chapter describes a data literacy competency framework, which includes the right technical skills, soft skills, and mindsets for data literacy, based on the role you play with data and the level of experience you are starting at.

In this chapter, we're going to cover the following main topics:

- Data literacy competency framework
- Data literacy skills
- Learning about data literacy best practices

Data literacy competency framework

Many of the definitions of data literacy, even our own, include the word *ability*, but data literacy is not just an ability that individuals have. It is more than that. It includes skills and mindsets as well. Abilities refer to being able to do something, whereas a skill refers to the effective use of an individual's knowledge and abilities that can be measured. These words often are used interchangeably but the key aspect as it relates to this definition is that skills can not only be measured but can also be gained through training or experience. Data literacy also requires individuals to not just have various skills but also a mindset for approaching data. Mindsets relate to our views and beliefs on certain topics and our willingness to apply them. For example, someone may have the skills to analyze data, but if they don't have the mindset to be open to getting diverse perspectives, then it's a moot point.

Putting this all together, to truly understand data literacy and identify how you can become more data literate, you need to identify the combination of skills and mindsets that allows individuals to find insights and meaning within their data to enable effective data-informed decision-making. This means aligning learning and education programs geared to increase data literacy with specific competencies.

Competencies are a broad set of knowledge, skills, and mindsets – being competent combines the acquisition of a skill with the mindset and behaviors to successfully execute it. In the context of data literacy, there are many situations where a person may have specific skills but are unable to apply them because of their mindset or the culture of their organization. For this reason, data literacy should be discussed in terms of competencies, so that people are enabled to apply their skills appropriately.

To establish the key competencies associated with data literacy, it is helpful to explore them through the lens of the full process behind turning raw data into insights. We've outlined the seven key phases that turn data into decisions, as shown in *Figure 11.1*, which we learned back in *Chapter 10, Turning Insights into Decisions,* and the competencies and sub-competencies linked to each of them:

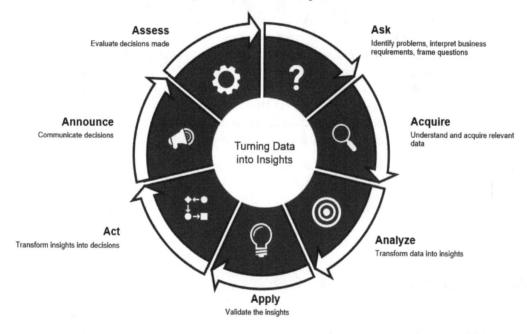

Figure 11.1 – Phases for turning data into insights

Identifying problems and interpreting requirements

The first phase defines the purpose of the decision being made. It starts by establishing the various use cases and expectations that organizations have with data, before putting processes in place to ensure the right questions are being asked that align with the business goals. It's important to lead with human thought and creativity here – after all, you know what your organization is trying to achieve by making this decision. Data should then be used to refine, validate, and inform these thoughts. Although many businesses follow the data as the first port of call, this often prevents the application of critical, creative, and collaborative thinking.

For this phase to be successful, it's crucial to identify the question, problem, or decision to be made and whether it can be solved using data. If it can, then set appropriate **key performance indicators (KPIs)** as a foundation and turn business questions into corresponding analytics questions. It's also important to translate these business requirements into a structured hypothesis.

This phase includes three competencies: problem identification, interpreting business requirements, and performance measurement.

Problem identification

A key part of a data analysis project is to identify the problem you are trying to solve. If you do not successfully do this, you will end up wasting a lot of time and resources. As the Cheshire cat said in *Alice's Adventures in Wonderland,*

"It does not matter where you are going if you do not know where you want to go."

Once the problem or decision to be made is established and confirmed by all, you need to *discern whether it can be solved by analytics*. Once it is determined that the problem or decision to be made can be solved by analytics, the next step is to properly *classify the decision* to be made, including the type of decision, its importance, and the time required for the decision.

Interpreting business requirements

Once you have identified a problem that can be solved with analytics, you need to continue gathering requirements from the business. The starting point for this is to *turn a business question into an analytical question*. Too often, people are asking questions such as *"How successful was my marketing campaign?"* While that may be a valid business question, it is not something that you can answer without asking more questions and getting more context. This involves interpreting business objectives, asking clarifying questions to get more specificity on the problem at hand, and then creating analytical questions from those business requirements.

Once you complete all your questioning and are confident the problem is scoped properly and you understand the true goals of the analysis you need, you should *translate business requirements into a structured hypothesis*. This approach helps you focus on the problem, but also in applying techniques to mitigate any bias that may creep into the decision-making process.

Performance measurements

There are situations where you are not reacting to ad hoc questions, rather you are proactively building out a measurement framework using **KPIs**, as discussed back in *Chapter 6, Aligning with Organizational Goals*. Measurement frameworks allow you to quantifiably assess how a part of the business is doing compared to something (such as the last period, or a benchmark target). This competency requires you to know how to *create good KPIs, including leading and lagging indicators*, and how to ensure they tie to the organization's goals and strategies.

Understanding, acquiring, and preparing relevant data

Next, there are specific skills and mindsets required to understand the concepts related to the question at hand, acquire the relevant data, and prepare it so it is in the appropriate format. Once you know the issue you are trying to solve, it's much easier to filter out irrelevant data. After the problem or question is identified, relevant concepts and data must be identified and prepared in a way that makes it accessible and suitable for further use.

This means understanding which data points are appropriate for the task at hand, using a systemic perspective. It also means developing an overview of how to retrieve data, as well as how to join, clean, transform, and create new data. This enables you to use the raw materials at your disposal to explore the challenge at hand more deeply.

This phase includes three competencies – identify relevant data, access data, and prepare data:

- **Identify relevant data**: Before you can access data for analysis, you need to *identify what sources of data are relevant* to the task at hand. This competence requires you to understand issues of data availability and data accessibility. It also requires you to think systemically about all the sources of data that may be relevant, including internal and external sources, and quantitative and qualitative sources.

- **Access data**: Once you identify relevant data sources, you need the *ability to retrieve them*. The specific tasks depend on the type of data source and can range from SQL statements to ETL batch processing, or to using scrapers and APIs.

- **Prepare data**: Many data sources are not created for the sole purpose of analytics. They have other purposes as well. Once you have acquired your data, you will need to not only validate the quality of the data by performing data audits, but you will also have to join disparate data sources, and then clean and potentially transform the data to make it analytics-ready. This requires you to be able to clean noisy and incomplete data, have an understanding of why data cleaning is needed based on the organizational context, and transform data into various formats using data wrangling, data mining, data standardization, and data transformation techniques.

Keep in mind when performing tasks within this phase, it is important to think of the term data as broadly as possible. It is not just about numbers, it also involves qualitative data, such as surveys, feedback from customers, and statements made by experts in the field, just to name a few. For example, if you are trying to decide how to improve a product that is suffering from a high number of returns, identifying, accessing, and preparing comments from buyers in online marketplaces, or questions asked of customer service related to the product are extremely relevant.

The outcome of this phase is data that is in the right form to be analyzed.

Turning data into insights

This phase is where the real analysis comes in. The skills and mindsets required to do this effectively will allow you to infer insights such as causality and correlation but given the huge volumes of data used by today's businesses, analytics tools are a crucial ally to achieve this. These come in many forms – whether simple descriptive analytics, diagnostic tools to enable root cause analysis, or advanced predictive analytics.

From the perspective of the data practitioner, competency at this phase means knowing the right analytics and statistics to use, learning how to assess patterns and trends across diverse data, performing comparative analytics, visualizing data, probing for causality, and ultimately, drawing inferences and conclusions.

This phase includes three competencies – analyze data, apply advanced analytics, and communicate data and insights:

- **Analyze data**: This competency encompasses techniques for analyzing data to come up with insights. This includes the following six sub-competencies:

    - Choose the right analytics and statistics to use

    - Utilize descriptive statistics

    - Assess patterns and trends

    - Perform diagnostic analytics

    - Probe for causality

    - Draw inferences and conclusions

- **Apply advanced analytics**: This competency encompasses techniques for applying advanced analytics, including statistics and math, predictive analytics, and machine learning.

- **Communicate data and insights**: This competency encompasses approaches to visualize and verbalize data and insights. This includes choosing the most appropriate visualization type, based on the question being asked and the data used, as well as being able to explain the results of statistics and other analytics to non-technical stakeholders.

The outcome of this phase is insights. Insights are visualized and verbalized in a way that the relevant stakeholders can properly interpret what the insights mean.

Validating the insights

This phase is where individuals apply the human element of working with data to make decisions. Now the analysis is complete and the insights are compiled. But the data you have been processing only means so much in isolation. Before using those insights to make any decisions, it's crucial to consider the skills and mindsets required to *interpret* and *validate* the insights before drawing a conclusion. This starts with the following:

1. Interpreting analytic results

2. Challenging your assumptions

3. Mitigating fallacies and bias

4. Understanding the implications and consequences of your insights

5. Examining additional perspectives

It's important for organizations to understand how the insights they have uncovered could be misleading if taken out of context before considering the final course of action.

To carry out this phase effectively, it's important to be confident when interpreting data – whether visualized or verbalized – to identify a course of action. Issues of data provenance, such as understanding ethical issues and possible bias, are also crucial to ensure any assumptions are challenged.

This phase includes two competencies – interpret and analyze results, and validate the thought process:

- **Interpret and analyze results**: This competency encompasses the interpretation of the results of analysis and the insights gleaned from them. This includes *interpreting the results of a statistical experiment, interpreting the results of various data analyses,* and *interpreting data visualizations and verbalized data.* These topics include not only an understanding of statistical terminology such as statistical significance but also of how to avoid various biases and fallacies related to interpreting results.

- **Validate the thought process**: After you interpret and analyze the results, you need to validate your thought process. This is useful so you do not jump to poorly supported conclusions due to a cognitive bias or an incorrect assumption. This includes the ability to *challenge your assumptions*, as well as the ability to apply techniques to *mitigate any fallacies and biases* you may have in your thought process.

The outcome of this phase is insights that are validated and can be used to make decisions. There are times when the actions in this phase uncover some incorrect challenges or bias that was not mitigated. In those cases, the organization goes back to the previous phase to refine the insights provided.

Transforming insights into decisions

Now that the insights have been validated, this phase is where the insights are used to draw conclusions and make a decision. The insights themselves will not make the decision. To do that, the decision maker needs to understand the insights and how they work to help make the decision, focusing on things such as the possible decisions and outcomes, what elements are risk and what are uncertainty, and the ethical considerations with the decision.

This phase includes one competency: **draw conclusions**. Drawing valid conclusions from the insights obtained through the analytic process requires you to *identify possible courses of action* to take, *understand whether there are any ethical implications, consider all the other potential implications* from drawing this conclusion, and factor in *how you dealt with any uncertainty within the data*. This includes understanding how to take analytic results into the decision-making process and how to draw sound conclusions based on a combination of the results of the analysis and your experiences.

The outcome of this phase is commonly a decision or a set of decisions. There are times when the actions in this phase uncover that more information is needed to make a decision. In those cases, the organization goes back to a previous phase, potentially the acquiring relevant data phase.

Communicating decisions with data

Despite all the work and time invested so far, it means nothing if you can't create the *arguments* needed to communicate data-based decisions. All stakeholders impacted by the decision need to understand and support the results that led to the conclusion that was made. There is a range of skills and mindsets required to be successful here, including how to identify the right stakeholders, how to verbalize the decisions and actions, and how to effectively use visualizations to share the data insights in a tangible and accessible way.

This phase includes two competencies – identify stakeholders and communicate decisions:

- **Identify stakeholders**: Before you can communicate your decisions, you need to identify and understand all of the stakeholders related to this decision. This includes the ability to conduct a stakeholder analysis.

- **Communicate decisions**: Once you identify the stakeholders, you need to be able to present the insights and decisions to those stakeholders with an easy-to-understand approach. This includes the ability to explain the results using data visualizations but also creating a narrative that engages the stakeholders and persuades them to act, including tailoring the message specifically to each stakeholder group.

The outcome of this phase is that all relevant stakeholders have communicated any decisions in the right way so that they can understand the decision, and will be on board with any changes required as a result.

Evaluating the outcome of a decision

Finally, no good process is complete without an evaluation phase, and that is no different for data analysis, to consider the impact and effectiveness of the decision after it has been acted on. This includes ensuring there were no unintended consequences and that the outcomes were positive in addressing the question or problem at hand. If the results were unexpected, it's important to reassess the information used and whether any of it could have been missing or misleading in such a way that prevented a more informed decision.

This phase includes two competencies – measure and evaluate results and reassess your thoughts:

- **Measure and evaluate results**: This competency includes the ability to perform an evaluation of the results of the decision to be able to determine its effectiveness. This includes the ability to quantify the effectiveness and impact of the decision.

- **Reassess your thoughts**: If the decision was not what was expected, this competency focuses on the ability to reassess your thoughts to be open-minded to learning from the mistakes and updating your decision.

The outcome of this phase may be that no action needs to be taken. However, even if the decision did make a positive impact, it is still important to follow these steps to see whether the process could be improved. As we mentioned earlier in the book, just because a decision has a positive impact, it does not mean it was the right decision. It is equally important to review and assess the process used, rather than just assessing the impact of the decision.

Understanding data

Understanding data is a foundational competency within data literacy. This means that it applies to all the various stages in the process, and is not limited to just one. No matter what role you are in or in what stage of the process you interact with data, everyone should strive to have an understanding of data. This entails being able to identify the type of data (qualitative or quantitative), the classification of data (nominal, ordinal, interval, or ratio), various data properties (such as whether it is discrete or continuous), and various descriptive measurements (such as central tendency and dispersion). This also includes the ability to understand statistical terminology, including identifying real statistics versus speculative statistics.

A visual representation of the data literacy competency framework, which lists each competency and sub-competency organized by the stage in the process, is shown in *Figure 11.2*:

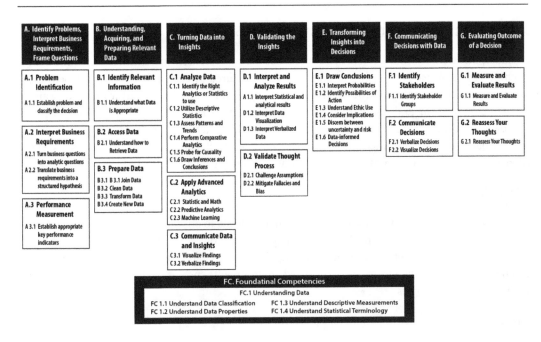

Figure 11.2 – Data literacy competency framework

Now that we have introduced the data literacy competency framework phases, let's move on to learn about the specific hard skills, soft skills, and mindsets that are included in the framework.

Data literacy skills

Current decision-making in business suffers from insight gaps. Organizations invest in data and analytics, hoping that will provide them with insights that they can use to make decisions, but in reality, there are many challenges and obstacles that get in the way of that process. One of the biggest challenges is that these organizations tend to focus on technology and hard skills only. They are definitely important, but you will not automatically get insights and better decisions with hard skills alone. Using data to make better data-informed decisions requires not only hard skills but also soft skills as well as mindsets.

When trying to find insights in your data, you need to use some technical skills such as **data extraction** and **data preparation**, as well as **data analytics** and **data visualization**, but if you are not critically challenging your insights to avoid any bias or incorrect assumptions, or if you are not actively listening to your colleagues' perspectives, you could end up inferring the wrong conclusion. This section will focus on identifying the technical skills, soft skills, and mindsets that are relevant to the data literacy competency framework.

Identifying data literacy technical skills

Individuals that want to embrace data literacy and use the competencies just mentioned require a set of technical skills. As we previously discussed, the skills required by each individual vary depending on their role in the data analysis process. These skills range from being able to start with raw data and then extract, transform, and standardize it, to skills related to performing analytics to find insights in the data. The set of technical skills we will discuss includes data extraction, data preparation, data analytics, data visualization, AI/ML, data science, interpreting statistical and analytical results, UX design, communicating with data, and understanding and using data effectively.

Data extraction

When an organization has an analytical question that it needs to answer, the key is understanding what data has information that will aid in answering that question. After the data is identified, it will need to be extracted and retrieved to be analyzed. This process can range from loading data from Excel files to extracting data from more advanced environments such as cloud service providers or data streaming technologies.

Data preparation

Data in its raw form is rarely ever ready to be analyzed. It is easier, and more robust, to store data in its raw form, and then prepare it for your analysis later. For example, if your organization works on wind turbines, you will most likely store measurements of the wind turbine speed as they are recorded. However, based on various questions you need to answer, you may need to aggregate the speeds, to show the daily average, weekly average, or similar. These tasks of aggregating the data, or potentially organizing it, cleaning it, and standardizing it, can take up to 80 percent of the total time spent making data-informed decisions. This shows how absolutely important it is that organizations have the right skills to not only be able to clean, transform, profile, tag, catalog, and standardize data, but also to know specifically which of those options are required based on the data you have, and the questions that are being asked.

Data analytics

Data analytics is used in the process of turning data into insights. It is not about finding questions but finding answers and gaining actionable insights for problems that we know or questions that we already have. Data analytics is the discipline used when you have an existing analytical question, such as *"What was the conversion percentage from our marketing campaign this quarter, compared to this quarter last year?"*

Data analytics often involves using descriptive analytic and diagnostic analytic capabilities.

Data visualization

A key component of data analytics is also data visualization. We separate those skills here because data visualizations are not only useful when you are trying to transform data into insights, but also when you are trying to communicate those insights and decisions to others. Data visualization is the process of putting data and information into a visual form. Using visuals over text aids in many ways, including how to analyze, interpret, and eventually communicate the insights.

Data science

Data science, much like data literacy, has had multiple definitions over the years. In this book, we will define it as a larger umbrella of disciplines including data analytics, data mining, machine learning, probability, predictive modeling, and much more. We separate data analytics from the preceding definition as the skill of data analytics can be applied independently through the process.

The main difference between data analytics and data science is that the purpose of data science is to uncover insights and patterns, typically from very large datasets. These patterns and insights are for problems that we do not currently know. Data analytics, on the other hand, is typically used when there is a need to find insights and answers to already existing and known questions. Both disciplines are part of the same phase in the process, transforming data into insights, but tackle the situation differently based on whether there is an existing analytics question that needs an answer or not.

Common foundational skills that data science requires are a working knowledge of applying statistics, using calculus and algebra, as well as machine learning.

Artificial intelligence and machine learning

Artificial intelligence and machine learning are also commonly included under the definition of data science, but we will separate those skills here. Data science typically deals with the process of processing, analyzing, and visualizing large amounts of data to find patterns and then make predictions from them. Artificial intelligence, on the other hand, deals with implementing predictive models to forecast future events. Data science uses statistical algorithms and techniques, and artificial intelligence generally uses computer algorithms.

Machine learning is a subset of artificial intelligence. It takes artificial intelligence one step further because its performance improves over time as it is exposed to more and more data. The goal of machine learning is for the algorithm to continue to learn and improve its decision-making without any alteration.

Let's take a look at a simplified process for machine learning:

1. The first step is determining what situation you are trying to decide on or predict and then choosing a machine learning algorithm to make the decision. For example, assume a bank wants to decide whether or not it should provide a loan to a loan applicant. The algorithm chosen to help with this decision is a logistic regression algorithm (which is used to analyze multiple variables and determine whether the bank should provide the loan). This algorithm will try to predict whether a loan applicant would default on their loan.

2. The second step in machine learning is to acquire the data. In our bank example, the bank would acquire all the historic data it has on the people who did receive a loan and whether or not they defaulted.

3. The next step is to run the algorithm using the data. In our example, the bank will then run the logistic regression using the data to determine the variables from the data that best predict whether the loan will default. When the bank does that, it will then have a model it can use with future loan applicants.

Using machine learning, the bank's algorithm will continuously try to evaluate and improve this model, even after it is in production.

Interpreting statistical and analytical results

While individuals who are trying to make decisions based on insights obtained by others do not need to have technical skills such as data analytics and data science, they do need to be able to interpret the results of the statistics, analytics, and visuals used. These individuals need knowledge of key statistical figures such as mean values and percentages, and their significance and limitations. They need to be knowledgeable about statistical terminology to be able to properly interpret the results of a statistical experiment. They also need to be knowledgeable in the business related to the questions being asked. This contextual information is critical for interpreting the results and trying to make decisions from them.

Data communication

Communicating with data, as discussed in greater detail in *Chapter 10, Turning Insights into Decisions*, is a vital skill that applies across multiple stages of the process. Communicating with data is commonly done using an approach called analytic storytelling. Analytic storytelling helps bring data to life using a combination of data, visualizations, and a narrative. This skill requires you to do all this at the right level. You do not want to overwhelm or bore your audience, but you also do not want to overload them with information. You should not only present the data but also add it in the appropriate context.

Understanding and using data effectively

As we previously discussed, the technical skills required by each individual vary depending on their role in the data analysis process. However, all skills and mindsets are underpinned by a core understanding of data. No matter at what phase in the process, everyone interacting with data should have this baseline understanding – including which properties and classifications the data represents (such as quantitative or qualitative), as well as the various levels of measurement of data (nominal, ordinal, interval, and ratio). With these skills, anyone can apply themselves to any phase of the broader process.

Figure 11.3 highlights the technical skills we just discussed and parts of the process they are relevant to:

	Understanding, Acquiring, and Preparing Relevant Data	Transforming Data into Insights	Transforming Insights into Decisions	Communicating Decisions with Data
Data Extraction	▓			
Data Prep	▓			
Data Analytics		▓		
Data Visualization		▓		▓
AI/ML		▓		
Data Science		▓		
Data Communication		▓	▓	▓
Interpreting Statistical and Analytical Results		▓	▓	▓
UX Design		▓		▓
Understanding and Using Data Effectively	▓	▓	▓	▓

Figure 11.3 – Data literacy technical skills

Data literacy soft skills

Soft skills are critically important to individuals who want to become data literate. Soft skills are personal habits or traits that shape how an individual works and how the individual works with others. These are required skills to be able to think critically and look past symptoms to find the root causes of problems. Soft skills are required for individuals to work collaboratively to gain valuable insights by leveraging relationship building and active listening. Finally, these skills are required in order to transform data into stories that are memorable and that engage and persuade an organization's stakeholders and help them understand the decisions being made. These soft skills can be organized into four categories: understanding complex situations, teamwork and collaboration, adapting to change, and fundamental soft skills that are useful in all stages of the process.

A visual depiction of the various soft skills related to data literacy competencies is shown in *Figure 11.4*:

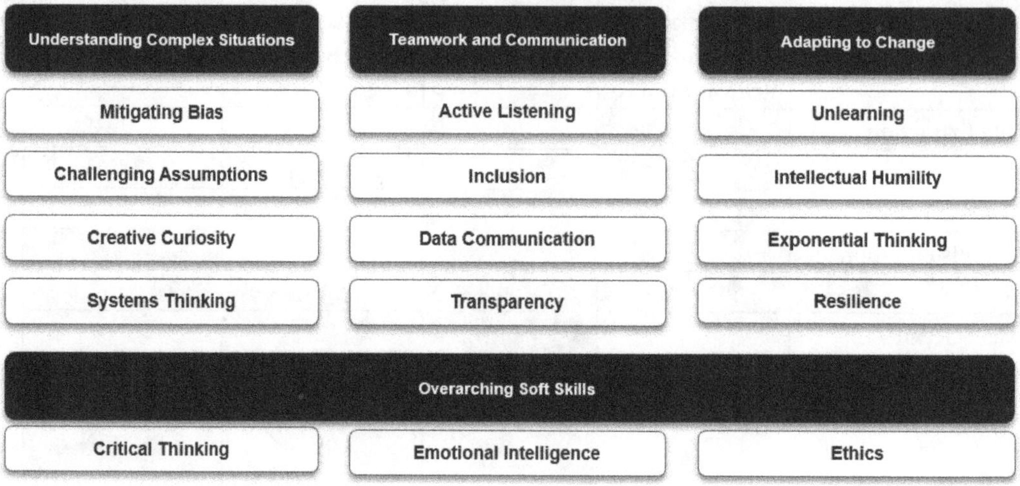

Understanding Complex Situations	Teamwork and Communication	Adapting to Change
Mitigating Bias	Active Listening	Unlearning
Challenging Assumptions	Inclusion	Intellectual Humility
Creative Curiosity	Data Communication	Exponential Thinking
Systems Thinking	Transparency	Resilience

Overarching Soft Skills		
Critical Thinking	Emotional Intelligence	Ethics

Figure 11.4 – Data literacy soft skills

These soft skills are not directly mapped to the seven-phase process as they are skills that apply to all phases of the process.

Understanding complex situations

While advances in automation and artificial intelligence have made it possible to automate more and more tasks previously accomplished by humans, machines still are way behind humans in the ability to apply logic, reasoning, understanding, and their experiences, as well as in their ability to leverage emotional and social skills. Therefore, understanding tasks such as how to mitigate bias and challenge assumptions, while maintaining creative curiosity and thinking systemically, will ensure that we can dig deeper into the story that data is telling us.

Mitigating bias

As discussed in *Chapter 8, Questioning the Data*, all human decision-making is susceptible to implicit bias, which can cause you to make less than rational decisions. We must learn about strategies to prevent those biases from negatively impacting our perspectives and decisions.

Challenging assumptions

As discussed in *Chapter 8, Questioning the Data*, our brains are all hard-wired to make assumptions. Challenging those assumptions is critical to understanding the true context and what the information is really trying to say.

Creative curiosity

The most important question we can ask is "*Why?*" This is how we all learn. However, we are always taught there is only one right answer, so we tend to stop looking for alternatives and we tend to stop asking why. In today's world, sometimes our culture puts a higher premium on answers rather than questions. It is no longer good enough to just be able to absorb information. It is about having the creative curiosity to ask questions and connect those questions and answers to what is important. This requires people to look for possible alternatives and answers, and look for different perspectives to gain a thorough understanding of the system.

Living in today's world, we are seeing tremendous innovation. Each cycle of innovation is more material than the last and closer together in time. The pattern is exponential. As this trend continues, and jobs continue to evolve, our creativity and curiosity will become our greatest asset. In a world where change is the only constant aspect, the ability to thrive in ambiguity, see around the corners, learn constantly, imagine a future, and then go and create it is key.

The reason we couple creativity and curiosity together is that we really need both. If someone was curious and not creative, they would want to come up with alternatives but would fail to do so. Whereas if someone was creative and not curious, they would be able to come up with obvious explanations and alternatives for problems with data, but they would not be able to think outside the box to help carry out real root-cause analysis into what is happening. There are always alternative ideas and approaches out there, but if we are not curious enough to find them or notice them, we will never use them.

Systems thinking

According to management consultant W. Edwards Deming, "*94 percent of problems in business are systems-driven, and only 6 percent are people-driven.*" Systems thinking is a different way of thinking that is useful when trying to manage complex problems. A basic principle is viewing a problem holistically in order to see connections and relationships that are not obvious. When applying systems thinking to problems, it helps us identify root causes versus just symptoms of the problems. In addition, thinking systemically also helps with organizational sensitivity. That is, being able to recognize the influence and consequences of a decision and how that impacts the rest of the organization.

Teamwork and communication

We have said repeatedly that data literacy is a team sport. The seven phases described earlier in the book and earlier in this chapter are typically not accomplished by the same individuals. The output from one phase is passed in as input to the next phase. Therefore, it is absolutely essential that all individuals have the ability to understand what stakeholders really want. This is where "forever skills" such as active listening, inclusion, and communicating with data come into play.

Active listening

Throughout all the phases in the process described, individuals are exposed to data and information. It could be raw data, requirements, insights, or even feedback. All individuals will take that data and information and try to apply meaning to it, and eventually draw a conclusion from it. That meaning is strongly influenced based on our own cultural and personal perspectives and experiences. This is why it is essential to actively listen to other individuals to ensure you hear their perspectives and experiences, as they may give you a better picture of the situation and lead you toward making a better decision.

Active listening involves a person not only listening to what another person is saying but also consciously making an effort to listen to the complete message being communicated. This involves paying attention and not being distracted or losing focus or interest in what the other person is saying.

Inclusion

We discussed the power of inclusion back in *Chapter 7, Designing Dashboards and Reports* when we introduced Scott E. Page and his book *The Difference*. As a reminder, Page highlights that

"Diversity trumps ability: diverse groups generally do better than 'high-ability' groups at problem-solving or prediction. These are not political statements; they are mathematical truths".

Data communication

Communicating with data was mentioned earlier under the *Technical skills* section. It is also listed here, as it has components that are technical and components that leverage soft skills. For example, the ability to select the appropriate data and create the most appropriate visualization for the stakeholders are technical skills. But the ability to create a narrative that is memorable, engaging, and persuasive requires this soft skill.

Transparency and accountability

Transparency may appear as an odd fit to be included in a data literacy book, but it is not. Transparency, along with accountability, helps decision-makers make clear and consistent decisions. Decision-makers using data should be open about not only the data they are using but also the question or problem they are trying to solve, as well as the decision itself. Transparency helps teach everyone on the team that they can trust each other to help provide insights into the decision and that decision-making is a team sport.

Adapting to change

The world continues to rapidly evolve and technology is constantly changing the way we work. What is required to stay up to date is not just learning the latest technology, but the ability to unlearn outdated ones, and to be resilient and adapt to the changes. This year, "forever skills" such as unlearning, intellectual humility, and exponential thinking, will become more valuable as we evolve our skillsets to meet the demands of a changing world.

Although we are sometimes presented with too much information, becoming data literate enables us to distinguish between signals and noise, as well as anticipate and evaluate incoming and current realities. As we've discussed, this isn't necessarily just about nurturing technical skills – developing the forever skills outlined here can be just as valuable when data is so ubiquitous.

Unlearning

Futurist Alvin Toffler once said:

The illiterate of the 21st century will not be those who cannot read and write, but those who cannot learn, unlearn, and relearn.

As we go through life learning new concepts, behind the scenes, our brains are always trying to connect these new concepts to the old ones we already know. This works really well when we are continuing to learn about the same concepts, just adding more advanced approaches.

But when learning about new concepts that contradict previous knowledge, our brains make it hard to forget the old, outdated knowledge. The practice of unlearning helps us discard something from our memory. This is very similar to how people try to unlearn bad habits, except in this case, it is not necessarily a bad habit, but rather an outdated skill or outdated mental model.

Sounds simple, right? Not really. In a famous experiment, engineer Destin Sandlin attempted to ride a backward bike. A backward bike is one on which the handlebars turn the bike in the opposite direction. Turning the bars to the left will turn the bike to the right, and vice versa. It took Destin over 8 months of riding the backward bike for 5 minutes each day before he was able to ride it without falling off. What is interesting is that after he mastered this skill, he was no longer able to ride a normal bike.

This example highlights that when change happens, some mental models that were accurate before the change will now be obsolete. In those scenarios, we have to unlearn the old mental models before we can learn about the new way forward. The example also highlights that unlearning an older mental model—even when the person is aware it needs to be done—takes time.

Intellectual humility

Intellectual humility is the recognition that the things you believe in might in fact be wrong. Not knowing the scope of our ignorance is part of the human condition. The ability to be aware of what we do not know and our ignorance and admit when we are wrong is a critical skill to allow you to move past it and come up with additional suggestions or decisions.

When an individual truly embraces data literacy, they are embracing intellectual humility, where decisions are not always made by the most senior person in the room or based on a "hunch" but by a collective exploration of the facts and figures.

Exponential thinking

You may be familiar with Moore's law, which states computer processes will continue to exponentially increase in capacity, by doubling every two years. Well, the same holds true for many other modern technologies such as storage, bandwidth, the Internet of Things, artificial intelligence, blockchains, and machine learning, just to name a few.

While all this technology is great, the majority of digital transformation projects fail to meet expectations. In fact, some reports highlight as many as 90% fail. Why? Obviously, it's complex and there are multiple reasons, but one common theme is that organizations struggle because they believe the technology alone will deliver exponential results.

While the world is evolving at an exponential rate, we are trained to think linearly and incrementally. Exponential thinking is hard. As Albert Einstein once famously said,

We cannot solve our problems with the same thinking we used when we created them.

When you have exponential technology but apply incremental thinking, organizations only end up with incremental results.

What does this mean for us as an organization and as leaders? For breakthrough results, we do not need to just change what we do, but we need to change and evolve how we think. Just take a look at how things have changed due to the COVID-19 pandemic. Estimates say it brought us forward around 10 years in digital transformation and required all of us to think outside the box to learn how to work in this new era.

Resilience

Today's world is **volatile**, **uncertain**, **complex**, and **ambiguous (VUCA)**. Not only is it VUCA, but it is constantly VUCA. Humans are wired for fight-or-flight reactions, which are short-term responses to crises or change. In today's world, this is not short-term, it is long-term and chronic. It is easy to get overwhelmed. Resilience helps us maintain balance long-term while at the same time embracing change so that we can keep positive and turn challenges into opportunities and successes.

Resilience is an individual's ability to adapt to various changes that cause some adversity. When someone is resilient, they not only adapt to those changes, but they learn and grow and improve from their experiences going through the change. Some people believe that individuals either have resilience or don't, but it has been proven scientifically that it is a skill that can be learned, developed, and improved.

Foundational soft skills

In addition to the soft skills just mentioned, there are also three foundational soft skills. These are considered foundational soft skills because they are useful across all the various phases in the process. These skills are critical thinking, emotional intelligence, and ethics.

Critical thinking

Decision-makers are constantly provided data in the form of numbers or insights, or similar. The challenge is that we tend to believe every number or piece of data we hear, especially when it comes from a trusted source. However, even if the source is trusted and the data is correct, insights from the data are created when we put it in context and apply meaning to it. This means that we may have put incorrect meaning to the data and then made decisions based on that, which is not ideal. This is why anyone involved in the process needs to have the skills to think critically about the data, to try to understand the context, and to understand the complexity of the situation where the answer is not limited to just one specific thing. Critical thinking allows individuals to assess limitations of what was presented, as well as mitigate any cognitive bias that they may have.

While we will not provide exhaustive coverage on critical thinking as a foundational soft skill, it is important to understand where in the process critical thinking skills should be applied. Toward that end, *Figure 11.5* lists the various critical thinking skills and what phases of the process they are relevant to:

	Identifying Problems and Interpreting Requirements	Understanding, Acquiring, and Preparing Relevant Data	Transforming Data into Insights	Transforming Insights into Decisions	Communicating Decisions with Data	Evaluating Outcomes of Decisions
Questioning	█					
Observation		█				
Analysis			█	█		
Numeracy			█			
Interpretation				█		
Reasoning				█		
Inference				█		
Evaluation				█		
Explanation					█	
Reflection						█

Figure 11.5 – Critical thinking components

Let's next move on to **emotional intelligence**.

Emotional intelligence

Emotional intelligence is a set of competencies, or abilities, in how an individual is aware of themselves, manages themselves, has confidence in their abilities and inherent value, is aware of others, manages their relationships with others, and accepts and values others. This skill involves an individual understanding the meaning of their emotions and feelings and how they affect other people.

As mentioned in the definition, there are six components of emotional intelligence. Those components are split between how an individual is aware of their own emotions, and how they are aware of others' emotions. They are also split between their behavior, feelings, and attitudes (see *Figure 11.6*):

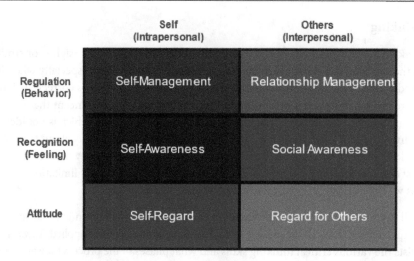

Figure 11.6 – Emotional intelligence components

We won't dive deep into all six components but we want to dive into one to highlight why this skill is critical for data-literate individuals. Consider relationship management, which is an individual's interpersonal skills and social effectiveness. Decisions should consider multiple perspectives from other people. This requires decision-makers to collaborate with others in order to explain the situation and obtain their perspectives. That collaboration depends on the quality of the relationships between the individuals as they work through the process together. This skill is not just useful in the final decision-making phase. It is also required for gathering requirements, coming up with the right analytical questions, identifying and communicating with stakeholders, and gathering feedback from stakeholders to assess the decision.

Emotionally intelligent individuals have various traits and skills that help them manage situations that come up. That list is organized by the six components just introduced (see *Figure 11.7*):

Self-Awareness	Self-Management	Self-Regard	Social Awareness	Relationship Management	Regard for Others
Openness	Impulse Control	Self-Confidence	Empathy	Accountability	Flexibility
Self-Knowledge	Resilience	Self-Respect	Awareness	Conflict Management	Interdependence
Integrity	Stress Tolerance	Optimism	Anticipation	Influence	trustworthiness
Introspection	Authenticity	Motivation	Mindfulness	Emotional Stability	Collaboration

Figure 11.7 – Emotional intelligence traits and skills

Ethics

Ethics is another critical soft skill when it comes to data literacy that needs to be developed. How can you work to ethically collect, store, and use data? What considerations do you have to make in your decision-making process about the ethical use of the data? These topics and more are discussed in great detail in *Chapter 9, Handling Data Responsibly*.

Data literacy mindsets

One of Amazon's 14 leadership principles is to "dive deep" and to remain skeptical until you can validate an opinion with data. We are best served (in life and in our jobs) when we make decisions based on data. If you can't quantify it, it's hard to leave your implicit bias out of the decisions (our implicit bias is often in our blind spot).

But, even when you base decisions on data, you need to ask these questions:

- Are you sure you are using the right data?

- Are you sure you are asking the right questions about the data?

- Are you sure you are challenging any assumptions you have of the data?

- Are you sure you have enough context from the data to ensure it is not telling you only part of the story?

Data literacy is more about obtaining a new mindset than anything else. Sure, there are tools and technologies that will make us more data literate. And those are critical. But we are in need of a mind shift as we transition from the information age to the knowledge age. In the information age, many have the belief that some data is better than none. In reality, some data can be very harmful.

As we move to the knowledge age, we need to think critically about data and information. We need to understand what data is relevant and what is not. We need to learn how to interpret the results to avoid any implicit bias. Data needs to become a native language. If someone says something we think is incorrect or misleading, we need to question it. We need to be open to being wrong and have the intellectual humility to admit that and explore alternatives. We need to not play it safe and avoid failure.

So, how can we best achieve this new mindset? We need to learn not only about the right data and analytic best practices and leverage the right tools and technologies, but we also need to have a data-informed mindset that shifts us from just looking for data and information to looking for insights and knowledge. This new mindset is a combination of three established mindsets: the growth mindset, open mindset, and promotion mindset (see *Figure 11.8*):

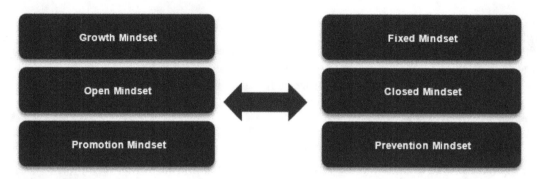

Figure 11.8 – Data literacy mindsets

Growth mindset

Individuals with growth mindsets believe that our abilities and understanding can be developed over time. Individuals are eager to learn, adapt to new situations, and embrace challenges. The opposite end of this spectrum is a fixed mindset. Individuals with fixed mindsets believe that our abilities and understanding are relatively fixed.

A growth mindset is essential for anyone who wants to be data literate. In today's world, we are constantly disrupted by technological innovation and advancements. We learn one way to work, and then a new technology forces us to unlearn and learn a new skill. This requires not only resilience but also an appetite to learn and adapt with the mindset to believe that we can. If an individual working with data did not have a growth mindset, they would more likely fail to see other perspectives than their current one, and would likely not learn about any of the latest technology and innovation that helps them with their data.

Open mindset

An open mindset is related to a growth mindset but different in one key area. Whereas a growth mindset relates to the degree that we believe our abilities and understanding can be developed, an open mindset relates to the degree that our minds are open to new ideas and suggestions. Individuals with an open mindset are willing to consider other perspectives and try out new experiences.

The opposite end of the spectrum is a closed mindset. Individuals with a closed mindset believe that they know what is best, are fearful of being wrong, and want to be seen as the authority on a given topic. When individuals have a closed mindset, it can result in an increase in bias in their thinking process, and it can also suppress the perspectives of others around them.

When it comes to data literacy, being intellectually humble and inclusive while being open to the perspectives of others is important. Not only are individuals with an open mindset open to different perspectives, but they also actively seek them out for fear of missing important information. In addition, being able to work in new environments and new experiences and challenges is critical, given the state of evolution and change we are facing in today's workplace.

Promotion mindset

A promotion mindset is related to the degree to which an individual orientates their goals around trying new things, advancing their values, and working outside of their comfort zone. The opposite end of the spectrum is a prevention mindset. Individuals with a prevention mindset focus more on meeting their responsibilities while taking as few risks as possible. They focus on trying to avoid mistakes and problems. That may sound like a positive thing, but due to that mindset, those individuals tend to operate in a way to intentionally avoid difficulties. As we have learned, a data-literate individual should embrace failure as a learning opportunity. They should strive to innovate and evolve, which is only possible when you are open to going beyond the status quo and taking some risks. Obviously, individuals need to weigh the risk assessment properly, so a promotion mindset does not mean blindly taking unnecessary risks all the time. Rather, it means the opposite – not blindly ignoring any potential risk all the time.

Summary

While many people are familiar with the term **data literacy**, very few are sure what competencies are related to data literacy, and even fewer people are aware of which of those competencies are relevant to their role. Individuals and organizations alike all highlight the importance of data literacy, but few have offered targeted data literacy education. Part of the reason for this is it is a combination of technical skills and soft skills, as well as mindsets, and those components are not typically taught together.

In this chapter, we defined what a data literacy competency framework is as well as what skills and mindsets are relevant for each competency. We also learned which of the seven phases of the process of interacting with data each competency falls under. This is important as it gives a structured framework to learn from. You can now understand which competencies are relevant to your role with data, and start finding relevant training courses or similar content.

In the next chapter, we will learn how we can assess our data literacy against these competencies at an individual level, as well as at an organizational level.

References

1. Armand Ruiz, *The 80/20 Data Science Dilemma*, (InfoWorld, September 26, 2017).

2. W. Edwards Deming, *Out of the Crisis* (Cambridge, Massachusetts: The MIT Press, 2018).

3. Scott E. Page, *The Difference: How the Power of Diversity Creates Better Groups, Firms, Schools, and Societies* (Princeton, NJ: Princeton University Press, 2008).

12
Assessing Your Data Literacy Maturity

As you've seen throughout this book, data literacy is both an individual construct and an organizational one. There is a common misconception about data literacy and data-informed decision-making that it is mostly focused on learning the right tools and using the right technologies. However, there is much more that is required. Even with the best data strategy and the right tools, it still requires the people who make the decisions to turn the data and insights into good decisions. That process requires a combination of skills and mindsets.

On top of that, organizations are looking to leverage data to drive transformation and modernization to help them get closer and adapt to their customer's needs, as well as obtain and sustain a competitive advantage. They cannot do this just by having an army of data-literate individuals. The organization requires the right strategy and processes, the right tools, and, of utmost importance, the right culture to support and foster data literacy.

Throughout this book, we have provided details about what makes organizations and individuals more data literate, and how you can increase your data literacy. However, to track your progress, you should start by assessing your current level, and then use that assessment to understand what competencies or programs to focus on next.

This chapter will introduce how you can assess your data literacy skills and then how to interpret the results of that assessment to personalize your educational journey. It will also cover how you can assess the maturity of your organization's data literacy to learn where and how you can improve.

The following topics will be covered in this chapter:

- Assessing individual data literacy
- Assessing organizational data literacy

Assessing individual data literacy

As per our belief, data literacy is not one-size-fits-all. Not only is it specific to the role that you play with data, but there are also different levels. Therefore, a single data literacy assessment that is used by everyone, regardless of their level or how they interact with data, is not practical or useful. Assessing someone's skills around preparing data is not relevant to a person whose role with data involves only reviewing insights generated by others.

However, it is very useful for people new to data literacy to have a simple way to assess their foundational data literacy skills and mindsets, regardless of what role they play with data. In this chapter, we will provide you with such an assessment. In the end, we will provide you with a link to a more robust assessment you can complete online if you want to go deeper.

This 22-question self-assessment, shown in *Figure 12.1*, can be completed in about 15 minutes. For each statement listed, you should score it between 1 and 5 using the following descriptions:

1. Strongly disagree with the statement (1 point)

2. Slightly disagree with the statement (2 points)

3. Neither agree nor disagree with the statement (3 points)

4. Slightly agree with the statement (4 points)

5. Strongly agree with the statement (5 points)

Understand Data	
This section assesses how well you understand raw data, including its type, classification, and any properties, as well as how well you understand the simple statistical terminology of various descriptive statistics, as discussed in *Chapter 2, Unfolding Your Data Journey*.	
1	Can identify whether data is qualitative or quantitative.
2	Can identify what level of measurement (nominal, ordinal, interval, ratio) a given piece of data has.
3	Can identify whether data is discrete or continuous.
4	Can understand simple statistical terminology and interpret the results of simple descriptive stats such as distributions, frequencies, ranks, percentiles, means, medians, modes, ranges, standard deviation, and interquartile ranges.
5	Can apply means, medians, and modes and how to choose the right one based on the data and the question.
6	Can identify data security, data privacy, and data ethics concerns related to the data being used.

Interpret Business Requirements

This section assesses how well you can understand the question being asked, identify relevant data, and how you can create proper **key performance indicators (KPIs)**, as discussed in *Chapter 6, Aligning with Organizational Goals*, and *Chapter 10, Turning Insights into Decisions*.

7	Can transform a business problem into a quantifiable form as an analytics question.
8	Can create KPIs that adhere to the characteristics of a KPI.
9	Can identify whether data is relevant or not relevant to the decision to be made.

Create and Interpret Data Visualizations

This section assesses how well you can both create and interpret data visualizations. Given this is a basic foundational data literacy assessment, the focus is only on basic visualizations, as discussed in *Chapter 8, Questioning the Data*.

10	Can select and create a basic visualization.
11	Can apply appropriate design components of visualizations, including the use of color, annotations, and preattentive attributes.
12	Can understand what information a basic visualization is meant to convey.
13	Can identify and describe simple patterns and trends in a visualization.

Apply the Human Element of Data Literacy

This section assesses how well you understand cognitive bias and its impact on your perspective of data and information, as well as how well you can identify and apply techniques to mitigate the impact of bias, as discussed in Chapter 7.

| 14 | Can describe cognitive biases and how they can impact interpreting data and insights. |
| 15 | Can apply techniques to help mitigate cognitive bias. |

Communicate with Data

This section assesses how well you can communicate insights and decisions using data, as discussed in Chapter 10.

| 16 | Can determine the appropriate method and mechanism for communicating the decision. |

Mindsets

This section assesses whether you have the right mindset to work with data.

17	Willingness to ask additional and clarifying questions.
18	Openness to new insights, even if they contradict your previous convictions.
19	Willingness to question your contextual knowledge and its influence on the interpretation of the data and insights.

20	Openness to the fact that your interpretation of the data and insights may be influenced by cognitive bias.
21	Willingness to question the significance of the results for the data or insights presented.
22	Objectivity in representing data, including no conscious manipulation to misrepresent the information to consumers.
TOTAL (Add up all the scores from above)	

Figure 12.1 – Foundational data literacy assessment

You can use the table shown in *Figure 12.2* to assess your foundational data literacy based on your total score:

Total Score	Foundational Data Literacy
0-44	You need to work on multiple skills and mindsets to increase your foundational data literacy.
45-69	You have some foundational data literacy skills, but still have a way to go to become foundationally data literate.
70-94	You have a majority of the foundational data literacy skills, but there is still room for growth in a few areas.
95-110	You have optimized all the foundational data literate skills. Congratulations! You can now look at the next level and grow from foundational skills to more intermediate and mastery levels.

Figure 12.2 – Foundational data literacy assessment scoring

If you are looking at areas to improve your data literacy, start by focusing on the statements and categories where you answered below a 4 or 5. Ideally, you should strive to have a score of either 4 or 5 for all of these 25 statements.

If you are interested in either a more comprehensive individual assessment that covers all roles, or if you are looking at going beyond foundational data literacy to more intermediate and advanced levels, then this is available at http://www.kevinhanegan.com/dataLiteracyAssessment.

This assessment leverages the following seven phases of how data is interacted with, from raw data to the decision being made with the data:

- Identifying problems, interpreting business requirements, and framing questions

- Understanding, acquiring, and preparing the relevant data

- Turning data into insights

- Validating the insights

- Transforming insights into decisions

- Communicating decisions

- Evaluating the outcomes of decisions

In this comprehensive assessment, you must select which parts of the data journey relate to your role. Then, you will be asked to complete the assessment for those related competencies out of the total 16 competencies and 37 sub-competencies. You will get results that show you your data literacy level for those competencies, with recommendations on areas you can work on.

Assessing organizational data literacy

There are 2 options for anyone looking to perform an organizational data literacy assessment. We have a simple 16-question assessment that you can use to get an understanding of where your organization is in terms data literacy, and we have a more robust assessment organized into 5 dimensions and 25 subdimensions. This chapter will introduce you to both assessments.

Basic organizational data literacy assessment

This 16-question assessment, shown in *Figure 12.3*, can be completed in about 10 to 15 minutes. For each statement listed, you should score it between 1 and 5 using the following descriptions:

1. Strongly disagree with the statement (1 point)

2. Slightly disagree with the statement (2 points)

3. Neither agree nor disagree with the statement (3 points)

4. Slightly agree with the statement (4 points)

5. Strongly agree with the statement (5 points)

Organizational Culture and Strategy	
This section assesses how well-suited the organizational strategy is to data literacy, including how well it supports a culture of data literacy, as discussed in *Chapter 4, Implementing Organizational Data Literacy* and *Chapter 6, Aligning with Organizational Goals.*	
1	An executive sponsor exists within the organization for data literacy.
2	The majority of the leaders within the organization promote data literacy in their processes, including the ability for employees to openly question and challenge data.
3	Your organization has defined and communicated its data and analytics vision and ambitions.
4	Leverages KPIs for strategic and departmental goals.

Organizational Processes

This section assesses organizational processes that relate to how they use and support data, as discussed in Chapters 4, 7, 9, and 10.

5	Decisions that are communicated include data, visualizations, and insights.
6	Decision-making processes that use both data and a human element are present within the organization.
7	The organization has processes and resources in place to support data security and data privacy.
8	The organization has processes and resources in place to monitor and improve data quality.
9	The organization has processes and education in place to foster the ethical handling of data.

Data and Analytics

This section assesses how the organization uses and provides access to data and analytics, as discussed in Chapters 2, 4, and 5.

10	Data is accessible to the majority of the organization to use in a self-service manner.
11	The organization has an established data strategy, including data management and data governance.
12	The organization leverages more than just descriptive analytics (including diagnostic, predictive, and prescriptive).
13	Data and analytics are embedded into the daily operations of the organization.

Tools and Technology

This section assesses the organization's portfolio of tools and technology to support data literacy.

| 14 | The organization invests in tools and technology that support the data journey and makes it easier for decision-makers to leverage data. |
| 15 | The organization invests in technical integrations that bring the data and analytics to the right users within their work environment with minimal manual intervention (this includes mashups and embedded dashboards and analytics, alerts and notifications, and tools to integrate the data with the analytics). |

Knowledge and Learning Programs	
This session assesses the organization's approach to how it educates, upskills, and supports its employees on their data literacy journey, as discussed in *Chapter 4, Implementing Organizational Data Literacy.*	
16	The organization provides support in the form of training, coaching, or community discussions so that employees can upskill on data literacy, as well as the time for employees to take advantage of the support.
TOTAL (Add up all the scores from above)	

Figure 12.3 – Basic organizational data literacy assessment

You can use the table shown in *Figure 12.4* to assess your organization's data literacy based on your total score:

Total Score	Organizational Data Literacy
16-32	Immature. Your organization does not have a lot of focus on data literacy.
33-44	Developing. Your organization has some areas that support organizational data literacy but it still has a long way to go to maximize the value data literacy can provide to an organization.
45-69	Managed. Your organization sees the value in data literacy and has a focus on some key areas of organizational data literacy, but there are a few additional focus areas that can make a difference.
70-80	Mature. Your organization ranks as a fully mature data-literate organization that has a focus on just about all of the key areas of organizational data literacy.

Figure 12.4 – Basic organizational data literacy assessment scoring

If you are looking at areas to improve your organizational data literacy, start by focusing on the categories or statements where you answered below a 4 or 5. Ideally, you should strive to have a score of either 4 or 5 in all of these 10 statements.

If you are looking for a more robust organizational data literacy assessment that can highlight more specific strengths and weaknesses, along with recommendations, you can use the assessment covered in the next section.

Robust organizational data literacy maturity assessment

Our more robust organizational data literacy assessment will assess your organization's maturity with data literacy initiatives in 5 dimensions and 25 total subdimensions.

The list of subdimensions can be seen in *Figure 12.5*:

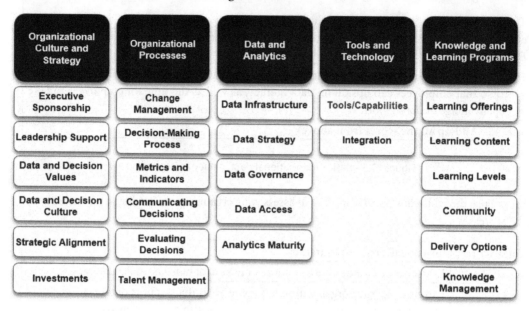

Figure 12.5 – Organizational data literacy dimensions and subdimensions

Ideally, the assessment would be filled out by someone in the organization with a good overview of the organization's culture and strategy, processes, data and analytics, metrics, skills, technology, data-driven culture, leadership, strategy, execution (of processes), analytical integration, analytical empowerment of employees, and education programs.

It is highly likely, especially in large organizations, that a single person may not know enough of all the dimensions to complete the assessment themselves. In these situations, it is OK to split the assessment up so that multiple resources are involved in filling it out. For example, maybe the chief data officer fills out the sections on data and analytics, maybe the chief information officer fills out the sections on tools and technology, and maybe a leader in education fills out the sections on knowledge and learning programs. Another way to split up the assessment would be to have a single individual or team responsible for the entire assessment, but rather than answering the questions themselves, they conduct interviews and perform audits and gather information to properly complete the assessment.

Let's move on to the actual assessment, which is organized by dimensions. The assessment is provided in this chapter but can also be taken online at `http://www.kevinhanegan.com/maturityAssessment`.

Organizational culture and strategy

There are six subdimensions within the organizational culture and strategy dimension:

Executive Sponsorship

An executive sponsor is critical to an organization's data and literacy maturity. Three of their main tasks are active and visible participation, communicating support and the importance of data literacy, and building a coalition. Select the number that best represents the status of the executive sponsorship of data literacy in your organization:

1. No executive sponsor exists. (1 point)

2. The executive sponsor is only evident through funding authorization and resource allocation. (2 points)

3. There is an executive sponsor who provides active and visible participation. (3 points)

4. There is an executive sponsor who provides active and visible participation, builds a coalition, and communicates support to promote data literacy. (4 points)

Score	

Leadership Support

Beyond the executive sponsor, there needs to be buy-in and support from other leaders, including actively using data to make decisions. Select the number that best represents the status of the leadership support of data literacy in your organization:

1. Managers have some awareness of the uses of data, but they don't see the value of it, and they don't believe data literacy is important for everyone. (1 point)

2. Many managers know data and data literacy is important, so they are interested in it, and they even use data from time to time, but they are not convinced and do not practice the principles required (that is, they do not allocate time for their team to upskill on data literacy). (2 points)

3. Most managers are engaged with data and ask the right questions about the data to harness the value in it. (3 points)

4. Most managers understand how data can improve their organization and actively use it to drive questions and influence their decisions. Leaders communicate using data and let the data inform and drive their own decisions. Leaders hold teams accountable for decisions they make if they are using just opinions and not data. (4 points)

Score	

Organizational Values

Organizational values guide your business decisions. Three organizational values specific to data literacy organizations are as follows:

1. Data-informed decision-making is valuable.

2. Democratization of data across the organization is important.

3. Sharing knowledge about data is recommended and seen as valuable.

Select the number that best represents the status of the organizational values of data literacy in your organization:

4. None of the characteristics listed exist. (1 point)

5. One of the characteristics listed exists. (2 points)

6. Two of the characteristics listed exist. (3 points)

7. All three of the characteristics listed exist. (4 points)

Score	

Data and Decision Culture

Culture is the way values are implemented in businesses. The following characteristics apply the data and decision culture for a data-literate organization:

1. A test and learning environment.

2. Hierarchies do not matter when it comes to decision-making.

3. Leaders should not have the ability to impose an instinct-based veto (not using data).

4. Data is openly questioned and challenged across the organization.

5. Users can ask questions and get answers without having to ask a data expert or similar.

Select the number that best represents the status of the data and decision culture at your organization.

6. None of the characteristics listed exist. (1 point)

7. One of the characteristics listed exists. (2 points)

8. Two of the characteristics listed exist. (3 points)

9. All of the characteristics listed exist. (4 points)

Score	

Strategic Alignment

The following characteristics are true for data-literate organizations in terms of the strategic alignment of data literacy:

1. A vision exists for where your organization wants to end up on its data literacy journey.
2. Specific data literacy objectives have been created.
3. A link has been made between data and staying ahead of the competition.
4. Data is seen as an organizational asset.
5. Shows a clear ROI on data investments.

Select the number that best represents the status of the data and decision culture in your organization:

6. None of the characteristics listed exist. (1 point)
7. One of the characteristics listed exists. (2 points)
8. Two of the characteristics listed exist. (3 points)
9. All of the characteristics listed exist. (4 points)

Score	

Investment

Data-literate organizations don't just talk about the importance of data and analytics and data literacy – they action it with investments to support those initiatives. Select the number that best represents the investments for data literacy in your organization:

1. Most of the investment in data and analytics is budgeted on a project-by-project basis. (1 point)
2. Most of the investment in data and analytics is budgeted within each department. (2 points)
3. Most of the investments in data and analytics come from a centralized budget in IT or similar. (3 points)
4. Most of the investments in data and analytics come from a centralized budget specific to data and analytics. (4 points)

Score	

Assessment score for organizational culture and strategy

Add up the total number of points for your responses across all six subdimensions and calculate the average score for this dimension, as shown in *Figure 12.6*. If you decided to get multiple people to complete the same sections of the assessment, calculate the average score:

Dimension: Organizational Culture and Strategy		
1	Executive Sponsorship	1-4
2	Leadership Support	1-4
3	Data and Decision Values	1-4
4	Data and Decision Culture	1-4
5	Strategic Alignment	1-4
6	Investments	1-4
Total Dimension Score (Add all scores and enter total)		
Average total (Divide the "Total Dimension Score" by 6)		

Figure 12.6 – Organizational culture and strategy scoring

Organizational processes

There are six subdimensions within the organizational processes dimension:

Change Management

As we mentioned earlier in this book, the biggest obstacles and adoption barriers that organizations face when they try to become data-literate are managerial and cultural. Both of these require strong change management. Select the number that best represents the change management in your organization:

1. Little or no change management practice exists. (1 point)

2. Some elements of change management are applied to some projects. (2 points)

3. Comprehensive change management exists, but only for some projects. (3 points)

4. Change management is seen as an organizational competency with not only an organization-wide standard but also a dedicated team and is used at all levels of the organization. (4 points)

Score	

Decision-Making Process

An organization is only truly data literate if it can use data to influence and inform decisions. This requires a decision-making process. Select the number that best represents the decision-making process in your organization:

1. Very little structure, if any at all, in a decision-making process. (1 point)

2. Some structure in the decision-making process but mostly in terms of terminology, not the actual process. (2 points)

3. There's a structured decision-making process in some departments but not all. (3 points)

4. There's a structured decision-making process that's used everywhere in the organization and tied to KPIs, performance data, and resource allocation. (4 points)

Score

Metrics and Indicators

Data-literate organizations leverage data everywhere, including running the business based on metrics and KPIs. Select the number that best represents the status of the metrics and indicators in your organization:

1. Has no established KPIs. (1 point)

2. Has KPIs but only for strategic organizational performance. (2 points)

3. Has KPIs for organizational and strategic performance, as well as departmental, but the departmental ones are not horizontally aligned. (3 points)

4. Has KPIs for organizational and strategic performance, as well as departmental, and a deliberate practice is in place to trickle down and across all KPIs for vertical and horizontal alignment. (4 points)

Score

Communicating Decisions

Data-literate organizations are highly skilled in communicating data and insights. Select the number that best represents how your organization communicates with data:

1. No organizational processes exist for communicating decisions with data and insights at any level. (1 point)

2. Decisions on select projects are communicated using data and insights but only in an ad hoc manner. No formal process exists. (2 points)

3. A process exists for communicating decisions using data and insights, but it is only used on select projects or within a subset of departments. (3 points)

4. A process exists and is used everywhere across the organization for communicating decisions using data and insights. (4 points)

Score	

Evaluating Decisions

Data-literate organizations have processes to evaluate and learn from decisions after they are made. The following characteristics apply to how data-literate organizations evaluate decisions:

1. The process is evaluated, not just the decision.

2. Post-mortem on major decisions.

3. Information is collected and analyzed related to the decision after it is made.

4. A process exists for evaluating decisions after they are made.

Select the number that best represents the status of evaluating decisions in your organization:

5. None or one of the characteristics listed exists. (1 point)

6. Two of the characteristics listed exist. (2 points)

7. Three of the characteristics listed exist. (3 points)

8. All four of the characteristics listed exist. (4 points)

Score	

Talent Management

Data-literate organizations properly manage their organization's talent as it relates to data literacy. Less focus is put on the specific job and role, and more focus is put on the relevant competencies and skills. The following characteristics apply to how data-literate organizations think about talent management:

1. The Criteria for assessing potential employees includes looking for specific data literacy competencies and skills.

2. The organization has a list of competencies and/or skills that are required to meet organization goals.

3. The organization has a method for analyzing employees against required competencies and/or skills.

4. The organization has an approach for closing the competency and skills gaps via learning opportunities.

Select the number that best represents the status of evaluating decisions in your organization:

5. None or one of the characteristics listed exists. (1 point)

6. Two of the characteristics listed exist. (2 points)

7. Three of the characteristics listed exist. (3 points)

8. All four of the characteristics listed exist. (4 points)

Score

Assessment score for organizational processes

Add up the total number of points for your responses across all six subdimensions and calculate the average score for this dimension, as shown in *Figure 12.7*:

Dimension: Organizational Processes		
		1-4
1	Change Management	1-4
2	Decision-Making Process	1-4
3	Metrics and Indicators	1-4
4	Communicating Decisions	1-4
5	Evaluating Decisions	1-4
6	Talent Management	1-4
Total Dimension Score (Add all scores and enter total)		
Average total (Divide the "Total Dimension Score" by 6)		

Figure 12.7 – Organizational process scoring

Data and analytics

There are five subdimensions within the data and analytics dimension:

Data Infrastructure

Data-literate organizations require a proper data infrastructure to be able to process, analyze, and act on data. Select the number that best represents the data infrastructure in your organization:

1. Data is collected on an ad hoc basis with disparate tools. (1 point)
2. There are a few people who understand how data is accessed in the organization. (2 points)
3. Data is accessible to the majority of the organization, but it is not readily discoverable, compliant, understood, or actionable throughout the organization. (3 points)
4. There's trusted centralized storage with quality data that is discoverable, trusted, understood by the business, and accessible. (4 points)

Score	

Data Strategy

Data-literate organizations require a solid data strategy to define how they manage data as a strategic asset. Select the number that best represents the data strategy in your organization:

1. No strategy in place. (1 point)
2. Departments have their own data strategies. (2 points)
3. Organization-wide data strategy. (3 points)
4. An organization-wide data strategy with its own organization, leader (CDO), and budget. (4 points)

Score	

Data Governance

Data-literate organizations require an effective data governance strategy to ensure the data is usable and protected so that it is trusted. Select the number that best represents the data governance in your organization:

1. There are no data quality rules and processes and no documented strategy for data governance. There is no centralized approach to data, leading to redundant data. (1 point)

2. Various departments have implemented rules and processes for data quality and governance, but nothing exists across the entire organization. (2 points)

3. A centralized approach to data quality and governance exists, but either not all the departments utilize it or the centralized approach is only used for specific projects. (3 points)

4. A centralized approach to data quality and governance exists, and the entire organization has embraced it, providing users with a trusted single source of truth when it comes to data and insights. (4 points)

Score	

Data Access/Data Democratization

The following characteristics apply to how employees within data-literate organizations access data:

1. Data is accessible across the organization to use with self-service analytics tools.

2. Internal and external integration.

3. Defined schemas of inputs.

4. Identifiable catalog of datasets.

5. Derivability of data.

Select the number that best represents the status of data access in your organization:

6. None or one of the characteristics listed exists. (1 point)

7. Two of the characteristics listed exist. (2 points)

8. Three or four of the characteristics listed exist. (3 points)

9. All five of the characteristics listed exist. (4 points)

Score	

Analytics Maturity

Data-literate organizations leverage the full range of analytic capabilities to help come up with insights. These range from more simple descriptive analytics to more advanced predictive and prescriptive analytics. Select the number that best represents the analytics maturity in your organization:

1. Basic analytics is used in some parts of the organization, but not everywhere. The analytics are typically in the form of descriptive analytics via ad hoc reporting on historical data. (1 point)

2. Analytics includes diagnostic analytics as well. (2 points)

3. Analytics includes predictive analytics as well. (3 points)

4. Analytics includes prescriptive analytics as well. (4 points)

Score	

Assessment score for data and analytics

Add up the total number of points for your responses across all five subdimensions and calculate the average score for this dimension, as shown in *Figure 12.8*:

Dimension: Data and Analytics		
1	Data Infrastructure	1-4
2	Data Strategy	1-4
3	Data Governance	1-4
4	Data Access	1-4
5	Analytics Maturity	1-4
Total Dimension Score (Add all scores and enter total)		
Average total (Divide the "Total Dimension Score" by 5)		

Figure 12.8 – Data and analytics scoring

Tools and technologies

There are two subdimensions within the tools and technologies dimension:

Tools

The following tools and capabilities should exist within a data-literate organization:

1. Data Storage Tools
2. Data Integration Tools
3. Master Data Management Tools
4. Data Mining Tools
5. Data Catalog
6. Data Visualization Tools
7. Analytics Tools
8. Advanced Analytic Tools
9. Artificial Intelligence/Machine Learning
10. Decision Intelligence Tools

Select the number that best represents the status of tools and capabilities in your organization:

11. Up to 3 of the tools and capabilities listed exist. (1 point)
12. 4 or 5 of the tools and capabilities listed exist. (2 points)
13. 6 or 8 of the tools and capabilities listed exist. (3 points)
14. 9 or 10 of the tools and capabilities listed exist. (4 points)

Score	

Integrations

Having the right tools and technology is important, but data-literate organizations require that those tools and technologies be integrated into the workflow of the users. This helps empower employees by bringing the insights to them in an environment they are used to, rather than them having to switch between multiple applications.

Select the number that best represents the maturity of technology integrations in your organization:

1. Data and insights are provided manually in the form of reports. Very little integration exists. (1 point)

2. Some levels of automated reports and dashboards exist within the organization, but they are not embedded; rather, they are emailed. (2 points)

3. A few key analytics are embedded directly into workflows and applications. The rest are handled via manual or automated reports and dashboards. (3 points)

4. The majority of analytic capabilities are embedded directly into workflows and applications that the users use. (4 points)

Score	

Assessment score for tools and technologies

Add up the total number of points for your responses across the two subdimensions and calculate the average score for this dimension, as shown in *Figure 12.9*:

Dimension: Tools and Technologies		
1	Tools and Capabilities	1-4
2	Integration	1-4
Total Dimension Score (Add all scores and enter total)		
Average total (Divide the "Total Dimension Score" by 2)		

Figure 12.9 – Tools and technologies scoring

Knowledge and learning programs

There are six subdimensions within the knowledge and learning programs dimension:

Learning Offerings

Data-literate organizations provide various learning options for their employees to upskill their data literacy. Select the number that best represents the maturity and diversity of data literacy learning offerings in your organization:

1. No offerings are provided or recommended. (1 point)

2. Third-party offerings are recommended but they must be completed on your own time. (2 points)

3. Offerings are built into the company's L&D programs and certain employees are allowed to take them during work hours (but not all employees). (3 points)

4. Organization-wide data upskilling programs are open and available to all employees to take during work hours. (4 points)

Score	

Content Included

The following types of learning content should exist within a data-literate organization:

1. Learning about data and analytics tools and technology.

2. Learning about industry and business knowledge.

3. Learning about organizational knowledge.

4. Learning about soft skills.

Select the number that best represents the status of data literacy learning content in your organization:

5. Data and analytics tools and technology training only. (1 point)

6. Data and analytics tools and technology training plus either industry, business, organizational knowledge, or soft skill training. (2 points)

7. Data and analytics tools and technology training plus two of the following: industry, business, organizational knowledge, or soft skill training. (3 points)

8. All four types of learning content exist. (4 points)

Score	

Levels and Assessments

A data-literate organization has learning offerings that contain various learning levels to allow individuals to learn what they need at the time (that is, awareness, understanding, application, and expertise). Select the number that best represents the levels of data literacy learning offered in your organization:

1. No learning levels. Just one level of training. (1 point)
2. Two learning levels (for example, basic and advanced) exist but there's no assessment to validate you learned what you needed at the current level. (2 points)
3. Three or more learning levels exist but there's no assessment to validate you learned what you needed at the current level. (3 points)
4. Three or more learning levels exist with an assessment to validate what you learned at each level. (4 points)

Score	

Community

Data-literate organizations provide mechanisms for employees to get informal learning and ask questions to peers in their moment of need. This can include forums, a coach or mentor, or a community of practice, as examples. Select the number that best represents the support for data literacy communities in your organization:

1. Forums exist but no one is accountable for monitoring them. (1 point)
2. Forums exist and there are employees dedicated to monitoring them. (2 points)
3. A coaching or mentoring program for data literacy exists. (3 points)
4. Communities of practice or similar exist. (4 points)

Score	

Learning Delivery Options

Data-literate organizations should provide multiple delivery options for employees to consume data-literate training. Those delivery options can include the following:

1. Instructor-led

2. Self-paced

3. Workshops

4. Webinars

5. Blended learning

Select the number that best represents the status of learning delivery options in your organization:

6. None exist. (1 point)

7. One or two exist. (2 points)

8. Three exist. (3 points)

9. Four or five exist. (4 points)

Score	

Knowledge Management Practices

Data-literate organizations provide a mechanism to capture the insights, knowledge, and wisdom of employees in an organizational knowledge base. Select the number that best represents the maturity of knowledge management in your organization:

1. No mechanism exists. (1 point)

1. A mechanism exists, but only in certain departments. (2 points)

2. A mechanism exists for the entire organization, but adoption is low. (3 points)

3. A mechanism exists for the entire organization, and the entire organization uses it. (4 points)

Score	

Assessment score for knowledge and learning programs

Add up the total number of points for your responses across all six subdimensions and calculate the average score for this dimension, as shown in *Figure 12.10*:

Dimension: Knowledge and Learning Programs		
1	Learning Offerings	1-4
2	Learning Content	1-4
3	Learning Levels	1-4
4	Community	1-4
5	Delivery Options	1-4
6	Knowledge Management	1-4
Total Dimension Score (Add all scores and enter total)		
Average total (Divide the "Total Dimension Score" by 6)		

Figure 12.10 – Knowledge and learning programs scoring

Analyzing the maturity score

Once the assessment is completed, the organization can analyze the results. The goal of this step is to identify the most important areas to start working on improving.

In the online assessment, each dimension's score is calculated on a range from 1 to 10. With a consistent range for each dimension, we can plot them all together in a radar plot, as shown in *Figure 12.11*, to see where your organization's data literacy strengths and weaknesses are:

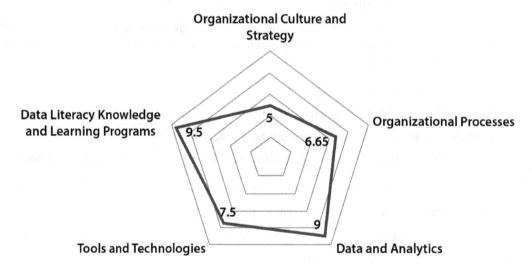

Figure 12.11 – Organizational data literacy assessment results

If you are not using the online assessment and are scoring this manually, just use the average scores from each dimension. As an example, *Figure 12.12* shows the scores from a completed manual assessment. Here, you can see the average scores from each dimension listed:

Average of the Organizational Culture and Strategy Dimension	2.0
Average of the Organizational Process Dimension	2.66
Average of the Data and Analytics Dimension	3.6
Average of the Tools and Technologies Dimension	3.0
Average of the Knowledge and Learning Programs Dimension	3.8
Overall Organizational Data Literacy Maturity Score (Take the average of all the dimension averages)	3.01

Figure 12.12 – Sample organizational data literacy assessment scoring

The table displayed in *Figure 12.13* shows the maturity level for each dimension calculated from the average score. The same table can be used to show the overall maturity level of the organization if you use the overall average score across all the dimensions:

Dimension Average Score	Maturity Level
1.00 – 1.59	Ad Hoc
1.60 – 2.19	Developing
2.20 – 2.79	Managed
2.80 – 3.39	Advanced
3.40 – 4.00	Optimized

Figure 12.13 – Organizational data literacy maturity levels

There is no common answer to the question of *what area we should focus on improving first*. All of the dimensions that have been assessed are important for organizations. However, we believe it is near impossible to mature in your organizational data literacy without the right strategy, support, and culture, so it makes sense to look for opportunities to increase your score in that dimension. Beyond that, the online assessment will give you more specific feedback and recommendations of where to start regarding your areas of improvement based on your scores.

However, if you are scoring the assessment manually and not using the online assessment, you should first focus on which dimensions are lower than the others. *Figure 12.14* shows the results of the sample assessment:

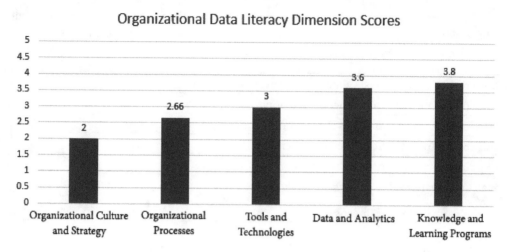

Figure 12.14 – Organizational Data Literacy dimension scores

The results highlight that **Organizational Culture and Strategy** is the lowest scoring dimension with a score of **2.0** on the higher end of the results compared to **Knowledge and Learning Programs**, which has a score of **3.8**. In this case, the recommendation would be to drill down into the **Organizational Culture and Strategy** dimension and start to make improvements there first.

To drill down into a dimension, you should look at each subdimension's score compared to the average across all the scores. For example, if you have identified you need to improve on your **Organizational Culture and Strategy** dimension, you can use the chart shown in *Figure 12.15* to visualize your scores for each of its six subdimensions and identify which you should prioritize first:

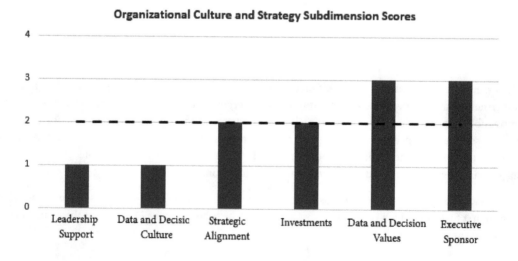

Figure 12.15 – Organizational Culture and Strategy Subdimension Scores

Addressing the subdimensions with the lowest scores would make the most sense as a place to start. Those subdimensions most likely need immediate attention. Once those subdimensions have been selected, the organization should meet and kick off a plan to address the weaknesses. In the example shown in *Figure 12.15*, the lowest subdimensions are **Leadership Support** and **Data and Decision Culture**.

Summary

In this chapter, we learned how to assess both the data literacy maturity of an organization as well as an individual's data literacy competency level. For both, we provided a very simple assessment that should take no longer than 15 minutes, along with more robust assessments that will give you more specifics on your gaps and where to focus next. Ideally, you will take the assessments initially so that you have a baseline and then retake the assessment at future intervals – for example, every 6 months or every year – to see how well you are closing the gaps.

In the next and final chapter, we will focus on how you should approach data and analytics projects within your organization, as well as what risks to look out for.

13

Managing Data and Analytics Projects

In this chapter, we'll talk about how data and analytics projects are different from other types of projects, why it's important to take care of typical data and analytics risks, and why it's a good idea to find out who your stakeholders are. Then, we'll talk about how to write a good (short, strong) data and analytics business case.

By the end of this chapter, you'll understand how data and analytics projects work, how to identify and manage stakeholders, and how to handle common data and analytics risks. We will also advise and guide you through the process of writing your data and analytics business case and conducting a complete financial analysis.

In this chapter, we will cover the following topics:

- Discovering why data and analytics projects fail
- Understanding four typical data and analytics project characteristics
- Understanding data and analytics project blockers
- Unfolding the data and analytics project approach
- Unfolding the data and analytics project framework
- Mitigating typical data and analytics project risks
- Determining roles in data and analytics projects (and teams)
- Managing data and analytics projects
- Writing a successful data and analytics business case
- Finding financial justification for your project

Discovering why data and analytics projects fail

We have discovered various research articles on the topic of data and analytics projects over the last 2 decades (yes—we've been dealing with data for more than 2 decades). As we all know, **business intelligence** (**BI**) projects can begin with a straightforward purpose and then fail for a variety of reasons, including:

- They involve multiple stakeholders

- They involve multiple actors

- They involve multiple suppliers

- Users do not adopt what we have created

Not just from our own experience, but also from the findings of several researchers, we discovered that the failure rate of data and analytics initiatives is quite high:

- According to Gartner, just 20% of data and analytics projects will actually generate business outcomes. (`https://blogs.gartner.com/andrew_white/2019/01/03/our-top-data-and-analytics-predicts-for-2019/`)

- The same is true for data science projects; according to TechTarget, 85% of those programs fail to meet their objectives. (`https://www.techtarget.com/searchbusinessanalytics/feature/How-to-increase-the-success-rate-of-data-science-projects`)

From what we know, do, and witness, data and analytics projects just begin with a simple purpose and no actual plan. Organizations just simply begin, and then it apparently goes in a number of different directions from there. There are numerous reasons why data and analytics projects can fail, resulting in money being lost and the need to acknowledge sunk costs.

Understanding four typical data and analytics project characteristics

When beginning data and analytics projects, it is necessary to investigate who your stakeholders (internally and externally) are, as these projects span organizations, teams, and even **business units** (**BUs**). We also have to deal with multiple suppliers. This typical first characteristic is an important factor that is frequently overlooked.

The second typical data and analytics project characteristic is that we would like to do a project for our BU or a smaller type of organization. We often forget that these types of projects will have a mix of technological and strategic issues, as well as significant internal political issues. When we return to *Chapter 1, The Beginning – The Flow of Data*, and discuss the disciplines of data and analytics, we see that our strategic management must embrace data and analytics for our organization. If not, and senior management do not embrace data and analytics—or worse, do not use it during management meetings—projects will definitely fail!

The third characteristic is data. Data is created internally from our processes, and perhaps we even need external data and combine it with internal data. It is also possible that we have to deliver data externally. This involves, again, a large number of internal —and in some cases, even external—stakeholders. We should investigate where the data is coming from, which data should we use, and so on.

Finally, the fourth characteristic is that data and analytics projects differ from most other projects. Therefore, we must consider a variety of risks, considering not only the usual project and organizational risks but also the "typical" data and analytics risks. We have the following phrase that we frequently use in our discussions, lectures, and presentations:

Think big. Act small. Scale fast.

If we can find the right variety of steps within a data and analytics project, combine different project methods, keep our scope in mind, and never forget to assist our business users, our projects will be a success! Let us take a step back and examine some common data and analytics project blockers that may arise during our data and analytics projects in the next section.

Understanding data and analytics project blockers

Every self-respecting organization recognizes the importance of data. There are a lot of webinars, books, blogs, articles, and so on to be found on the internet. Every one of them actually underlies the importance of data and how it can help to reach a promising future with data-informed decision-making. The truth, however, is that we see little results in practice. Why is it so?—you ask. Is it due to the fact that we use the wrong tools? Do we have poor data quality? Are our expectations too high, or is our company (and even personal) culture behind? In this section, we will discuss four types of data and analytics issues.

Pitfalls in data and analytics projects

Let's run through a list of pitfalls that occur in data and analytics projects:

- There is no business involvement; it is an IT party.
- Several suppliers (tools, hardware, services) are required, and there is no clear structure.
- When we start too big, the company has to wait too long for results, and we lose commitment.
- There is no one-size-fits-all solution; we lose commitment, and requirements change.
- There is no good project approach; how do we deal with independencies or changing requirements, and how do we avoid a scope creep?

Changes within data and analytics projects include the following:

- During the project, when the solution we create comes to life, the requirements mostly become clear. As a result, manageability decreases, priorities shift, and a scope creep occurs.

- When changes occur, project control can face challenges in terms of planning and staff availability. Technical issues can also arise; we typically see issues with a large amount of rework, as well as technical glitches with environment scalability.

- A company strategy changes, resources leave, dirty data was not identified, and so on.

Let's move on to cover lack of expertise next.

Lack of expertise

Lack of expertise in data and analytics includes the following:

- Data and analytics projects are frequently complex and require a wide range of knowledge.

- When a data project begins, it frequently begins by reinventing the wheel again and again. Good ideas (best practices) are rarely secured or taken care of.

- Despite limited knowledge, we see that projects tend to deliver insights, but solution maintenance is difficult and expensive. It is frequently caused by not using coding conventions, documentation, incorrect technology, insufficient scalability, or programming errors that result in performance issues. Often, organizations require specialized expertise for solutions to keep running.

The technical architecture

Let's go through the scenarios related to the technical architecture:

- Often, a drop of oil isn't enough to save a project. Organizations simply bought the wrong set of gears. Or, the tooling is simply insufficient for the organization's needs, or it is far too complicated. "*Building a beautiful castle in the clouds also requires a good architect*", as said by one of our mentors (RIP—David Bolton).

- Another scenario is that we purchased an incorrect set of gears, and the components of our data and analytics environment are unable to communicate or collaborate. When this happens, we'll need a lot of money to fix the problems.

Time and money

Project delivery times are lengthy, costs are excessively high (higher than expected), and the following pain points can occur:

- The deliverables are conflicting and ambiguous.

- An incorrect project strategy.

- Leadership and ownership of data or (K)PIs are neglected or not known.

- The project isn't providing actionable insights; we measure just because we can measure.

- There are no good data integration plans in place; data quality issues arise and no one takes responsibility.

- There is no plan in place for maintenance and development, or—even worse—there is no implementation planned (such as instructions on how to use the dashboard, learn to analyze, and how they can answer their use cases).

By understanding the issues that can occur during the different stages of data and analytics projects, it is easier to understand how a project should be set up and how you can manage and approach those types of projects.

Unfolding the data and analytics project approach

To be successful and manage data and analytics projects, we need a strategy that includes more than just a mix of project methods. A data and analytics project should always begin with a business question and from a business standpoint. When we examine organizations systematically, we can identify four approaches for data and analytics projects that we should include in our project strategy:

- **Vertical-driven**: The strategic objectives are leading

- **Horizontal-driven**: The core processes are taking the lead

- **Market-driven**: The market in which an organization specializes is leading

- **Data-driven**: When we don't know where to begin, we let the data guide us

When it comes to an organization as a system, it's all about the big picture (strategic), making sure all parts of the system are working together (horizontal), and keeping an eye on external factors (market-driven). You can also use the data-driven approach if you're not sure what value data can provide. It's common to start your projects with one of these four approaches (or a combination of them) and be able to identify and collect the most important data. This is something that should be addressed early on in the project when you're writing your business case.

It is critical to have agility in place to use the organization as a system and make data-informed decisions quickly. We may be able to develop into an intelligent performing organization if we are successful. To accomplish this, the source systems must be in place (documented, perfectly integrated, and so on), the culture must be open and transformative, and responsibilities must be clearly written.

We will help you understand the goals of an organization and how KPIs are built and need to be aligned to the objectives of an organization in our organizational goals chapter (*Chapter 6, Aligning with Organizational Goals*). From an organizational standpoint, we must consider gaps in processes or systems, as well as the fact that processes and systems are cross-organizational.

To illustrate, consider *Figure 13.1*. The pyramid represents the strategic, tactical, and operational objectives. The activities for those objectives are described (for the most part) in process descriptions, which are supported by our source systems. Looking at the example in *Figure 13.1*, it is clear that there is a gap in processes (not all are covered) or that there is an overlap in processes. However, the harsh reality is that our process activities are not fully supported by our source systems:

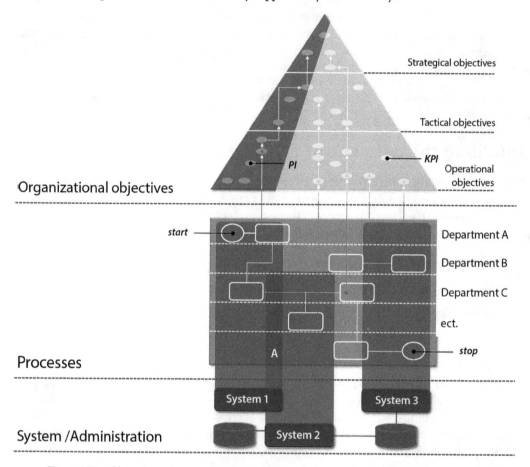

Figure 13.1 – Objectives, processes, and supporting systems such as a CRM, ERP, and so on

In this section, we explained several business approaches that we can consider for our data and analytics projects. If we look at those approaches none of them is 100% steadfast; every one of them has some gaps or some typical risks. What we do know is that we have to listen to our customers or users to find the correct approach or even a correct mix of approaches.

It is fine to start with a horizontal business approach (as we did with our "*Call to Balloon*" example) and plot the strategic objectives of the process or combine them from scratch. Or, even start with only a raw set of data and find out what could be measured and create strategic objectives at a later stage. In our opinion, when a company has no experience in defining strategic objectives, it is okay to practice and learn!

In the next section, we will discuss the project framework that we have used over time in our data and analytics projects.

Unfolding the data and analytics project framework

As stated earlier, there are two elementary sides to the advised project approach:

- Traditional "Waterfall" and the incremental/iterative/Scrum/Agile way
- A "multi-disciplinary" project team

Those two elements are so critical that a project will almost certainly fail if they are not present. *Intermezzo 2* contains a story about how to be successful with a specific project approach. And there is still a lot written about this topic by many experts; best practices are good ideas that you can tweak to fit within your organization.

Intermezzo 2 – successfully managing a data and analytics project

At a relatively large organization, a couple of years ago, we started out with a new team and centralized our data and analytics projects. We knew from the start (written in an implementation plan) that data and analytics projects needed a specific approach. The way in which the team was designed and the proactive approach on the part of the management and the underlying teams were somewhat unique in this more traditional organization as shown in *Figure 13.2*:

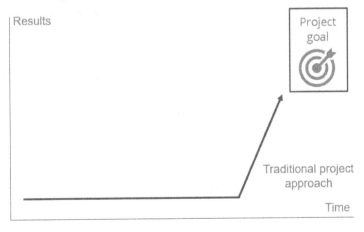

Figure 13.2 – Traditional project approach

We found out that a big bang project approach was not a good way to approach data and analytics projects. To be honest, at that time, the big bang scenario project approach was happening all around the world—big bang projects took too long, the targeted results were not met, and scope creep occurred, but the main thing was that the demand that was originally stated changed due to new economic situations or new laws that were installed.

When we thought of the new approach, we found out that the planning and starting phases were steps that were in a kind of sequence as first steps, but to get the buzz going within the organizations, we needed to actually show them to our business users. This approach (see *figure 13.3*)made a total difference in our projects. The main point as ever (and still now), we need a short **time to market** (**TTM**), and the information is needed now, not in a year's time!

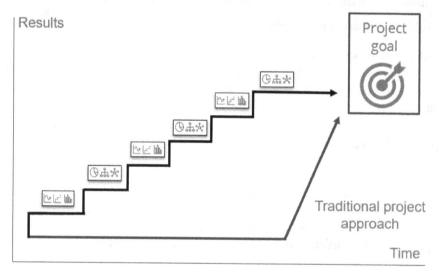

Figure 13.3 – Traditional projects versus agile/iterative projects

Important note

The story that is written is a real-life story. Out of respect for the organizations, we will not mention their names.

There are currently good methods for managing your projects, and the method could be set up in a **Scrum** (mostly somewhat tailored) manner, an agile way, or—as we used to say in the early days—with incremental stages. Data and analytics projects are not the same as process or system implementations. Our business users frequently do not know what insights they require. Typically, a project begins with an HR report (sick leave, headcount, and so on) or some financial reports. The data and analytics buzz will begin when we work on those ideas and turn them into the first insights for their data-informed decision-making. When this moment arrives, their desires and demands become more clear, and their backlog or list of new insights grows.

This is difficult from the standpoint of project planning; we can estimate the amount of work that needs to be done. The tricky part about data and analytics projects is that a scope creep can occur quickly. As a result, we can't estimate larger projects that well; it is advisable to overstate (roughly estimated) and plan and work in smaller increments. We can better manage our projects this way. When we work in smaller increments, we can divide the work more easily and manage scope creep more effectively.

To make this clearer, it is interesting to have the differences between the two approaches in place:

	Big bang approach	Phase (incremental) approach
Complexity	Higher	Lower
Risks	Bigger (and more)	Smaller (and fewer)
Organizational pressure	Higher	Lower
Benefits	All at once	In time (more phased)

Figure 13.4 – Differences in data and analytics projects

Let's move on to discovering typical risks in data and analytics projects.

Mitigating typical data and analytics project risks

What are the common risk factors that we have to manage in our data and analytics projects? When it comes to data and analytics projects, we have some typical risks to take care of. We can divide them into four categories:

- Project risks
- Technical risks
- Culture risks
- Content risks

Managing the risks of projects is important. It's not only difficult to discuss, collect, and describe the project risks—you'll also have to think about how to avoid them and address countermeasures. We mention high potential risks in our plans (project plan and business case), but we will have a risk register for all risks. We do this with the following method: what is the chance that this risk will occur and what is the impact of that risk when it occurs? From a project management point of view, managing risks is complex and can be challenging.

Project risks

Project risks are common risks that can occur in all kinds of projects. To mention some: scope creep, low performance, high costs, time crunches, stretched resources, operational changes, a lack of clarity, and hidden stakeholders, to name a few.

Technical risks

There are several situations (risks) that can occur from a technical point of view. The quality of the source systems can be an issue. Connections that you need to extract data from are not functioning accordingly to plan, such as the complexity of using APIs (connecting protocols) or other custom connections.

There can also be risks with the collection of data, and the amount of data collected. In today's world, there is so much data that an organization may have to make choices based on what it wants to extract and how to use it to measure its organizational goals.

Data from multiple sources is another risk. It is hard to have all kinds of data stored in several databases in all kinds of programming languages. Combining data manually is time-consuming and takes a big toll on your project. **Extract, transform, and load** (ETL) is a complex workload. Gartner says that 70% to 80% of its work is on the data integration side of dashboarding and reporting. The setup of the data and analytics environment is no longer suitable (for example, there is a lack of scalability).

What to do with data that can't be used due to the fact that it's inaccessible is another consideration. Retrieving data is sometimes complicated due to all kinds of connected issues. Sometimes, though, it is really inaccessible—for example, due to supplier rules or other reasons, it can happen that you need to pull the plug on the project.

Last but not least is a data warehouse environment that is built by the IT department, and the business is not consulted or is not in the lead with its business questions.

Cultural risks

Pressure from the top is one risk. Top leaders such as CFOs or other executives demand more results and drive value from data and analytics projects. This type of stakeholder needs special attention in order to keep expectations in place (expectation management).

Lack of support is another issue. We need support from the organization to be successful in our data and analytics projects. In the end, it is our business user: the reason we do our projects. We need that support from the top but also from the business itself. The moment the team (top and bottom) understands the benefits that data and analytics projects can bring, it is more likely to cooperate in your projects.

People can get confused or experience anxiety when they have to work with data and analytics. As we data literacy geeks say, people shouldn't be pushed to work with data and analytics—they should do this because they want to. Therefore, you need to address the educational, implementation part of your data and analytics project.

Visualizations that are not understood present another risk. To be successful with data and analytics, we need visualizations that are presented in a clear meaningful way. If we do not take care of the data literacy levels within an organization, we might lose our public. Therefore, it is necessary to think of the risk of overwhelming our readers/viewers.

A shortage of skills or a lack of data literacy skills should also be considered. Some organizations struggle with the data literacy skills that are needed on several levels within an organization. When employees do not have the capability to read, write, and argue with insights created from data, we need to address this in a risk assessment and help them to educate themselves.

An *island culture* should be avoided. When a bigger organization has multiple departments, working together is important. The problem occurs when departments think they can work separately from each other. Every department (and this also involves data management) probably has its own definitions and its own data and analytics tools to use.

Power and making decisions on gut feelings is something else to watch out for. Some organizations have a (financial) culture in which there is less transparency or decisions are made on gut feel (back pocket financial books, or various complex Excel reports). People tend to be afraid of transparency.

Content risks

Poor quality of data is a risk. Nothing is worse and more harmful for your data and analytics projects than inaccurate data. When bad data comes in, bad insights come out (garbage in is garbage out). Bad data quality can lead to many negative consequences and even pulling the plug on your data and analytics project. The result is that you have to start at the base and start with the processes around data management. In *Chapter 5*, *Managing Your Data Environment*, you'll find more information about this topic.

When inconsistent data, a lack of data, or data without any context arises, this is actually a risk that we can't avoid, as we need data (good data) for data-informed decision-making. In *Figure 13.6*, we explain that it's possible that the data isn't available as it's not being registered or the data hasn't got any context (or it is not known).

Inconsistent data (we have source system A and B, and A has another definition than B, while the subject is the same) is a problem that can occur. This can be the case when the organization uses multiple source systems for its activities that need to be registered but there is no common data management or data register in place.

As mentioned, besides these typical data and analytics issues or risks, there are more risks to think of. A risk register is a good way to begin—discuss, collect, and describe risks in the register, and manage them well. When risks are not addressed, it is likely that the project team will end up in many discussions, or reinvent the wheel over and over again.

Determining roles in data and analytics projects (and teams)

The field of data and analytics is shifting. From our point of view, it's not a project that can be done by just one person anymore. The roles are different; in this current era, we need more specialists in specific areas. The roles within a project can differ, and a person can have multiple roles in a project (or in their daily activities in the data and analytics team).

We see the following basic roles for data and analytics projects:

- Data and analytics manager/CDO
- Project manager/leaders (overall and technical)
- Product owner/Scrum master
- Data and analytics architects
- Data analyst/business analyst
- Data integration specialists
- Data visualization specialists
- Privacy and security specialists
- Data stewards
- Data owners/process owners
- Usability experts
- Trainers
- Business analysts and business users (we need them to have that buy-in within the organization)
- Other stakeholders that come up and are involved in the data and analytics project

The roles are dependent on the size of the organization and how data and analytics are incorporated into the strategic plans of the organization. More or less, we see those roles and a combination of roles more often in somewhat bigger organizations, which have a certain maturity level in the data and analytics field. Smaller organizations just use integration specialists in combination with a visualization specialist, and they report to the management. These core roles will work well initially, and then more roles can be added as the organization's data and analytics maturity develops.

Managing data and analytics projects

To run a data and analytics project, you must consider several factors in your project approach. We will walk you through the data and analytics approach that we have used over time in *Figure 13.5*:

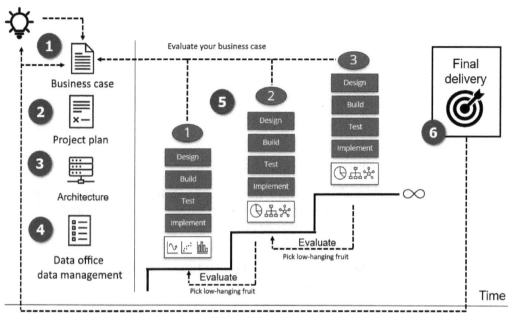

Figure 13.5 – Data and analytics project approach

In the visualized project approach, we defined several steps that we will now explain in more depth:

1. **The idea – the data and analytics business case**: Every initiative should begin with a business goal in mind. It should also be included in a business case if you want to calculate the value and **return on investment** (**ROI**). You will describe your idea in your business case using several options or scenarios, a financial analysis, and details of potential high risks.

   In the *Writing a successful data and analytics business case* section, we will walk you through the steps of creating a data and analytics business case and conducting a thorough financial analysis.

2. **Project plan**: After the business case has been approved, the project plan must be written. This plan can be written as a **project initiation document** (**PID**) or in other formats.

   The following elements should (and can) be described in a project plan:

   - Reasons for your project (introduction, problem definition)

   - Objectives, results, and the strategic value for your organization

   - Scope—what is in and what is out of your project

   - A high-level approach to the project

- The different phases of your project
- Project team (organization and tasks)
- Risks (project, organization, data, and analytics)
- Project planning
- Financial planning (the basis is written in your business case)
- Quality assurance
- Project control/communication

3. **Architecture check**: Discuss the tools you'll need and ask your architects whether the current environment is scalable or suitable for your project. When there is no data and analytics environment available, a tool selection must be performed. Your architects can assist you in determining the most appropriate architecture for your data and analytics environment.

   The following elements should be thought of and need to be discussed (as it can cause surprises when you depend on your hardware suppliers):

   - Data flow questions
   - Dataset size, available connections, privacy checks, expected row count, and so on
   - Data consumption
   - Is the current environment up to date, is it future-proof, are there enough licenses, is the environment scalable, and so on?

4. **Data office/data management**: Some organizations do not have a data office or data management in place. Data management and data quality are mostly handled by data and analytics (project) teams. Taking care of your data elements by documenting the metadata (the definition of your user data elements) and looking for the owners of that data in order to address data quality and the responsibilities that come with it.

   When a data office is in place (usually in larger organizations), seek its assistance, definitions, and knowledge of the source systems from which you want to extract and transform valuable information. Your data office is aware of the specifics of the data you wish to use, as well as the process owners, data owners, and data stewards. They can assist you and your project in achieving success!

5. **Increments or sprints**: The number of sprints is mostly unknown because the business users' wishes and demands are not always clear. Backlogs, lists with additional demands, and desires are difficult to manage. It is necessary to prioritize the tasks at hand and reduce the length of sprints (the most-often-made mistake is that sprints or increments are made too big).

A sprint consists of repeating steps:

- **Design** (the measurement plan): Keep in mind that the increment sprint should not take more than 2 weeks to complete. In this design or measurement plan, analyze what is required to be built and how it supports the objectives of the organization (or teams, units, and so on). Analyze the data quality and present the findings to the business. Create a concept report that is more engaging for your business users.

- **Build**: This step involves data extraction and the creation of first insights for your business users (the biggest success factor here is to show your business users the first results). Show the initial results to your business users and ensure that they understand the visualizations you created for them.

- **Test**: Not only from a programming standpoint but also asking your business users to assist you with testing. They will embrace it and carry the insights in this manner, and they will be your sponsors as a result.

- **Implement**: From our experience, the most common mistake is not guiding your business users on how to use dashboards and reports. Take some time for instruction on the insights that are created to become successful. Assist them in comprehending the use cases and guiding them through the filtering and analyzing processes. This way, they will be encouraged and excited for what is to come.

Our recommendation is to evaluate your increment delivery using the STARR methodology (described under *Final delivery*, next) in order to improve your approach and become even better at project delivery.

Low-hanging fruit are quick adjustments that you can make in the next increment to directly add value to your organization. But the amazing thing about low-hanging fruit is that the required informatics will become more and more specific and linked to the processes in the organization and that knowledge can be carried forward to the next increment or sprint.

6. **Final delivery**: When the project is completed, it must be transferred to the supporting team that manages the data and analytics environment. This team must manage the dashboard and ensure its performance, management, and maintenance.

After the final delivery, it is time to evaluate your project and learn how to do things better the next time. We can use the **STARR** method to help you evaluate in a methodical manner:

- **S – Situation** (what was the situation?): Describe the situation of your work, why, who was involved, where, and so on

- **T – Task** (what did you want to achieve?): Describe the assignment, and describe what your role in the project/situation was

- **A – Action** (what did you do?): Describe the approach that you have used (activities, tools, preparations, and so on)

- **R – Results** (what effect did it have?): How were the results assessed?
- **R – Reflect** (what would you do differently the next time?): How do you look back at your actions and results and what should you do differently?

In the *Appendix A – Templates* section, you will find a template for this type of evaluation.

To conclude the typical data and analytics approach, we have found out that we need to be aware of some important elements to eventually be successful in our data and analytics projects:

- The business processes and objectives should lead your data and analytics strategy
- Use a combination of waterfall and incremental (sprints, agile)
- Business and IT need to work together as much as possible
- Think big (have that dot on the horizon), start small, and scale fast

To conclude this section, we do hope that we have given you a good set of pragmatic data and analytics project tips, what to take care of, which risks to manage, and so on. In the next section of this chapter, we will help you to understand and write a data and analytics business case.

Writing a successful data and analytics business case

Building or writing a business case is not difficult; in most cases, business cases are lengthy documents that are written once and then filed away in a desk drawer. We never seem to finish our projects and are constantly checking the business case and results of our data and analytics project. Why? Our project management plan does not include it. Actually, we should review the business case after each phase to see whether-we're still on track and the revenue and costs are still as expected.

If we are not discussing the initial business case during our project, it could be for several reasons:

- There is no good project management strategy (changing requirements, the source systems we rely on are not that well-documented, or the knowledge is not available)
- In our project board, there are no superusers or business users
- Our project is being led by IT, but the business representatives are not on the same page
- Because we made our project too big, we had to wait too long for our first results
- We must work collaboratively with multiple vendors (services, tools, and hardware)
- If no quality assurance is in place, when will we know that the project was a success?

A business case, according to **PRINCE2**, justifies the execution of a project, program, or portfolio. It evaluates the benefits, costs, and risks of various options before recommending one.

With our business case, we want to see whether data and analytics, as well as our project, can provide the value we expect. Are the investments justified by the expected value or revenue?

A chapter layout for your business case

A business case should include the following elements:

- **Reasoning for your project**: A brief introduction, a description of the problem, and the project's main goal (why).

- **Options or scenarios**: To solve the problem that we discussed in the first chapter, we must describe a few options (usually, three to four options/scenarios). This shows our readers, board, or other decision-makers that we have considered a variety of solutions and scenarios to solve the problem. The *"Do nothing"* option is the first option or scenario.

  The following elements create a scenario: an introduction, pros and cons, and strategic contribution. *Figure 13.6* shows an example of how to write your scenarios or options:

Option 1	"Do nothing"
Description	We will not do anything with this option; the current data and analytics situation will remain unchanged, and we will not work on new developments. The ad hoc decision-making process will remain unchanged, and it will be carried out directly from the source systems.
Pros	<ul><li>There is no financial investment</li><li>No innovation or impact on the current situation</li><li>Our end users do not need to invest any time, and no training facilities are required</li></ul>
Cons	<ul><li>The information gap will remain and broaden</li><li>KPIs exist, but there is no way to use dashboards and reports interactively to make data-driven decisions</li><li>We will be unable to assess the performance of our teams</li><li>We won't be able to see how our clients thrive and work</li><li>We will remain an ad hoc decision-making organization</li><li>We won't be able to respond to changes as quickly if we don't have daily reports and dashboards</li></ul>
Strategical contribution	The control information for management and achieving our service objectives have not changed. However, in the long run, a negative impact on the organization (loss of image) may occur, and as a result, it is possible that we will lose clients due to a lack of information.

Figure 13.6 – Option or scenario description

- **Qualitative benefits**: Try to emphasize the advantages that your project will bring to your company (without the financial calculations for now). You might consider the following enhancements:

  - Improvements in efficiency (cost savings—for example, process improvements)

  - Improvements in efficiency (increased revenue, higher margins—for example, new product launches)

  - Other quality improvements (better use of our staff instead of removing them, and so on)

- **Risks**: Which high-impact risks did you identify? There are several risks that we should investigate, control, and describe, as stated in *Chapter 9, Handling Data Responsibly*.

  - What is the probability of that risk occurring in your project? (Place them in a table and give them a value from 1 to 5. 1: it is not likely that this risk will occur; 5: most likely this risk will occur.)

  - What effect will this risk have on my project if it actually occurs? (Place them in a table and give them a value from 1 to 5. 1: it is not likely that this risk will occur; 5: most likely this risk will occur.)

  - The next step is to multiply the value from the chance and impact values to get the final score. Every score that is higher than 18 will be a high-impact risk that needs to have a place in your business case.

  - Below our table (or next to the noted risk), we have to describe the measures that we have to take to mitigate the risks.

As an example, we have noted two risks in this table, along with mitigating measures:

Nr.	Risk	Chance	Impact	Score
1	Extracting historical data can cause performance issues.	5	5	25
2	Inconsistent data from several sources does not align. Therefore, the insights will not be trusted.	4	4	16

Figure 13.7 – Risk table

Risk mitigation measures include:

- **Risk 1**: In order to avoid problems when extracting historical data from the source systems, we will extract the data (in batches if necessary) during nightly hours.

- **Risk 2**: When extracting data from various sources, we must first check for consistency. The next step is to discuss the discovered inconsistencies with our business users.

It is not difficult to write a solid business case, but it does require practice. Take special care of documents that are long, cloudy, or difficult to read (once at a company, business cases were more than 50 pages long). Make it solid, easy to understand, and to the point!

When is a business case sufficient? When it adds value to your organization's strategic goals. Following that, when the project assists the organization in improving and growing into a higher-performing organization.

Finding financial justification for your project

There are a few things to consider when conducting a thorough financial analysis of your project. It not only makes all project costs visible, but it also explains why you need to include them in your budget. The same principle applies to the future value that your business case can provide. Always plan 3 years ahead of time, and consider the costs of maintaining dashboards and reports. The majority of the benefits will be quantitative (in euros/dollars), but some will be qualitative. Those details must be included in your business case!

We'll guide you through a financial analysis of a project and how to build a cost argumentation in this chapter. The following are the elements of a financial analysis:

- One-time project costs
- Yearly recurring costs
- The quantitative benefits
- The quantitative analysis (benefits minus the costs)

In the next example, we will guide you through a financial analysis for a fictive small project:

QUANTITATIVE ANALYSIS	YEAR 1	YEAR 2	YEAR 3	TOTAL
One-time project costs				
Information analysis (80 hours * 100 USD)	$ 8.000			$ 8.000
Data integration specialist (160 hours * 100 USD)	$ 16.000			$ 16.000
Data visualization specialist (120 hours * 1.000 USD)	$ 12.000			$ 12.000
Project management (120 hours * 125 USD)	$ 15.000			$ 15.000
Training for our business users (16 hours * 100 USD)	$ 1.600			$ 1.600
Communication hours (16 hours * 100 USD)	$ 1.600			$ 1.600

License expansion (25 new users * 600 USD)	$ 15.000			$ 15.000
TOTAL ONE-TIME PROJECT COSTS	$ 69.200	$	$	$ 69.200

Figure 13.8 – One-time project costs

Argumentation for one-time project costs

It is important to not only think about, address, and calculate the costs or benefits—it is just as important to describe the argumentation about it as well so that your readers will be able to understand your calculations. Here's an example of how to do this:

- The information analysis will be performed by an internal colleague and will be communicated to our management team

- The team has hired an external data integration specialist from one of our suppliers

- The data visualization specialist is an internal colleague, and he will also perform the training for our business users

- The communication hours are necessary for our SharePoint environment, but also for the newsletter that we will send once every 2 weeks

- After a discussion with our internal architects and our procurement department, they advised an expansion of our licenses

By adding your arguments, it is more clear to the readers and decision-makers who will (hopefully) accept the calculated costs.

In the next section of your business case, we will address the recurring annual cost that will occur after implementing the data and analytics project.

Annual recurring costs

As an organization, we always plan our budget in July and August for the following year, including any additional costs for licenses or work that needs to be done. When the project is delivered to the data and analytics team for further maintenance, we must calculate the additional costs. Here's an overview of this:

RECURRING COSTS	YEAR 1	YEAR 2	YEAR 3	TOTAL
Maintenance of dashboard and reports (32 hours * 85 USD = 2.720 per month, per year 32,640)	$ 5.440	$ 32.640	$ 32.640	$ 70.720
Yearly maintenance and support license fee (20% of 15,000 euro = 3.000 USD per year)	$ 0.00	$ 3.000	$ 3.000	$ 6.000
TOTAL RECURRING COSTS	$ 5.440	$ 35.640	$ 35.640	$ 76.720

Figure 13.9 – Annual recurring costs

Argumentation for annual recurring costs

It is necessary to add argumentation for those recurring annual costs in this example that we have written, including some argumental phrases so that it's easy to understand why and what we mean by this. Here's an example of what this could include:

- The project will be delivered in the month of October, therefore we have calculated 2 months' maintenance and support hours for the data and analytics team.

- The yearly maintenance and support fee for our software vendor is included in the project costs. This maintenance fee needs to be paid on a yearly basis. The new licenses and the annual maintenance and support fee are discussed with our procurement department.

In the next section of our example business case, we have to address the qualitative and quantitative benefits of our project.

The quantitative benefits

We can determine what our data and analytics improvements will deliver by analyzing the quantitative and qualitative benefits. We should always be able to determine what improvements we can make and attempt to quantify them. It is not always simple, but with logic, you should be able to get there. It can be difficult to qualify for benefits, especially in government organizations. This type of organization will primarily reason in qualitative terms:

- **Quantitative:** The right focus on the right things, improving processes, efficiency improvements, and so on

- **Qualitative:** Better control, proactive versus reactive, improvement of procurement processes, and so on

Let's visualize the quantitative benefits in the following table:

QUANTITATIVE BENEFITS	YEAR 1	YEAR 2	YEAR 3	TOTAL
OPBRENGSTEN				
2*40 hours per month in staff savings; the average internal hourly rate is 85. (2*40*85 USD = 6.800 monthly/annual 81.600)	$ 13.600	$ 81.600	$ 81.600	$ 176.800
5% efficiency improvement in our processes. Yearly budget 3.6 million USD: 3.6 million/100 * 5% = 180.000 USD per year. 180.000/12 * 2 months = 30.000	$ 30.000	$ 180.000	$ 180.000	$ 390.000
Total benefits	**$ 43.600**	**$ 261.600**	**$ 261.600**	**$ 566.800**

Figure 13.10 – Quantitative revenue

Argumentation for quantitative benefits

As we stated earlier, with addressing the one-time costs for the project and the annual recurring cost, we need to give information on how we have calculated the values and what argumentation we use for that in this example business case. Here's how we can do this:

2*40 hours per month saving in delivery of handmade Excel reports. All reports will be automated and interactive and available for our employees. As the project is delivered in October, the saving of hours will start this year (2 months 2*40*2 = 6.800 USD per month). We have calculated this with an average internal hourly rate of 85 USD.

Efficiency improvement in our processes will save up to 5% of our annual budget. 5% of 3.6 million USD is 180.000 USD annually. For the current year, this efficiency improvement will be 30.000 USD.

The last section of our business case financial analysis is to perform quantitative analysis to see whether our business case has a positive outcome.

The quantitative analysis

We will look at the costs and the value of the benefits in this final step of the financial analysis and subtract them from each other. We can immediately see whether and when our project will deliver the value we expect, as well as define the project's ROI. Have a look at the following example:

QUANTITATIVE ANALYSIS	YEAR 1	YEAR 2	YEAR 3	TOTAL
BENEFITS				
Total of Benefits	$ 43.600	$ 261.600	$ 261.600	$ 566.800
TOTAL BENEFITS	$ 43.600	$ 261.600	$ 261.600	$ 566.800
COSTS				
ONE-TIME PROJECT COSTS	$ 69.200			$ 69.200
RECURRING COSTS	$ 5.440	$ 35.640	$ 35.640	$ 76.720
TOTAL COSTS	$ 74.640	$ 35.640	$ 35.640	$ 145.920
NET TO BENEFITS (+) / COSTS (-)	$ -31.040	$ 225.960	$ 225.960	$ 420.880

Figure 13.11 – Quantitative analysis

Let's move on to ROI next.

ROI

ROI is an English term that literally means "return on your investment". This method allows you to quickly determine whether or not you should invest. Simply divide the total project revenue by the project investment amount to arrive at the solution. The result is expressed as a percentage, and if it is negative, it makes no sense to invest in the projects.

There are several ROI formulas that you can use to calculate your ROI. However, there is one ROI formula that is most commonly used:

$$ROI = \text{Expected Revenue} - \text{Costs of Investment} \Big/ \text{Costs of Investment} * 100\%$$

Figure 13.12 – ROI

If we calculate the ROI for our example financial analysis, we can do it as follows:

$$ROI = \quad 566.800 \; - \; 145,920 \; = \; 420,880$$

$$420,880 \; \Big/ \; 145,920 \; = \; 2,88432018 * 100\% = 2,88 \text{ (Rounded)}$$

Figure 13.13 – Calculating our project example ROI

Our ROI calculation is, therefore, this: (566.900 – 145.920) / 145.920 *100% = 2.88

In concrete terms, this means that every euro you invest gives you a rounded profit of 2.88 dollar cents. When we have calculated a negative percentage? Then, it means that every euro you invest causes x loss in dollar cents.

Conclusion and advice

You have written the introduction, the problem analysis, and the project's main objectives to conclude this paragraph and the aspects of your business case. Then, you wrote down the various options and their strategic contributions. You've considered the value of your project and potential risks and have conducted a financial analysis. It's time to wrap up the business case and recommend an option to your board of directors' management team.

An option is to use a table such as the one in *Figure 13.14*. With this table, we are able to make a thorough choice and advise the client:

	Option 1	Option 2	Option 3	Option 4
Description	No changes	Having a new tool	Change existing visualizations	Complete new infrastructure and Cockpit
Benefits	None	High	Medium	High/medium
Cons	High	Low	Medium	Very high
Strategic contribution	None	High	Medium	Medium
Actors	None	4	5	8
Implementation- time	None	4 sprints of 2 weeks	2 sprints of 2 weeks	6 sprints of 2 weeks
Costs	None	Medium (write the value of your financial analysis here)	Low (write the value of your financial analysis here)	Very high (write the value of your financial analysis here)
Maintenance	None	Medium (write the value of your financial analysis here)	Low (write the value of your financial analysis here)	High (write the value of your financial analysis here)

Figure 13.14 – Conclusion and advice for our data and analytics project

Let's summarize the chapter next.

Summary

After reading this chapter, we now have a better understanding of data and analytics projects, as well as the project approach that we can take. With those skills, you can manage and practice them in projects, identify typical risks in data and analytics projects, and define mitigating measures.

We discussed the steps within and approach toward data and analytics projects, as well as the setup of the first part of a project using the waterfall method and combining it with an incremental approach after the planning phase. We also addressed the need for multiple people, or actors, in your projects. The most important step in delivering increments (or sprints) and finishing your project is to evaluate and learn how to do things even better in the future. We discussed the STARR methodology, which can help you reflect and evaluate in a structured manner.

In the final section of this chapter, we discussed the business case and walked you through the various steps of writing a solid business case. We showed you how to conduct a thorough financial analysis and how to convert it into an ROI calculation. We concluded this chapter with an introduction to gathering all of the information from your business case in order to make an informed decision and advise your decision-makers on which option to take.

We will provide you with a number of templates and documents that we used throughout this book in the following chapter. You are free to use them (even digitally) as knowledge must be shared! This book's final chapter contains inspirational materials, books, websites, and so on. Throughout our careers, we have gained knowledge through reading, learning, and doing, and books and websites are included.

Appendix A – Templates

We have used a variety of templates throughout this book.

The following templates are the ones that are all available. Please feel free to use these ideas as best practices, as *best practices are good ideas*:

- Project intake form
- Layout for a business case
- Layout for a business case scenario description
- A business case financial analysis
- Layout for a risk assessment
- Layout for a summary business case (for the conclusion and advice)
- Layout information and measure plan
- Layout for a KPI description
- Table with the Inmon groups and a description of their roles

Project intake form

Part I – To be completed by the client

Project	
Name:	
Adjustment for existing application(s)	☐ Yes, name:
	☒ No

Client details	
Organizational unit client	
Cost center number client	
Client (budget manager)	
Client role	
Delegated client	
Role delegated client	
Contact person client	
Role contact person	
Relationship with other project(s)	☐ Yes, name: ☒ No

Project description
Briefly describe what the client wants to see realized.

Description of business unit

Briefly describe the function of the business unit for which the application is intended.

Non-functional requirements	
Number of expected users	<10 | 10-50 | 50-100 | 100-250 | >250
Expected frequency of use	ad-hoc | daily | weekly | monthly | quarterly | yearly
expected mode of use	Standard reporting | Search interactively
Up-to-datedness of the data (refresh rate)	ad-hoc | daily | weekly | monthly | quarterly | yearly
Addition and or explanation	

Data security check

A data security incident is a serious security breach. When protected, sensitive, or confidential data is stolen, used, viewed, stored, or transmitted by someone who is not authorized, a breach occurs. Other security concerns include data leaks, information leaks (who can see what), sensitive information leaks, and data spillage. As a result, when it comes to data and information usage, we must identify some specific elements.

Application/model/app Dashboards and reports are critical for any organization, team, or department. The work cannot be completed without this information.	Essential | Important | Desirable | Unclassified
Confidentiality The dashboards and reports are private and only available to a select group of managers and employees.	Essential | Important | Desirable | Unclassified
Access Control What type of access control is required when confidentiality is required? What are the rules that we must follow? (Manager of team A – can see information about team A, and so on).	Add information:
Integrity Incorrect information will not be tolerated (accountable environment). The organization suffers significant damage if the information is incorrect, incomplete, or late. Inaccurate data, such as inaccurate financial transactions, undermines trust in the organization.	Essential | Important | Desirable | Unclassified
Availability Dashboards and reports are essential. The organization will suffer severe consequences if the information is not available.	Essential | Important | Desirable | Unclassified
Addition and or explanation	

Data privacy check

Some countries have special legislation and regulations when it comes to data usage and data privacy. For example, in the Netherlands, there is a regulation called **General Data Protection Regulations (GDPR)**. When it comes to regulations in the US it is a patchwork of rules. There is actually no specific privacy law except in relation to children but in the State of California, they have implemented data privacy regulations.

When it comes to using personal data we should take care and be aware upfront that we need to consider the privacy regulations for our project. There are several categories that we have to identify and classify.

Name, address, and city data (Name, address, postal code, city of residence)	☐ Yes ☒ No
Identification data (Passport, driver's license, or social security number)	☐ Yes ☒ No
Application details (Application letters, resume)	☐ Yes ☒ No
Contact details (E-mail address, phone or fax number)	☐ Yes ☒ No
Salary details (Salary details, social payments, income taxes, expense reimbursement)	☐ Yes ☒ No
Social media accounts (LinkedIn, Twitter, WhatsApp, Facebook)	☐ Yes ☒ No
Image and sound recordings (Video, photos, passport photographs)	☐ Yes ☒ No
Payment details (Bank name, account number, name of account holder)	☐ Yes ☒ No

Addition and or explanation When a checkbox is answered with "yes" it is advised to arrange a legislation and regulations check with your Privacy Officer.	
Legislation – regulations check	
Is privacy impact analysis needed?	Essential | Important | Desirable | Unclassified
Is a register of data needed?	Essential | Important | Desirable | Unclassified
Addition and/or explanation	

	Data ethics checklist	
	Data generation, use, collection, analysis, and dissemination are all aspects of data. We can do this with both unstructured and structured data. When we do so, there is a chance that the decisions we make will have an impact on individuals and the world. As a result, we must be open about how we use data in our projects.	
1	**Do we have to take care of laws and regulations in this data and analytics project?** The first critical step is to determine whether any legalizations or regulations are applicable to the project.	☐ Yes ☒ No Write any additional information here:
2	**Is the data that we want to use available in an ethical manner and is this data suitable for usage?** We must be mindful of who owns the data and ensure that it is used in the manner intended by the owner!	☐ Yes ☒ No Write any additional information here:
3	**Is it possible to identify and check bias in the data that we have collected or used for our models?** People can be biased by their origin, and the same is true for data and the application of algorithms and business rules. The data we collect and store is not as objective as we believe! When using algorithms and business rules, we should be aware that the data we use to train the models can have an impact on people and possible human bias can be magnified, which results in undesirable outcomes. To conclude, we must be able to identify, test, verify, and discuss the results.	☐ Yes ☒ No Write any additional information here:

4	**Can we identify and demonstrate bias in our created model or in the data used?** When we use data and apply various models, we may have used data that is biased. When we use that specific data set and apply the learning models, the model produces biased results. For example, a bias based on gender, age, equality, or racial elements. We need to be aware that we must consider documenting, discussing, and evaluating our data usage choices. The message here is to avoid doing things simply because you can!	☐ Yes ☒ No Write any additional information here:
5	**Can the legal rights of individuals be impinged by the use of data?** When an individual's legal rights are at stake, the organization must have permission and the right to use data for specific purposes. As an example, suppose an organization provides data to its direct partners, but different privacy conditions than the internal data usage may be addressed here. In the event of an incident, for example, they know the addresses and more detailed information from people, but certain data is not shared to protect those people's privacy (such as names, address details, and other things on which someone can be individually identified). It could also happen internally, for example, by logging information that is known at the employee level but is shared with users at the department or concern level. We should be aware of this in order to protect the privacy of each individual employee.	☐ Yes ☒ No Write any additional information here:

6	**Are we able to understand that the data we want to use is suitable for the purposes of our project?** When we begin an analytics or data science project, we must understand and ensure that the data we intend to use is appropriate for the purpose of our projects. Following that, we should be able to verify and validate the data for our project. For example, when records or values are missing, the outcome or our algorithms and business rules can have a significant impact on the results, potentially producing a biased result.	☐ Yes ☒ No Write any additional information here:
7	**Do we have a multi-disciplinary team present to discuss the present dilemmas, and explore the possible usage of algorithms and the possible outcomes?** When it comes to assessing and discussing our own work, we need to focus on the dilemma and the outcomes that can occur with a multi-disciplinary team.	☐ Yes ☒ No Write any additional information here:
8	**Explainable AI by design? Are we able to define the role of an algorithm used and what processes are being followed (procedural transparency)?** It is critical for data engineers and data scientists who train models to understand the model's behavior in order to detect errors or weaknesses. This is why we must correctly describe the used algorithms or business rules. When data scientists and data engineers train a model, it is critical to understand the model's behavior. They must be able to identify any flaws or errors.	☐ Yes ☒ No Write any additional information here:

9	**Explainable AI. Are we able to explain the algorithm or business rules to the guardians, stakeholders, and others whom it concerns?** Explainable AI is defined as the ability of a person to comprehend the reason for a decision. The decision is influenced by algorithms and business rules. To be able to understand the model's decision, we must be able to explain the decision. We can do so by design, but we can also do it post-hoc by using an algorithm to understand the black-box model.	☐ Yes ☒ No Write any additional information here:
	Addition and/or explanation	

Risks	
Are organizational changes to be expected that could affect the progress of the project?	☐ Yes ☒ No
Has a project manager/leader/coordinator been appointed on the client side?	☐ Yes ☒ No
Is the contact person present full-time? Or is there a full-time backup?	☐ Yes ☒ No
Can a response time to questions of a maximum of 3 days be guaranteed?	☐ Yes ☒ No
Does the contact person have knowledge of the source systems and the source data?	☐ Yes ☒ No
Is all data available in the source systems?	☐ Yes ☒ No ☒ No, but the development/adaptation of the source systems is planned and will be released on the following date:
Are there interfaces with the source systems?	☐ Yes ☒ No ☒ No, we have to arrange this
Are there dependencies with external suppliers?	☐ Yes ☒ No
Are there dependencies with external suppliers?	☐ Yes ☒ No

Source system data (per source system)	
Source system name	
Source system type	☐ Database ☐ Interface, an automated connection ☒ File, manual (e.g. MS Excel, CSV, and so on) ☐ Cloud ☐ Other
Owner source system (department)	
Internal/external management organization	☒ Internal – name: ☐ External – name:
Contact person	
Is the source system data model available?	☒ Yes ☐ No
Are field definitions available?	☐ Yes ☐ No
Particularities	
Size of data delivery (number of files)	
Number of expected rows	
Additional information	

Source system data (per source system)	
Source system name	
Source system type	☐ Database ☒ Interface, an automated connection ☐ File, manual (e.g. MS Excel, CSV, and so on) ☐ Cloud ☐ Other
Owner source system (department)	
Internal/external management organization	☒ Internal – name: ☐ External – name:
Contact person	
Is the source system data model available?	☒ Yes ☐ No
Are field definitions available?	☐ Yes ☐ No
Particularities	
Size of data delivery (number of files)	
Number of expected rows	
Additional information	

Part II – to be completed by the contractor/internal supplier, and so on.

Other project data	
Project number	
Date of intake	
The appointed project manager or project leader	
Date intake forwarded to the contact person	
Name of the person who did the intake	
Relationship with other projects?	☐ Yes, name of project: ☒ No

The first functional requests that are known

Indicate in the table below as completely and concretely as possible which functional requirements you set for the application. The MoSCoW method is used to set priorities:

- Must have this – this requirement must be delivered in the final result

- Should have this if at all possible – this requirement is highly desirable

- Could have this if it does not affect anything else – this requirement should only be addressed if there is enough time

- Would have this – this requirement will not be discussed now, but could be interesting in the future and is noted in the backlog

Complexity:

- Low/middle/high/very high

- The standard level of change complexity is middle

Description of the functional requirements	MoSCoW	Complexity	Intended for the type of use?

Other elements that were agreed upon

STARR TEMPLATE

Name project   :

Name project member   :

Date   :

S   Situation

Describe the circumstances under which the your project took place (reason, parties involved, where, etc.)

T   Task

Describe the exact assignment you worked on (and who was your project leader, client), or that you assigned to yourself. Indicate what your role/position was in this project

A   Activities

Describe the approach you used (activities; tools; preparation)

R   Results

> How was the result assessed, by whom and on what basis?

R   Reflect

> Why do you consider this your best practice, how do you look back to the work that you have done? Relate to the complexity of the situation and/or development in feedback you've received.

Layout for a business case

1. *Reasons for your project* – A brief introduction, a description of the problem, and the project's main goal (why).

2. *The options or scenarios* – The following elements create a scenario: an introduction, pros and cons, and strategic contribution. *Figure 13.10* shows an example of how to write your scenarios or options.

3. *Qualitative benefits* – Try to emphasize the advantages that your project will bring to your company (without the financial calculations for now).

4. *Risks* – Which high-impact risks did you identify? There are several risks that we should investigate, control, and describe.

5. *Financial analysis* – There are a few things to consider when conducting a thorough financial analysis of your project. It not only makes all project costs visible, but it also explains why you need to include them in your budget. The same principle applies to the future value that your business case can provide. Always plan three years ahead of time, and consider the costs of maintaining dashboards and reports. The majority of the benefits will be quantitative (in eurodollars), but some will be qualitative.

6. *Conclusion and advice* – It's time to wrap up the business case and recommend an option to your board of directors and management team.

Layout for a business case scenario description

Name	
Option 1	
Description	
Pros	
Cons	
Strategic contribution	

A business case financial analysis

In the next example, we will guide you through a financial analysis for a fictive small project. In *Chapter 13, Managing Data and Analytics Projects*, the business case is described in more detail.

Describe and calculate the one-time project costs:

QUANTITATIVE ANALYSIS	YEAR 1	YEAR 2	YEAR 3	TOTAL
One-time project costs				
	$ 0,00	$ 0,00	$ 0,00	$ 0,00
	$ 0,00	$ 0,00	$ 0,00	$ 0,00
TOTAL ONE-OFF COSTS	$ 0,00	$ 0,00	$ 0,00	$ 0,00

Describe and calculate the annual recurring costs:

RECURRING COSTS	YEAR 1	YEAR 2	YEAR 3	TOTAL
	$ 0,00	$ 0,00	$ 0,00	$ 0,00
	$ 0,00	$ 0,00	$ 0,00	$ 0,00
TOTAL RECURRING COSTS	$ 0,00	$ 0,00	$ 0,00	$ 0,00

Describe and calculate the quantitative benefits:

QUANTITATIVE BENEFITS	YEAR 1	YEAR 2	YEAR 3	TOTAL
Value				
	$ 0,00	$ 0,00	$ 0,00	$ 0,00
	$ 0,00	$ 0,00	$ 0,00	$ 0,00
TOTAL BENEFITS (VALUE)	$ 0,00	$ 0,00	$ 0,00	$ 0,00

When one-time costs, recurring cost, and the possible value is calculated it's time to perform a quantitative analysis. With this analysis, you will be able to determine if the project could be of value to your organization.

QUANTITATIVE ANALYSIS	YEAR 1	YEAR 2	YEAR 3	TOTAL
BENEFITS				
Total of benefits	$ 0,00	$ 0,00	$ 0,00	$ 0,00
	$ 0,00	$ 0,00	$ 0,00	$ 0,00
TOTAL BENEFITS	$ 0,00	$ 0,00	$ 0,00	$ 0,00
COSTS				
ONE-TIME PROJECT COSTS	$ 0,00	$ 0,00	$ 0,00	$ 0,00
RECURRING COSTS	$ 0,00	$ 0,00	$ 0,00	$ 0,00
TOTAL COSTS	$ 0,00	$ 0,00	$ 0,00	$ 0,00
NET BENEFITS (+) / COSTS (-)	$ 0,00	$ 0,00	$ 0,00	$ 0,00

Layout for a risk assessment

Which high-impact risks did you identify? Rate their chance of occurring from 1-5, along with the potential impact also from 1-5, and multiply to get the total score.

Nr.	Risk	Chance of occurrence	Impact	Score
1	Extracting historical data can cause performance issues.	5	5	25
2	Inconsistent data from several sources that do not align. Therefore, the insights will not be trusted.	4	4	16
3				
4				
5				

Layout for a summary business case

The following is an example of using a table with the business case elements to make a thorough choice based on an array of advice.

	Option 1	Option 2	Option 3	Option 4
Description	No changes	Having a new tool	Change existing visualizations	Complete new infrastructure and cockpit
Benefits	None	High	Medium	High/medium
Cons	High	Low	Medium	Very high
Strategic contribution	None	High	Medium	Medium
Actors	None	4	5	8
Project duration	None	4 sprints of 2 weeks	2 sprints of 2 weeks	6 sprints of 2 weeks

Costs	None	Medium (write the value of your financial analysis here)	Low (write the value of your financial analysis here)	Very high (write the value of your financial analysis here)
Maintenance	None	Medium (write the value of your financial analysis here)	Low (write the value of your financial analysis here)	High (write the value of your financial analysis here)

Layout information and measure plan

Elements that should be written down in an information measure plan are as follows:

1. An introduction:

    A. A short description of your information measure plan

    B. A problem analysis

    C. The objectives of your project

    D. The scope (what are you going to do and what not)

2. The information necessity for management:

    A. Describe the KPIs and reports that are needed

    B. Who your users are (have a look at *Figure 7.16, Chapter 7*)

    C. Describe the desired level of granularity (the level of detail)

    D. Describe the nonfunctional requirements (see the intake form that we added here in the template chapter)

3. User stories/use cases/requirements:

    A. User story 1

    B. User story 2

    C. And so on

4. Data sources:

    A. Desired sources

    B. Data quality check

    C. Describe the missing data

    D.   Describe the metadata

5.   The solution:

    A.   Describe the dashboard and reports (follow the DARs principle – see *Chapter 7*)

    B.   Describe and sketch the data flow

    C.   Design the dashboard (using the chatting and sketching technique that is described in *Chapter 7*)

6.   Appendix : A

    A.   Design decisions

    B.   Remarks

Layout for a KPI description

Name of KPI	
Definition of KPI	
Owner of KPI	
What is the purpose of usage?	
Frequency	
Department	
Type of graph	
Additional information	

Unit of measure	
Data source	
Required tables	
Reporting period	
Data owner	
Data steward	
Date of KPI approval	
Norm	
KPI	

Table with the Inmon groups and a description of their roles

Who is my public?	Farmers	Tourists	Explorers	Miners
Managing board	X			
Middle management	X			
Team manager		X		
Team lead				
Controller			X	
Process advisor			X	
Business analysts			X	
Analysts			X	
Data analysts			X	
Data scientists				X

A short description of the Inmon classifications used in the table: **Farmers** have defined, predictable requirements. **Tourists** are practically equivalent to farmers, but they must utilize filters to look at the data differently and understand the findings. **Explorers** seek to examine existing indicators from several perspectives (dimensions) and interact thoroughly with dashboards and reports for data-informed decision-making. **Miners** are more of a scientific field; they are our data scientists, and they want a lot of freedom to investigate anomalies in the data (looking for the golden egg).

15

Appendix B – References

Throughout this book, we have cited or referred to additional materials to help you on your data literacy journey. This appendix serves as a single collection of all these resources. They are categorized as follows:

- *Inspirational books* – Books that we believe are valuable to read to help you increase your data literacy journey.

- *Online articles and blogs* – This is a collection of useful articles and blog posts on topics that are also covered in this book. They can be used to expand your knowledge.

- *Online tools* – This is a collection of helpful online tools that you can use in your various data and analytics projects.

- *Online sites* – This is a collection of websites where we believe you will find useful content related to data literacy.

This list is also available at www.kevinhanegan.com/dataliteracyinpracticereferences. This is especially helpful for people who have the paperback version of this book, so you can click on any of the URLs directly.

Inspirational books

- *Cruise. Control (Dutch)* by Merlijn Gillissen and Charles van der Ploeg

- *De Intelligente, datagedreven organisatie* (Dutch) by Daan van Beek

- *De Big Data Revolution (Dutch)* by Viktor Mayer-Schonenberger and Kennetrh Cukier (also availale in English)

- *Data Strategy* by Bernard Marr

- *Datacratisch Werken* (Dutch) by Daan van Beek

- *Data Quality. The Field Guide* by Thomas C Redman Ph. D

- *Designing Regenerative Cultures* by Daniel Wahl

- *Everyday Bias: Identifying and Navigating Unconscious Judgments in Our Daily Lives* by Howard Ross

- *Lateral Thinking Puzzles* by Paul Sloane

- *Leading Change* by John P Kotter

- *Now You See It* by Stephen Few

- *Out of the Crisis* by Edward Deming

- *Show Me the Numbers* by Stephen Few

- *The Difference: How the Power of Diversity Creates Better Groups, Firms, Schools, and Societies* by Scott Page

- *The Fifth Discipline Fieldbook: Strategies and Tools for Building a Learning Organization* by Peter Senge

- *Thinking with Data* by Max Shron

- *Turning Data into Wisdom* by Kevin Hanegan

Online articles and blogs

- *6 Reasons Why BI and Analytics Projects Fail and How to Avoid It* by Mark Tossel: `https://www.salesforceben.com/6-reasons-why-bi-and-analytics-projects-fail-and-how-to-avoid-it`

- *A Complete Guide to Bar Charts* by Mike Yi: `https://chartio.com/learn/charts/bar-chart-complete-guide/`

- *An Appeal to the Eye. William Playfair promotes his charts* by RJ Andrews: `https://infowetrust.com/project/breviary`

- *BitMetric's Visualization of Gartner's Business Analytics Magic Quadrant*: `https://qap.bitmetric.nl/extensions/magicquadrant/index.html` by Bitmetric

- *Business Intelligence and Analytics Image*: `https://www.researchgate.net/figure/Business-intelligence-and-analytics-Source-Davenport-and-Harris-2007_fig1_311962711`

- *Chapter 5 (The Big Bang: William Playfair, the Father of Modern Graphics) from A History of Data Visualization & Graphic Communication*: `https://friendly.github.io/HistDataVis/ch05-playfair.html`

- *Concave vs Convex*: `https://www.grammarly.com/blog/concave-vs-convex/`

- *Data on Old Faithful Geyser*: `https://www.nps.gov/yell/planyourvisit/exploreoldfaithful.htm`

- *Data Privacy and Security Statistics*: `https://www.vpnmentor.com/blog/data-privacy-security-stats`

- *Data Tables Design Basics* by Taras Bakusevych: `https://taras-bakusevych.medium.com/data-tables-design-3c705b106a64`

- *Data Visualization Overview* by Kate Brush and Ed Burns: `https://www.techtarget.com/searchbusinessanalytics/definition/data-visualization`

- *Diagram of the Causes of Mortality in the Army in the East*: `https://www.historyofinformation.com/image.php?id=851`

- *How to Increase the Success Rate of Data Science Projects*: `https://www.techtarget.com/searchbusinessanalytics/feature/How-to-increase-the-success-rate-of-data-science-projects`

- *Important Examples of Prehistoric Rock Art*: `https://www.spain.info/en/places-of-interest/caves-altamira`

- *Moneyball (the movie)*: `https://en.wikipedia.org/wiki/Moneyball_(film)`

- *Netherlands Data Protection Authority Publishes 2021 Data Breach Report*: `https://www.dataguidance.com/news/netherlands-ap-publishes-2021-data-breach-report`

- *Our Top Data and Analytics Predictions for 2019* by Andrew White: `https://blogs.gartner.com/andrew_white/2019/01/03/our-top-data-and-analytics-predicts-for-2019/`

- *Policy Brief: Principles for Responsible Data Handling*: `https://www.internetsociety.org/policybriefs/responsible-data-handling`

- *QlikView Case Study: Uitvoeringsinstituut Werknemersverzekeringen (UWV) Competence Center builds more than 50 applications in just 2 years and provides 1,650 people with reporting & analysis capabilities*: `https://www.qlik.com/us/-/media/files/customer-success/global-us/uwv-success-story-en.pdf` and `http://docplayer.net/30148188-Disqover-uwv-qlikview-competence-center-qcc.html`

- *The 7 Most Pressing Ethical Issues in Artificial Intelligence*: `https://kambria.io/blog/the-7-most-pressing-ethical-issues-in-artificial-intelligence`

- *The Lost Art of Questioning* by Kevin Hanegan: `https://www.qlik.com/blog/the-lost-art-of-questioning`

- *Torn… Between Two…* by Angelika Klidas: `https://www.linkedin.com/pulse/torn-between-two-angelika-klidas`

- *Visual Battle: Table vs Graph* by Cole Nussbaumer: `https://www.storytellingwithdata.com/blog/2011/11/visual-battle-table-vs-graph`

- *VizLib Library: Supporting data literacy for all*: `https://home.vizlib.com/vizlib-library-supporting-data-literacy-for-all/`

- *What to Consider When Creating Tables: Dos & Don'ts of Table Design* by Lisa Charlotte Muth: `https://blog.datawrapper.de/guide-what-to-consider-when-creating-tables`

- *Why Do So Many BI Initiatives Fail?* `https://www.silvon.com/blog/bi-initiatives-fail` by Pat Passet

- *Why Visual Literacy is Essential to Good Data Visualization* by Ben Dexter Cooley: `https://towardsdatascience.com/why-visual-literacy-is-essential-to-good-data-visualization-5b9dffb5aa6f`

Dutch articles and blogs

The following list includes articles and blogs written in Dutch:

- *13 Vision Statement Examples* by Jasper Bronkhorst: `https://www.geldreview.nl/leiderschap/visie-statement-voorbeelden`

- *Call to Balloon – Insight into the Chain of Acute Myocardial Infarction Care (Dutch)* by Guus Schrijvers: `http://guusschrijvers.nl/wp-content/uploads/2016/10/Martin-Smeekes-Meten-en-weten-in-de-spoedzorgketen.pdf`

- *How You Become the Most Inspiring Organization in your Industry (Dutch)*: `https://www.identitive.nl/hoe-ook-meest-inspirerende-organisatie-branche-worden`

- *Increase in infections continues, number of new corona patients in hospitals fluctuate (Dutch)*: `https://www.telegraaf.nl/nieuws/2012726519/stijging-besmettingen-zet-door-aantal-nieuwe-coronapatienten-in-ziekenhuizen-schommelt`

- *Predictive Analytics: Five Inspiring Examples (Dutch)*: `https://biplatform.nl/517083/predictive-analytics-vijf-inspirerende-voorbeelden.html`

- *Small Online Discovery Tour in Stasi Museum*: `https://www.pieterjanssen.eu/2020/04/06/kleine-online-ontdekkingstocht-in-stasi-museum`

- *Transition Process of the Stasi Documents in Full Swing*: `https://www.pieterjanssen.eu/2020/06/15/transitieproces-van-de-stasi-documenten-in-volle-gang`

- `https://mijngemeente.vrnhn.nl/verhalen/call-balloon-tijdwinst-bij-patienten-met-een-hartinfarct`

- `https://www.rd.nl/artikel/479438-in-2020-produceert-de-wereld-40-zettabytes-aan-digitale-data` by Reformatorisch dagblad

Online tools

The following list includes the online tools you can use:

- *Adobe Color* – Online color wheel and color theme generator: `color.adobe.com`

- *Coolors* – Online color palette generator: `coolors.co`

- *Financial Times Chart Doctor* – A repository for images related to the Financial Times Visual Vocabulary: `https://github.com/Financial-Times/chart-doctor/tree/main/visual-vocabulary`

- *Palette Generator* – Create color palettes based off uploaded images `palettegenerator.com`

- *Sketch App Sources* – Design files and other UI/UX resources and templates: `www.sketchappsources.com`

- *Statista* – Site that shows statistics around the volume of data and information created and consumed: `www.statista.com/statistics/871513/worldwide-data-created`

Online sites

You can find the following sites and information online:

- *Alberto Cairo's website* – Content related to information design and data visualization: `www.albertocairo.com`

- *Dataversity* – Data Education for Business and IT Professionals: `www.dataversity.net`

- *Freecode Camp* – Educational site for learning web development: `www.freecodecamp.org`

- *IBM* – Helps organizations become data-driven businesses: `www.ibm.com`

- *IDC* – A global market intelligence firm: `www.idc.com`

- *Perceptual Edge Data Visualization Consultancy*: `www.perceptualedge.com`

- *Qlik* – Data and Analytics Software Company: `www.qlik.com`

- *SAS Analytics Academic Programs* `https://www.sas.com/nl_nl/learn/academic-programs.html`

- *The Data Literacy Project* – A community dedicated to creating a data-literate world, with blogs, assessments, courses, and more: `thedataliteracyproject.org`

- *The Power of AI and IoT* – AI and IoT Knowledge Base (Dutch): `thepowerofai.nl`

Index

Packt.com

Subscribe to our online digital library for full access to over 7,000 books and videos, as well as industry leading tools to help you plan your personal development and advance your career. For more information, please visit our website.

Why subscribe?

- Spend less time learning and more time coding with practical eBooks and Videos from over 4,000 industry professionals

- Improve your learning with Skill Plans built especially for you

- Get a free eBook or video every month

- Fully searchable for easy access to vital information

- Copy and paste, print, and bookmark content

Did you know that Packt offers eBook versions of every book published, with PDF and ePub files available? You can upgrade to the eBook version at packt.com and as a print book customer, you are entitled to a discount on the eBook copy. Get in touch with us at customercare@packtpub.com for more details.

At www.packt.com, you can also read a collection of free technical articles, sign up for a range of free newsletters, and receive exclusive discounts and offers on Packt books and eBooks.

Other Books You May Enjoy

If you enjoyed this book, you may be interested in these other books by Packt:

Time Series Analysis with Python Cookbook

Tarek A. Atwan

ISBN: 978-1-80107-554-1

- Understand what makes time series data different from other data
- Apply various imputation and interpolation strategies for missing data
- Implement different models for univariate and multivariate time series
- Use different deep learning libraries such as TensorFlow, Keras, and PyTorch
- Plot interactive time series visualizations using hvPlot
- Explore state-space models and the unobserved components model (UCM)
- Detect anomalies using statistical and machine learning methods
- Forecast complex time series with multiple seasonal patterns

Codeless Time Series Analysis with KNIME

Corey Weisinger, Maarit Widmann, Daniele Tonini

ISBN: 978-1-80323-206-5

- Install and configure KNIME time series integration
- Implement common preprocessing techniques before analyzing data
- Visualize and display time series data in the form of plots and graphs
- Separate time series data into trends, seasonality, and residuals
- Train and deploy FFNN and LSTM to perform predictive analysis
- Use multivariate analysis by enabling GPU training for neural networks
- Train and deploy an ML-based forecasting model using Spark and H2O

Packt is searching for authors like you

If you're interested in becoming an author for Packt, please visit `authors.packtpub.com` and apply today. We have worked with thousands of developers and tech professionals, just like you, to help them share their insight with the global tech community. You can make a general application, apply for a specific hot topic that we are recruiting an author for, or submit your own idea.

Share Your Thoughts

Now you've finished *Data Literacy in Practice* , we'd love to hear your thoughts! Scan the QR code below to go straight to the Amazon review page for this book and share your feedback or leave a review on the site that you purchased it from.

`https://packt.link/r/1-803-24675-8`

Your review is important to us and the tech community and will help us make sure we're delivering excellent quality content.

Download a free PDF copy of this book

Thanks for purchasing this book!

Do you like to read on the go but are unable to carry your print books everywhere? Is your eBook purchase not compatible with the device of your choice?

Don't worry, now with every Packt book you get a DRM-free PDF version of that book at no cost.

Read anywhere, any place, on any device. Search, copy, and paste code from your favorite technical books directly into your application.

The perks don't stop there, you can get exclusive access to discounts, newsletters, and great free content in your inbox daily

Follow these simple steps to get the benefits:

1. Scan the QR code or visit the link below

https://packt.link/free-ebook/9781803246758

2. Submit your proof of purchase
3. That's it! We'll send your free PDF and other benefits to your email directly